Healing and Peacebuilding After War

This book brings together multiple perspectives to examine the strengths and limitations of efforts to promote healing and peacebuilding after war, focusing on the aftermath of the traumatic armed conflict in Bosnia and Herzegovina.

The book begins with a simple premise: trauma that is not transformed is transferred. Drawing on multidisciplinary insights from academics, peace practitioners and trauma experts, this book examines the limitations of our current strategies for promoting healing and peacebuilding after war while offering inroads into best practices to prevent future violence through psychosocial trauma recovery and the healing of memories. The contributions create a conversation that allows readers to critically rethink the deeper roots and mechanisms of trauma created by the war.

Collectively, the authors provide strategic recommendations to policymakers, peace practitioners, donors and international organizations engaged in work in Bosnia and Herzegovina – strategies that can be applied to other countries rebuilding after war.

This volume will be of much interest to students of conflict resolution, peacebuilding, social psychology, Balkan politics and International Relations in general.

Julianne Funk is Research Fellow at the Hellenic Foundation for European and Foreign Policy (ELIAMEP), Greece, and Managing Editor of *Southeast European and Black Sea Studies*.

Nancy Good is a trauma therapist and international therapist consultant with The KonTerra Group and Portland Trauma Recovery. For 20 years she was faculty with Eastern Mennonite University's Center for Justice and Peacebuilding, USA.

Marie E. Berry is Assistant Professor and director, Inclusive Global Leadership Initiative at the Josef Korbel School of International Studies at the University of Denver, USA.

Healing and Peacebuilding After War

Transforming Trauma in Bosnia and Herzegovina

Edited by
Julianne Funk, Nancy Good and Marie E. Berry

Routledge
Taylor & Francis Group
LONDON AND NEW YORK

First published 2020
by Routledge
2 Park Square, Milton Park, Abingdon, Oxon OX14 4RN

and by Routledge
605 Third Avenue, New York, NY 10017

Routledge is an imprint of the Taylor & Francis Group, an informa business

British Library Cataloguing-in-Publication Data
A catalogue record for this book is available from the British Library

Library of Congress Cataloging-in-Publication Data
Names: Trauma, Memory and Healing in the Balkans and Beyond (2016 : Sarajevo, Bosnia and Herzegovina), author. | Funk, Julianne, 1975– editor. | Good, Nancy, 1952– editor. | Berry, Marie E., 1983– editor.
Title: Healing and peacebuilding after war : transforming trauma in Bosnia and Herzegovina / edited by Julianne Funk, Nancy Good, and Marie E. Berry.
Description: Abingdon, Oxon ; New York, NY : Routledge, 2020. | Series: Routledge studies in peace and conflict resolution | Includes bibliographical references and index.
Identifiers: LCCN 2020004584 (print) | LCCN 2020004585 (ebook) | ISBN 9780367027988 (hardback) | ISBN 9780429397745 (ebook)
Subjects: LCSH: Peace-building—Bosnia and Herzegovina—Congresses. | Collective memory—Bosnia and Herzegovina—Congresses. | Psychic trauma—Bosnia and Herzegovina—Congresses. | Yugoslav War, 1991–1995—Psychological aspects—Congresses. | Bosnia and Herzegovina—Politics and government—1992—Congresses.
Classification: LCC JZ5584.B5 T73 2020 (print) | LCC JZ5584.B5 (ebook) | DDC 362.1968/52100949742—dc23
LC record available at https://lccn.loc.gov/2020004584
LC ebook record available at https://lccn.loc.gov/2020004585

Typeset in Times New Roman by
Apex CoVantage, LLC

ISBN 13: 978-0-367-02798-8 (hbk)

DOI: 10.4324/9780429397745

Contents

Acknowledgments

This book has its origin in a conference held in Sarajevo in the summer of 2016, entitled *Trauma, Memory and Healing in the Balkans and Beyond.* As editors, we would therefore like first to thank Zilka Spahić Šiljak and TPO Foundation for initiating the event and envisioning a wide impact for the future of the region. Others at TPO Foundation in Sarajevo made the practical arrangements run smoothly. We are grateful for the conference participants' willingness to share their own work and foster an interactive and intimate setting where we engaged with trauma's great challenges to us as scholars and activists from all over the world. We wish we could have included all voices in this volume. We also wish to thank our blind reviewers, the editors of this series and Routledge for valuing this topic, and TPO Foundation for entrusting us with the editing of this book.

We would not have put in the effort to compile this book if we were not inspired by the neglected and often intangible work of local trauma-informed clinicians and peacebuilders who persevere in their often unappreciated efforts day in and day out. Two particular examples of expertise, innovative methods and advocacy for better practices in a context deeply lacking psychosocial support are Amela Puljek-Shank and Amra Delić; these two women's inputs to the book's contents were invaluable.

We are also grateful for the energy and hard work of research assistants at the Josef Korbel School of International Studies at the University of Denver as we were finalizing this book. In particular, Ariel Zarate provided feedback, edits, and suggestions to the authors and the editorial team. As the book went into production, Micaela Iveson helped finalize the chapters and move the manuscript to press.

Finally, we want to acknowledge all of the people of Bosnia and Herzegovina who are working every day to build a future of peace for their country. As three women from the US and Canada, we cannot know what it was like to experience the war in Bosnia and Herzegovina in the 1990s. Our different backgrounds – a peace activist and scholar, a trauma therapist and conflict consultant, and an academic – have allowed us to look broadly at the multiple ways war shaped Bosnian society as well as the multifaceted and innovative ways people have found to move forward in the aftermath. We offer this book with tremendous respect for the lived experiences – of pain and joy – of all who survived the war. We humbly hope it may help to bring more attention to the imperative need to foreground local solutions and trauma-informed practices in other violence-affected contexts.

Julianne Funk
Nancy Good
Marie E. Berry

Contributors

Marie E. Berry is Assistant Professor at the Josef Korbel School of International Studies at the University of Denver, where she is an affiliate of the Sié Chéou-Kang Center for International Security and Diplomacy. She is also the Director of the Inclusive Global Leadership Initiative (IGLI), an effort to catalyze research, education and programming aimed at elevating and amplifying the work that women activists are doing at the grassroots to advance peace, justice and human rights across the world. As a sociologist, her research focuses on violence, gender and politics. Her first book, *War, Women, and Power: From Violence to Mobilization in Rwanda and Bosnia-Herzegovina* (Cambridge University Press 2018), examines the impact of war and genocide on women's political mobilization in Rwanda and Bosnia. Her second book project explores women's participation in movements for social change across the world. Together with Dr. Milli Lake (LSE), she runs the Women's Rights After War Project. She received her PhD in sociology from UCLA in 2015.

Edita Čolo Zahirović is a psychologist and peace activist. She has worked on peacebuilding initiatives for Catholic Relief Services in Sarajevo for nearly a decade, focusing primarily on Bosnia and Herzegovina. She holds an MA in Social Work (2009) and a BA in Philosophy (2007) from the University of Sarajevo.

Stephanie C. Edwards holds a PhD in Theological Ethics from Boston College (2019) and a Master's degrees in Theological Studies and Social Work from Boston University (2011). Her dissertation presents a constructive ethics of memory rooted in the Christian tradition. Her research pivots around how we experience as well as inherit memories of trauma in the religious, sociocultural, historical and political realms, as well as how our brains themselves may play a role – in conversation with the emerging field of trauma epigenetics within neuroscience research. Her interest in interdisciplinary work has its roots in her "other" career as a social worker, and her extensive travel and work in the former Yugoslavia, El Salvador, and post-Katrina New Orleans. She currently serves as the Executive Director of the Boston Theological Interreligious Consortium.

Julianne Funk is Research Fellow at the Hellenic Foundation for European and Foreign Policy and Managing Editor of the Routledge journal *Southeast European and Black Sea Studies*. She is a social scientist and peace researcher focused on the Balkans, with specializations in Balkan religions, interreligious relations and faith-based initiatives as well as trauma/healing after mass violence. She speaks and teaches all over Europe and has been actively engaged with grassroots peace organizations in Bosnia and Herzegovina for the last ten years. Currently, she is conducting research about religious and cultural heritage and postwar ethnic relations in Kosovo, which is funded by the Kosovo Foundation for Open Society. She holds a PhD in Social Sciences and an MA in Peace and Conflict Studies from the Katholieke Universiteit Leuven, Belgium.

Nancy Good is a trauma-informed therapist, mediator and international consultant with The KonTerra Group and Portland Trauma Recovery. She provides organizational and individual support to international aid organizations offering staff care, psychological first aid and critical incident response in the aftermath of trauma and high-threat environments. For over 35 years, she has combined her expertise in the fields of mental health, trauma healing, organizational resilience and mediation with the aim to strengthen teams and build resilience, warding off secondary trauma, compassion fatigue and burnout. She served as faculty at Eastern Mennonite University (EMU) for more than 25 years, 15 of them at EMU's Center for Justice and Peacebuilding (CJP), specializing in trauma healing and transformation since 1997. The trauma course became a foundation for a Trauma Concentration at CJP as well as STAR, Seminars for Trauma Awareness and Resilience. Nancy is a founding member of USAID Staff Care Center for five years and continues to offer clinical services and training for staff working in chronic stress environments, country evacuations due to civil unrest or natural disasters and sudden loss or death after violence/war. She holds a Master's degree in Social Work from VCU (1982) and a PhD from Union Institute and University (2006); her dissertation, "Peacebuilders Healing Trauma: From Victim to Survivor to Provider," focused on Post-Traumatic Growth (PTG) and building resilience in the midst of trauma and peacebuilding.

Barry Hart is Professor of Trauma, Identity and Conflict Studies in the Center for Justice and Peacebuilding, Eastern Mennonite University. He has conducted workshops on peacebuilding, psychosocial trauma recovery and reconciliation for religious and secular leaders in multiple countries in Africa, Europe and the Americas. He lived and worked in the Balkans, where he developed and led trauma and conflict transformation programs for schools, communities and religious leaders. He helped develop a joint interreligious and peacebuilding Master's degree program across three departments at the University of Sarajevo, and as a Fulbright Specialist, is teaching courses in this program. He was also engaged in a three-year peacebuilding institute and curriculum development project between EMU and the University of Hargeisa in Somaliland (2008–2011). He is also a member of the International Council of Initiatives of

Change. He holds a Ph.D. in Conflict Analysis and Resolution from the Institute for Conflict Analysis and Resolution (ICAR), George Mason University.

Kristina Hook received her PhD in peace studies and anthropology from the University of Notre Dame. She holds MA degrees in Anthropology (2017) and International Development (2012) from Notre Dame and the University of Denver's Josef Korbel School of International Studies, respectively. A 2018–2019 US Fulbright fellow to Ukraine, Kristina's current project explores the dynamics and legacy of the Soviet-era Holodomor, including how these events influence modern interpretations of Ukraine's current armed conflict. Kristina has conducted extensive fieldwork in Ukraine, supported by USAID and the National Science Foundation's Graduate Research Fellowship Program (NSF-GRFP). Having worked in more than 20 countries, Kristina has published on topics including genocide causality, post-conflict reconstruction, trauma healing, humanitarian crises and sustainable development policies. Previously, Kristina served as a policy officer at the US Department of State and as a political/economic officer in a US Embassy abroad. In 2013, she was awarded a US Presidential Management Fellowship.

Alma Jeftić is a Research Fellow at the Peace Research Institute, International Christian University in Tokyo, Japan; an Ethics Committee member at the Memory Studies Association; and the Co-Chair of the Research Network on Transnational Memory and Identity in Europe (Council for European Studies at Columbia University). She taught Psychology at the International University of Sarajevo and worked as a Visiting Researcher at the School of Psychology, University of Sussex, and at the Centre for Southeast European Studies, University of Graz. Alma is the author of *Social Aspects of Memories. Stories of Victims and Perpetrators from Bosnia-Herzegovina* (Routledge, 2019).

Kathryn Mansfield is currently the lead trainer for the STAR (Strategies for Trauma Awareness and Resilience) program based at Eastern Mennonite University's Center for Justice and Peacebuilding. She is also finishing a PhD in Expressive Arts and Conflict Transformation, focused on arts-based, embodied learning for facing chronic violence. After eight years working in a multinational bank in New York and London, she has for the last 15 years focused on peace education in multiple contexts. Her learning journeys have included an undergraduate degree in US History from Harvard, an MA from Notre Dame's Kroc Institute for International Peace Studies, trainings as a yoga instructor, healing dance facilitator and practitioner of integrative energetic medicine. She hopes to complete her doctoral dissertation work with the European Graduate School in Switzerland in 2020.

Stephan Parmentier studied law, political science and sociology at the universities of Ghent and Leuven (Belgium) and sociology and conflict resolution at the Humphrey Institute for Public Affairs, University of Minnesota-Twin Cities (USA). He currently teaches sociology of crime, law and human rights at the Faculty of Law of the University of Leuven and since September 2017, serves as the Chairperson of the Interfaculty Council of Development Cooperation at the same university. Since July 2010 he is the Secretary-General of the International Society of Criminology, and for many years he has been a member of the Advisory Board of the Oxford Centre of Criminology and the International Center for Transitional Justice (New York). He is the founder and general editor of the international book *Series on Transitional Justice* (Intersentia Publishers, Cambridge/Antwerp) and editor of the *International Journal of Restorative Justice* (Eleven Publishing, The Hague).

Mina Rauschenbach holds a PhD in Social Sciences (University of Lausanne) and is Lecturer and Senior Researcher at the Institute of Social Sciences of the University of Lausanne, as well as a Research Associate at the Leuven Institute of Criminology (University of Leuven/KU Leuven). Her main areas of research interest concern the role of conflict-related narratives and beliefs in collective understandings of the past and how they shape different stakeholders' (e.g., victims, perpetrators, citizens, diaspora communities) justice perceptions and beliefs in the aftermath of serious human rights violations. She is Associate Editor at the Intersentia Series on Transitional Justice (Intersentia Publishers, Cambridge/Antwerp). She has recently been published in *Political Psychology*, *Transitional Justice Review* and *International Criminal Justice Review*.

Jessica M. Smith is a doctoral candidate at the School for Conflict Analysis and Resolution at George Mason University. Her research is focused on local experiences of agency in postwar peacebuilding and combines an action research methodology called photovoice with narrative and feminist ethnographic methods. The overall goal of her work is to elevate local knowledge into broader international policy and programming development. Jessica holds a Bachelor of Arts degree in Political Science with minors in Spanish and Psychology, as well as a Master of Arts degree in Social Justice and Human Rights, both from Arizona State University. She has worked with the International Rescue Committee, Catholic Charities, the United Nations, USAID and Oxfam GB. Currently, Jessica is the Research and Policy Manager for the Georgetown Institute for Women, Peace and Security and a research scholar at the Elliott School of International Affairs at the George Washington University.

Zilka Spahić Šiljak holds a PhD in gender studies, and the scope of her work includes addressing cutting-edge issues involving human rights, politics, religion, education and peacebuilding. She has more than 15 years of experience in academic teaching and work in the governmental and nongovernmental sectors. She teaches Cultural Studies at the University of Zenica and at the Center for Interdisciplinary Studies of the University of Sarajevo. She is also a research associate at Stanford University. Her publications include *Bosnian Labyrinth: Culture, Gender and Leadership* (2019); *Living Values: Global Ethos in Local Context of BiH* (2018); *Shining Humanity–Life Stories of Women Peacebuilders in Bosnia and Herzegovina* (2014); *Contesting*

Female, Feminist and Muslim Identities. Post-Socialist Contexts of Bosnia and Herzegovina and Kosovo (2012); *Women Religion and Politics*, 2010; *Women, Believers and Citizens* (2009). She also runs the Transcultural Psychosocial Educational Foundation in Sarajevo, which includes projects on trauma, memory and healing.

Maarten Van Craen holds a PhD in Political Science from the University of Leuven (Belgium) and is currently a postdoctoral researcher at the Leuven Institute of Criminology of the University of Leuven (supported by the Research Foundation Flanders–FWO). Previously, he conducted postdoctoral research on police legitimacy at Northwestern University in Chicago. His research interests include internal and external procedural justice, institutional legitimacy, citizen attitudes toward government institutions, policing and ethnic minorities. He has published widely in these areas, and his work has appeared in journals such as *Justice Quarterly*, *Journal of Experimental Criminology*, *Criminal Justice and Behavior* and *European Journal of Criminology*.

Figures and tables

Figures

Tables

1 Introduction

Julianne Funk and Marie E. Berry

It is our conviction that there can be no sustainable peace without working to heal trauma resulting from violence. Furthermore, trauma that is not transformed gets trapped and is often transferred into more violence. Trauma can become "stuck," held within our societies through cultural memory, in institutions through structural violence and even kept within our very bodies (see Mansfield in this volume; van der Kolk 2015). As such, like any other energy, it does not just evaporate but finds paths of release. These claims ground this book and the conference from which it arose: *Trauma, Memory and Healing in the Balkans and Beyond*, "organized by TPO Foundation" and held in Sarajevo in 2016. The international and local constituency of interdisciplinary scholars and practitioners considered seriously the nature and role of trauma as an obstacle to and opportunity for building peace in a variety of contexts, including postwar former Yugoslav states. This book seeks to do the same, with a particular focus on Bosnia and Herzegovina.

There is much to learn from the Bosnian case. Between 1992 and 1995, Bosnia and Herzegovina survived a three-and-a-half year war that produced no winners but many losers. As the first war to unfold on European soil since World War II, Bosnia and Herzegovina captured the attention of people across the globe. Rather than dismissing the violence as far away, out of sight from Western institutions and political elites, people across the world watched as massive civilian atrocities and bloodshed were captured as part of the 24-hour news cycle. Military, peacekeeping and humanitarian interventions led by the United Nations and NATO helped protect civilians and eventually led to the Dayton Peace Agreement, which formally ended the war. In the years since, international actors, in coordination with domestic organizations, have worked to establish security, promote justice and build peace in the devastated country.

Despite these efforts, however, peace remains fragile. The country remains divided into two semiautonomous political entities ensconced in the Dayton Accords, and political elites frequently elevate the victimhood of their own group to rally political support. Bosnia and Herzegovina is still a way from joining the European Union due to the need for significant political reforms, which remain inaccessible due to the postwar political structure and power sharing of the national groups. Elections in 2018 reflected much of the same ethno-national discourse that characterized the war years. While there are many examples of communities – and youth in particular – carving out spaces for cross-ethnic community building,[1] social distrust and ethnic segregation remain from the war 25 years ago. Recently, as Bosnia and Herzegovina has become a new route for migrants fleeing to Western Europe, new questions about state capacity and national identity are emerging alongside vivid wartime memories of displacement and flight. Unhealed trauma, combined with this political dysfunction and evolving pressures, leave the country vulnerable to future instability and insecurity.

How does the legacy of war trauma underscore these dynamics? How might we design more effective interventions to address the still unhealed individual and collective trauma in Bosnia and Herzegovina? And what does the Bosnian case teach us about how to successfully conduct trauma-informed peacebuilding in the aftermath of other cases of violence? The chapters in this book present some of the international and locally-led successes in addressing these legacies of war, while also underscoring the profound limitations to these responses. The peacebuilding interventions deployed in Bosnia and Herzegovina – which ranged from political and security reforms to the International Criminal Tribunal for the former Yugoslavia to local youth camps – helped to develop a peacebuilding "toolkit" that has been used in various contexts from East Timor to Nepal and Colombia. Yet as the authors in this book illustrate, examining the Bosnian case more than two decades after the war helps reveal the limitations of these interventions and calls for us to reexamine how we work to create positive, inclusive and durable peace after war. Throughout the book, the authors champion the importance of centering trauma healing in the process of working toward peace. They also offer some concrete ideas for innovations in peacebuilding, which will be useful to scholars and practitioners working in other postwar and insecure contexts.

Background to the Bosnian war

Before the war, Bosnia and Herzegovina was Yugoslavia's most ethnically "mixed" republic. During Tito's three-decade reign, ethnicity (or religion, its key determinant), was suppressed in favor of a unified Yugoslav identity. The three dominant religious groups – Orthodox Christians, Catholics, and Muslims – spoke the same language (with minor differences) and regularly intermarried (Ramet 2002). In the cities, people lived as next-door neighbors with those of other ethnic heritages, whereas in villages and towns, it was common for different ethno-religious communities to live side by side in separate neighborhoods (Bringa 1995). After Tito's death in 1980, a rising tide of ethno-nationalism swept the country, as political elites began to mobilize support by appealing to their ethnic constituencies (Ramet 2002).

Amid the end of the Cold War in the early 1990s and the collapse of the Soviet Union, Yugoslavia experienced its own collapse. In the context of economic decline and rising of ethno-nationalism, Slovenia and Croatia declared their independence from Yugoslavia in 1991. War in Croatia broke out between its newly independent government and "rebel" or autonomous Serb regions that did not wish to succeed from Yugoslavia and that received support from the Yugoslavia

National Army (JNA). Meanwhile, Bosnian Serb leaders similarly established Serb autonomous regions throughout the country, upholding their alliance with Yugoslavia (then consisting of Serbia, Montenegro and Macedonia, as well as Kosovo within Serbia; Mojzes 1994). Like the Serb regions, Bosnian Croats also sought autonomous "communities" on the territory of Bosnia and Herzegovina.

In 1992, Bosnia and Herzegovina conducted its own independence referendum, which passed with overwhelming support. However, most Bosnian Serbs, who comprised about a third of the population, boycotted the referendum (Ibid.). Bosnian Croat and Serb political leaders increasingly refused to participate in the Bosnian assembly and simultaneously made their own national claims against a united and independent state of Bosnia and Herzegovina until, in April 1992, the country's independence was welcomed by the European Community and the United States. This was a final straw and a trigger for war. Serb political elites of Bosnia and Herzegovina established Republika Srpska, which quickly captured the majority of the country's territory with support from the massive JNA and affiliated paramilitary groups. The Bosnian government was also engaged with the (Bosnian) Croatian defense forces (HDZ), supported by Croatia, over territory mostly in Herzegovina. Eventually, the Croatian defense and Bosnian government army were convinced to join forces to drive the Bosnian Serb army back to half of the territory (49 percent, to be exact; Silber and Little 1997).

The type, severity and duration of violence varied substantially across the country during the war. Sarajevo, the capital city, was subjected to a deadly siege for over three years, during which more than 11,000 city dwellers were killed. In other parts of the country, paramilitary forces, often with support from the JNA, conducted military campaigns aimed to force the non-Serb population into flight. This led to the term "ethnic cleansing," coined to refer to attempts to "cleanse" Serb parts of the country of any non-Serb residents (Toal and Dahlman 2011). Massive war crimes (e.g., the torture of prisoners, including civilians), crimes against humanity (e.g., slavery, deportations, mass rapes, the killing of civilians, ethnic and political persecution) and genocide also characterized the violence (see work by Woodward 1995; Burg and Shoup 1999; Stiglmayer 1994; Becirevic 2014).

The international community increasingly turned its attention to Bosnia and Herzegovina as reports of atrocities against civilians continued. In July 1995, the massacre of 8,000 boys and men around the UN "safe zone" of Srebrenica led NATO and UN officials to commence a new, more aggressive military intervention. After Bosnian Serb forces shelled a busy marketplace the following month, NATO launched Operation Deliberate Force, an aggressive campaign to harness air and ground power to defeat the Bosnian Serb forces. This campaign forced the various warring parties to the negotiating table in November 1995, where they reached the Dayton Agreement, a cease-fire bringing the war to a formal close. According to the International Criminal Tribunal for the former Yugoslavia (ICTY) and *The Bosnian Book of the Dead* (Tokača 2013), the war in Bosnia and Herzegovina resulted in approximately 100,000 people killed (of which 40 percent were civilians), thousands missing, and over two million refugees and internally displaced persons. In addition, an estimated 20,000 women, girls and men were victims of rape or other forms of sexual violence and sexual torture (Delić and Avdibegović 2015).

Legacies of war

The Dayton Peace Agreement was made possible by securing concessions from each of the warring parties. As a result, the Agreement divided the country into two semiautonomous entities, the Federation of Bosnia and Herzegovina, which comprises 51 percent of the country's territory, and the Republika Srpska, comprising 49 percent. The agreement also provides for consociational power sharing, including a rotating tripartite presidency and national veto power in the case that any of the three constituent groups perceive their national interests to be threatened. Additionally, an all-powerful High Representative, appointed by the European Community, was charged with overseeing the implementation of the Agreement rather than wait for the necessary internal collaboration of the recently warring groups (Merdzanovic 2015).

This political arrangement has been tremendously dysfunctional. Moreover, the postwar dynamics have rewarded many of the same political elites responsible for the war with continued political (and economic) power. Shadow and gray economics became the driving forces of the economy, as political elites and previously marginal economic actors made fortunes in weapons trafficking and other illicit transactions (Andreas 2011). A massive international aid response – estimated to have brought approximately 100,000 international actors to Bosnia and Herzegovina as the war came to a close – inflated local economics and created new power imbalances while bringing essential aid to the population (see Belloni 2001; Pugh 2005; Andreas 2009).

The war in Bosnia and Herzegovina caused tremendous devastation to the social fabric. Ethnic cleansing destroyed lives and livelihoods for the majority of residents. Homogenization and segregation have also meant the loss of the previously regular and usually friendly social interaction across what are now clear lines of ethno-national difference. Today it is rare to find close relationships across ethnic lines except in urban centers such as Sarajevo or Tuzla. Families also suffered division into "sides" (particularly ones with mixed marriages). The death of both soldiers and ordinary people who were simply living "in the wrong place" according to the wartime goal of homogenous ethnic areas contributed to the devastation of the community. During the war, trust for neighbors deteriorated due to experiences of "betrayal" through the indirect violence of silently fleeing (rather than notifying or defending one another) or direct violation. The dynamics of wartime provided a "soldier" mentality even to civilians under siege, where blaming the other group was a survival mechanism for many (Maček 2009).

The war also devastated general social trust, irrespective of ethnic belonging. A 2009 UNDP study showed that only 10 percent of all residents thought most people could be trusted, although a Bertelsmann Stiftung 2018 Country Report claims that social trust has increased in the last years. Mooren and Kleber (2001) define trust as the confidence one has in the predictability of other people, the future and life in general. Trust is an important and common loss due to violence and trauma. However, another sign of general distrust – in this case distrust of the system – is the mass evacuation and brain drain of Bosnia's young to the West, where more opportunity awaits. This migration is a clear reflection of the heavy and widespread pessimism about the country's current and future prospects. Such pessimism is not unwarranted; youth unemployment (among 15–24-year-olds) is the highest in Europe, at about 55 percent in 2017 according to the World Bank.

The legacy of the war is also profoundly felt in overall health and well-being. General well-being is seriously reduced by widespread poverty; according to World Bank statistics, GDP per capita is less than 400 US dollars monthly. The current economic situation, which is currently "skewed toward the public rather than the private sector" (World Bank 2017), provides financial security primarily via governmental positions, which are doled out according to party affiliation. Those who are not "inside" tend to struggle their whole lives to simply survive. For those returnees to prewar homes in locations where they are now minorities, discrimination, neglect and social ostracism are forms of indirect violence that they suffer daily – as such, many "returnees" do not actually reside in their prewar homes.

The country's residents suffer from poor mental health, especially among former soldiers and vulnerable civilian groups such as children, women and elderly people. According to clinical psychologist and psychotherapist Amra Delić, individual and community mental health in Bosnia and Herzegovina is focused only on severe schizophrenia, whereas trauma is not considered seriously. Many symptoms of trauma stem from wartime exposure to violence, and yet as Good and Funk discuss in Chapter 2, there is extensive evidence that trauma affects generations born after the war years. This intergenerational transmission of trauma reaffirms the importance of addressing the traumatic legacies of war directly, in order to support populations as they recover and rebuild.

These elements, among many others, provide residents little hope for the foreseeable future. In her research on a culture of trauma in her local community, journalist and scholar Belma Bećibašić has expressed pervading cultural trauma in terms of the remaining presence of the war as a sense of loss that also holds them captive:

> The war occupies a rather uncomfortable place in people's memories . . . for almost everyone it means loss, regardless of whether it is a real, tragic loss of close family members, material loss, [of one's] home, the places where we lived, the positions we enjoyed, whether it is economic loss, a loss of former ideals, or a breakdown of illusions not only from the time before the war, but rather of the post-war era, the loss of confidence in the political elite and the possibility of change. As a consequence there is an exhaustion or fatigue about the past, which also comes from a disbelief that justice will be served. . . . The war is often seen as the culprit responsible for everything that has caused the situation in which we find ourselves today, as a society and as individuals, and all of this, bearing in mind that the war ended 20 years

> ago, speaks to the present state of affairs and the omnipresent lethargy to tackle current challenges, injustice, or to resist policies that continue to prevail today.
>
> (Bećirbašić 2019)

This cultural trauma is inherently a collective, social issue, not just a task for one-on-one psychological help but a psychosocial challenge. While individuals have memories of their own specific suffering, we frame our memories within the stories of our communities, which tend to give the individual experience a sense of meaning within the whole. While such stories can revel in victimization such that a collective avoids acknowledging its own violators and violations, minorities' narratives are usually suppressed, leading to lacking frames of meaning for the suffering of those "others." On the other hand, individual memories, such as those publicly reported by the Mothers of Srebrenica, are co-opted by the collective for political maneuvering (see Spahić Šiljak's chapter in this volume; Berry 2017), too often resulting in that very individual's needs being lost or forgotten.

Another legacy of the war is a commonly held perspective that trauma is only PTSD (a severe form of trauma; and that treatment is only possible for those with PTSD symptoms (e.g., rape victims, former combatants). The flip side of this perspective is that the rest of the population escaped traumatization and therefore are not "crazy," or, in other words, in need of psychosocial support (see Good and Funk's chapter in this volume). Consequently, as the Funk was told by resident trauma practitioners, many common and everyday trauma symptoms (e.g., insomnia, anxiety, or avoiding places or people who raise difficult memories) are simply ignored or treated as a physical, medical issue rather than being addressed at their root. This, alongside a dearth of concern for postwar psychosocial well-being from interventions and donors, means that more 25 years after war, trauma is still active and commonly misdiagnosed as generalized depression and treated with antidepressants or antianxiety medication – or simply accepted as the new norm.

Despite the intervention of the international community and investments in postwar peacebuilding, there has been no great interest in individual mental health or collective post-traumatic conditions in Bosnia and Herzegovina. This has also been the case with local actors. Professional and scientific understandings of trauma and potential responses to it are also neglected. There is not enough context-specific research nor any significant initiative to promote the treatment of trauma. In a 2006 study (now more than a decade old) of 170 NGOs in Bosnia and Herzegovina and 23 public health institutions, only 13 NGOs and four public health institutions "responded that they do work in trauma healing" (Puljek-Shank and Puljek-Shank 2008, 186). An evaluation made by a trauma practitioner team from World Vision, after ten years of working with more than 11,000 children, expressed that trauma symptoms remain "strong many years after the war and among children who did not experience primary traumatization" (Ibid., 185).

Women-led organizations like Medica Zenica may be the most notable exceptions to this disinterest and neglect of trauma suffering and psychosocial help in postwar Bosnia and Herzegovina (see also the chapter by Spahić Šiljak in this volume). In a 2014 study of 51 women who suffered wartime rape and sexual violence and who used Medica Zenica's services during and after the war, the organization noted that the majority continue to suffer from "debilitating long-term effect[s]" and PTSD symptoms (Medica 2014, 10), while 70 percent said that the "rape still influences their lives completely, mostly in the form of constant distressing memories of the events, emotional problems such as fear or nervousness, health challenges, and serious problems in close personal relationships." This is alarming given the fact that they "all benefitted from a variety of psychosocial services from Medica Zenica that they described as having been very helpful" (Ibid.). Nevertheless, the study is also notable in juxtaposing simultaneously these women's chronic suffering with their "considerable ability to cope and recreate their lives and their relationships" (Ibid., 16). Participants noted that this was often made possible through Medica's holistic approach and comprehensive support: "Apart from taking care of their needs for professional medical and psychological care, housing and food, it was crucial to provide them with a space in which they could re-establish trust in human beings and create normal and stimulating inter-personal relationships in which they feel accepted, cared for and safe" (Ibid., 15). This is one example, among many to be found in this book, demonstrating the significance of addressing trauma in the mix of peacebuilding work. The need may often be invisible, but once awareness is raised, individual and collective trauma are present and active in the country's everyday reality.

Goals of the book

The TPO Foundation in Sarajevo decided to address this very significant lacuna of concern, policy, practice and scholarship on trauma via its 2016 conference in Sarajevo. The event gathered knowledge for dissemination to scholars and practitioners from the region and beyond – this book is one avenue of that dissemination. The conference's aim was to create an archive of information through a grounding analysis for trauma healing work in the Balkans that can serve as the basis for strategic recommendations for organizations and governmental agencies working in Bosnia and Herzegovina as well as other contemporary postwar contexts. In addition, the conference created a much-needed network of activists and scholars who share best practices for psychosocial trauma recovery and the healing of difficult memories. This book contributes to these goals by specifically:

- Raising awareness regarding the ubiquitous, ongoing, trauma-related facets of postwar life in Bosnia and Herzegovina, as well as in other conflict-affected contexts (local and global historic, economic, political and cultural realities).
- Fostering interdisciplinary learning that goes beyond regional group divisions through examining the existing truths constructed by previous generations and broadening these into new possibilities for collective healing.

- Opening processes for psychosocial healing and reenergizing dignity as part of recovery/healing. We recognize that this requires public deliberation, a conscious decision plus political will on all levels of society (government, local communities and individuals), a common and critical rethinking the deeper roots of collective trauma as well as sharing the experiences of these phenomena and expertise about their mechanisms.
- Developing just and non-harmful cultural memories, social solidarity and collaboration across the Balkan region. Non-Balkan scholars and practitioners are included in order to incorporate a range of thematic expertise and inputs.

Overview of the book

This book is divided to four parts, each dealing with a key issue related to trauma healing and the relationship between trauma, memory and the practice of peacebuilding as something seeking long-term benefits for society. The first part, "Incorporating Trauma Healing into Peacebuilding Practice," provides an overview of what trauma is, as well as the critical links between trauma healing and peacebuilding at the nexus of current scholarship and practice. As these fields of mental health and peace implementation after war are rarely considered together, the book begins by advocating for their synergy for the sake of both sustainable peace and true healing of traumatized populations. Nancy Good and Julianne Funk examine the basics of trauma – what is and what it is not – in Chapter 2. In Chapter 3, Kristina Hook draws from conflict research and integrated anthropological perspectives as a way to justify trauma interventions in peacebuilding contexts. She explains how expanding these efforts may enable populations to move forward toward a spectrum of recovery of physical and mental well-being, how untreated trauma may have both long-term societal and physical impacts and how trauma interventions may ultimately mitigate future conflict dynamics. In Chapter 4, Barry Hart considers what such expanded peacebuilding means, practically, in complex contexts of trauma. He asserts that it is necessary to rebuild communities affected by war and psychosocial trauma through creative, constructive, cross-sector planning and suggests a multidisciplinary peacebuilding framework that demonstrates a comprehensive picture of the needed transformation.

Part II, "How to Remember and Tell Stories of Trauma," addresses the deep ethnic divisions and negative historical narratives that are reinforced by the state and political actors in Bosnia and Herzegovina and which continue to inhibit reconciliation more than two decades after war. The chapters in this section also consider transformative remembrance practices. Stories of traumas are so often used to intensify hostility and revenge toward "others," slowing processes of healing and social reconstruction. One challenge of remembering trauma is implicit prejudice, which easily becomes an integral part of both individual and collective memory and therefore can be transmitted to subsequent generations. In Chapter 5, Alma Jeftić seeks to analyze the ways collective narratives have been created out of difficult memories that currently exist in postwar Bosnia and Herzegovina, as demonstrated by its three different history textbooks. She provides an original *Conflict Narrative Development Model* schematic to explain this process. Chapter 6 deals with the related challenge of competing narratives of suffering that inflame divisions after experiences of wartime trauma. Stephanie C. Edwards explores the potential of a method called "multidirectional memory" for the development of relational justice and peace, the creation of non-harmful cultural memories and shared literal and figurative spaces in Bosnia and Herzegovina. In Chapter 7, "Remembering Side by Side: Transforming Relationships through Storytelling," Edita Čolo Zahirović offers the example of two notable projects that enabled former soldiers and war survivors of different ethnic and religious backgrounds to publicly share their war stories, thereby moving from trauma victims to active peacebuilders.

Part III, "Women's Resilience," is concerned with the crucial gender dimension of the 1990s war in Bosnia and Herzegovina, where an estimated 20,000 women (not to mention men) were sexually assaulted. Many still live under a stigma and silence imposed by ethno-nationalist agendas, cultural and religious norms and their family's and nation's honor. Zilka Spahić Šiljak begins the problematization of this theme in Chapter 8, "Victim or Survivor? Choosing Identity after Wartime Sexual Violence," which explores body politics and the ethnicization of women's bodies as well as how the feminist debate and the language about victimhood, survivorship and agency (dis)empower women. Marie Berry complexifies the picture in Chapter 9. Moving beyond understanding violence as solely destructive, she considers war as an accelerated period of social change during and after which Bosnian women defined their experience not as victimization but rather as transformation and survival. Berry tells us about how violence, contrary to expectations, actually opened spaces for women to participate in new forms of social and political action, such as their key roles in grassroots community organizations. Then, in Chapter 10, Jessica M. Smith highlights how the dominant discourse of women's victimhood in Bosnia and Herzegovina has in many ways structured not only the speaking space but which types of stories can be told by whom; women are the *subjects of stories*, instead of the *storytellers*. Photovoice, an arts-based method Smith has used in her research, gives transformative space to women's narratives, bringing forth local wisdom and repositioning women as agents of change.

In Part IV, "From Justice to Artistic Expression: Practices of Working with Trauma," we consider the very different approaches from justice and arts-based realms as methods to respond to and recover from trauma. In Chapter 11, Mina Rauschenbach, Stephan Parmentier and Maarten Van Craen focus on transitional justice measures, which constitute a significant postwar peacebuilding component but at the same time seem to be a major source of contestation between and within ethno-national groups. The authors argue that despite this, symbolic (local, nonjudicial) forms of transitional justice have potential for acknowledgment, recognition of violence and social reconstruction, provided that they are mutual and inclusive, and that they reflect the needs and experiences of the justice stakeholders for whom they were meant. In Chapter 12, "Taking Play Seriously," Kathryn Mansfield explores how confronting the "stuckness" of trauma in our body-minds enables us to face chronic violence even in the aftermath of trauma. She considers practices she introduced at the conference in Sarajevo as ways to explore how and why engaging the physical body in movement and play raises somatic awareness and generates creative pathways for transforming – rather than transferring – trauma. In the book's Conclusion, we highlight some of the concrete programmatic and policy findings from this volume and consider the implications of the collection of essays for postwar conflicts beyond Bosnia.

Conclusion

War traumatization in Bosnia and Herzegovina has had catastrophic, profound and long-lasting effects on its primary and secondary victims. Fischer (2006) stated that justice and healing are also part of the process of conflict transformation and reconciliation, emphasizing that this is a task that requires proactive engagement by political decision-makers and the whole Bosnian society. However, facing the past in a just and truthful way also requires dealing with one's own responsibility. Sadly, this is still avoided at governmental and parliamentary levels, whereas many victims are subject to political exploitation and manipulation.

Many conditions have inhibited the processes of recovery, peacebuilding and reconciliation in Bosnia and Herzegovina and have heightened the risk of secondary victimization for various groups. These conditions include stigmatizing attitudes; the underestimation of individual suffering; inappropriate societal and institutional responses to helping traumatized people; a lack of political will to recognize the collective dimension of war traumatization and accountability; untiring ethno-national rhetoric; homogenized narratives; the slow pace of criminal justice; a lack of a systematic, interdisciplinary approach to healing historical wounds; and poverty and structural violence.

While innumerable efforts have gone into peacebuilding in Bosnia and Herzegovina for more than two decades, recognition of unhealed trauma as well as the processes supporting recovery from trauma are sparse. For a country that survived the immense violence of four wars during the 20th century, there can be no question of the presence of trauma not only individually but as a collective. Yet for most residents, only the most extreme cases of PTSD are perceived as trauma – and even these cases have insufficient support. The everyday symptoms as well as the consequences of such an experience for thousands of individuals and for their communities are not widely understood and go generally unaddressed today. Addressing the psychological and psychosocial aspects of peace is, we suggest, crucial for transforming the cycle of violent conflict to a durable, inclusive peace.

Note

1 https://wagingnonviolence.org/feature/student-protest-blocks-ethnic-segregation-plan-bosnia-herzegovina-jajce/.

References

Andreas, Peter. 2009. "Symbiosis Between Peace Operations and Illicit Business in Bosnia." *International Peacekeeping* 16.1: 33–46.

Andreas, Peter. 2011. *Blue Helmets and Black Markets: The Business of Survival in the Siege of Sarajevo*. Ithaca, NY: Cornell University Press.

Bećirbašić, Belma. 2019. "Interview by Dženana Karup Druško. Intervju, Belma Bećirbašić: Šutnja o problematičnim tačkama prošlosti [Interview with Belma Bećirbašić: Silence About the Problematic Points of the Past]." Avantgarda.ba, 27 April. www.mreza-mira.net/vijesti/razno/sutnja-o-problematicnim-tackama-proslosti/.

Becirevic, Edina. 2014. *Genocide on the Drina River*. New Haven, CT: Yale University Press.

Belloni, Roberto. 2001. "Civil Society and Peacebuilding in Bosnia and Herzegovina." *Journal of Peace Research* 38.2: 163–180.

Berry, Marie E. 2017. "Barriers to Women's Progress After Atrocity: Evidence from Rwanda and Bosnia-Herzegovina." *Gender & Society* 31.6: 830–853.

Bertelsmann, Stiftung. 2018. *BTI Country Report–Bosnia and Herzegovina*. Gütersloh: Bertelsmann Stiftung.

Bringa, Tone. 1995. *Being Muslim the Bosnian Way: Identity and Community in a Central Bosnian Village*. Princeton, NJ: Princeton University Press.

Burg, Steven L., and Paul S. Shoup. 1999. *The War in Bosnia-Herzegovina: Ethnic Conflict and International Intervention*. Armonk, NY: M.E. Sharpe.

Delić, Amra, and Esmina Avdibegović. 2015. "Shame and Silence in the Aftermath of War Rape in Bosnia and Herzegovina: 22 Years Later." Paper presented at the Symposium Interdisciplinary Perspectives on Children Born of War – From World War II to Current Conflict Settings, 4–5 June, Hannover.

Fischer, Martina. 2006. *Peacebuilding and Civil Society in Bosnia-Herzegovina: Ten Years After Dayton*. Berlin: Lit Verlag.

Maček, Ivana. 2009. *Sarajevo Under Siege: Anthropology in Wartime*. Philadelphia: Penn State Press.

Medica Zenica and Medica Mondiale e.V., eds. 2014. "We Are Still Alive: We Have Been Harmed but We Are Brave and Strong. A Research on the Long-Term Consequences of War Rape and Coping Strategies of Survivors in Bosnia and Herzegovina. Summary." *Zenica & Cologne*. doi:10.15498/89451.1.

Merdzanovic, Adis. 2015. *Democracy by Decree: Prospects and Limits of Imposed Consociational Democracy in Bosnia and Herzegovina*. Hanover: Ibidem-Verlag.

Mojzes, Paul. 1994. *Yugoslavian Inferno: Ethnoreligious Warfare in the Balkans*. New York: Continuum.

Mooren, G.T.M. and R.J. Kleber. 2001. "The Impact of War in Bosnia and Herzegovina: Devastated Trust." *International Journal of Mental Health* 30.2: 6–21.

Pugh, Michael. 2005. "Transformation in the Political Economy of Bosnia Since Dayton." *International Peacekeeping* 12.3: 448–462.

Puljek-Shank, Amela, and Randy Puljek-Shank. 2008. "The Contribution of Trauma Healing to Peacebuilding in Southeast Europe." In *Peacebuilding in Traumatized Societies*, edited by Barry Hart, 155–183. Lanham, MD: University of America Press.

Ramet, Sabrina P. 2002. *Balkan Babel: The Disintegration of Yugoslavia from the Death of Tito to the Fall of Milosevic*. 4th ed. London: Westview Press.

Silber, Laura, and Allan Little. 1997. *Yugoslavia: Death of a Nation*. New York: Penguin Books.

Stiglmayer, Alexandra, ed. 1994. *Mass Rape: The War Against Women in Bosnia-Herzegovina*. Lincoln: University of Nebraska Press.

Toal, Gerard, and Carl T. Dahlman. 2011. *Bosnia Remade: Ethnic Cleansing and Its Reversal*. Oxford: Oxford University Press.

Tokača, Mirsad. 2013. *The Bosnian Book of the Dead*. Sarajevo and Belgrade: Research and Documentation Centre and the Humanitarian Law Center of Serbia.

TPO Foundation is the Transcultural Psychosocial Educational Foundation based in Sarajevo, Bosnia and Herzegovina.

United Nations Development Programme (UNDP). 2009. *The Ties That Bind: Social Capital in Bosnia and Herzegovina*. National Human Development Report. New York: United Nations Development Programme.

Van der Kolk, Bessel A. 2015. *The Body Keeps the Score: Brain, Mind and Body in the Healing of Trauma*. New York: Penguin.

Woodward, Susan L. 1995. *Balkan Tragedy: Chaos and Dissolution After the Cold War*. Washington, DC: Brookings Institution Press.

The World Bank in Bosnia & Herzegovina. 2017. "Overview: Country Context." Last updated 26 October. www.worldbank.org/en/country/bosniaandherzegovina/overview.

Part I

Incorporating trauma healing into peacebuilding practice

2 Fundamentals of trauma

Confronting the myths and widening the spectrum for peacebuilding

Nancy Good and Julianne Funk

The raging intensity of war trauma and the urgency of its healing are both generally underestimated. History demonstrates that trauma that is not transformed gets transferred; if the wounds of trauma are not guided toward a safe, healing path, it is likely that the unhealed traumas may contribute to ongoing cycles of violence and thwart peacebuilding efforts. What are we to do with the explosive, painful energy and the aftermath from years of war? Trauma does not suddenly evaporate on its own. We see patterns where victims become the aggressors as unhealed trauma is externalized against others, or even more frequently, is turned inward toward oneself or one's group (e.g., in self-loathing, depression or internalized oppression).

Trauma has come into ordinary parlance in the last decades. In the midst of prolonged conflict, natural disasters or more episodic violence, trauma is increasingly recognized across a myriad of disciplines. This accompanies a growing recognition of how racism, discrimination, oppression and factors like economic deprivation associated with these phenomena often inflict prolonged trauma upon marginalized communities. Research points to the role such oppressions play in instigating conflict and contributing to its recurrence.

There are many stories we tell about trauma – what it is and what it is not – some of which are that time heals all wounds and that if we just get on with things, we will "get over it." Providing a foundation for the ideas to follow in the volume, this chapter aims to expand our understanding of trauma. We wish herein to move from our idea that trauma is about a single traumatic event to the phenomenon of complex and cumulative trauma. Trauma is not only individual; it is collective as well. Rather than seeing trauma as primarily the stigmatized diagnosis of post-traumatic stress disorder (PTSD), there are varied degrees of traumatic stress on the trauma spectrum, all of which are legitimate. We must resist the blaming and silencing of victims as if they themselves are responsible for what they suffered; instead, we must ask survivors what happened to them and how the traumatic memory still lives on in their bodies and brains. By considering the less-known Post-Traumatic Growth (PTG), we move from the pain of trauma to finding the gift in trauma. Trauma can be destructive, but it can also build strength and resilience. The more we become trauma-informed and increase our understanding of trauma, the more capable we are of developing new insights for how individuals and communities can move into peace practices, healing and rebuilding after war.

When war ends with the signing of the peace treaties, we do not question the need to rebuild buildings and bridges. However, when it comes to addressing trauma, why do we still need to make the case that trauma healing should be integrated into peacebuilding? One explanation for this difference is the tangibility and visibility of physical reconstruction. We are not well trained to see the invisible, bio-psychosocial wounds of trauma, and therefore they may seem easy to ignore. Thankfully, neuroscience is helping us to actually see the damage done when the brain is stuck in the survival mode of unhealed trauma. As is the case with Bosnia and Herzegovina more than two decades after the war's end, the lack of a sustainable, vibrant peace can be traced to invisible and yet somehow very tangible obstacles in the hearts and minds of people that are rooted deeply in the body and brain functions affected and altered by the violence.

This chapter seeks to deepen our understanding of the trajectory of trauma practice and the critical need for its integration in peacebuilding efforts. It considers the amnesiac emergence of the trauma field as well as commonly held myths about trauma, pointing out where these fail to grasp the proven reality of this phenomenon. It then offers a holistic understanding of trauma according to the Four B Model (Good 2009) and emphasizes the important relationship between the complementary fields of trauma and conflict/peace research.

1. Evolution of the trauma field

The field of trauma studies has floundered significantly in its development because too often trauma fails to be recognized, named and therefore acknowledged. According to psychiatrist Judith Herman, "The study of psychological trauma has a curious history – one of episodic amnesia. Periods of active investigation have alternated with periods of oblivion" (Herman 1997, 7). Cases of human-inflicted atrocities are often silenced or forgotten. This silence sometimes removes even the certainty that a traumatic event even happened. It seems that trauma overwhelms the human being so completely that our systems for dealing with it can shut down. Indeed, "The ordinary response to atrocities is to banish them from our conscience" (Ibid., 1). In this way, we know the "central dialectic" in trauma studies is a "conflict between the will to deny horrible events and the will to proclaim them aloud" (Ibid.). This is evidenced in the field's evolution.

Trauma went unnamed in the Western world for most of history. Before PTSD developed as a clinical term in the 1980s, experiences of trauma had not been named explicitly but were well documented, albeit described almost exclusively from a clinical perspective and relating to the context of combat (Trimble 1985). In the late 19th century, women who suffered from "hysteria" exhibited symptoms such as those induced by "altered states of consciousness" which Freud and Breuer recognized as a result of psychological trauma (Herman 1997, 12). They and other scientists found that rediscovering and describing feelings and memories could be cathartic as a treatment, and thus modern psychotherapy emerged.

Many of the stories arising from "hysterical" women's psychological analysis with Freud were regarding "sexual assault, abuse, and incest" (Ibid., 13). Herman notes that Freud eventually gave up on his investigations of hysteria due to the implications of the "endemic" presence of such "perverted acts against children" within respectable society (Ibid., 14).

In the 20th century, during and just after World War I, British soldiers' symptoms of traumatic stress were named "shell shock," which facilitated combat veterans' access to treatment and a disability pension. But quickly thereafter, the term was almost erased when British and the German doctors instead decided to treat the condition as a character defect and prescribed punitive, painful treatments. Servicemen who succumbed to such sickness were judged to be undisciplined and untrained soldiers. During World War II and thereafter, terms like "war neuroses" and "battle fatigue" were given to the traumatic stress resulting from armed conflict. But the medical professionals kept returning to blaming the soldier's character as originally weak rather than to what the soldier experienced. The long periods of silence and denial in between these sporadic recognitions can be understood as suppression of a dangerous idea. As psychiatrist and post-traumatic stress expert Bessel van der Kolk explains regarding the standard German approach in World War II, "Apparently awareness of the devastating effects of war on soldiers' minds would have constituted a threat to the Nazis' plunge into another round of insanity" (van der Kolk 2014, 188–189).

In the 1980s, posttraumatic stress disorder (PTSD) was named and included in the American Psychiatric Association's Diagnostic and Statistical Manual of Mental Disorders (DSM-III) after many stories from Vietnam veterans.[1] From a historical perspective, the significant change with the naming of PTSD was the shift away from assigning blame to the suffering individual for having an inherent weakness. The change allowed seeing the cause as outside the individual, such as a traumatic event. However, once again in the early 1990s, there was a turn toward the denial of trauma when many scholarly articles referred to False Memory Syndrome, where individuals allegedly created elaborate false memories, for example of sexual abuse, which had supposedly lain dormant for many years before resurfacing, but those "memories" were actually planted there by a therapist or a feminist. We have seen that blaming the victim for being weak or for making up false memories is combined with a poor scientific understanding of (repressed) memory. It is interesting to note, however, that the 1980s diagnostic criteria for PTSD actually recognized memory loss as a symptom: "an inability to recall important personal information, usually of a traumatic or stressful nature, that is too extensive to be explained by normal forgetfulness" (Ibid., 192).

The 1990s were also critical for expanding trauma studies from PTSD to include PTG, and from primary, firsthand trauma to incorporate also secondary trauma as a result of being exposed to stories or evidence of trauma. The 1990s also included the further development of our understanding of traumatic memory as a "dual memory system" (Ibid., 196), recognizing the fundamental difference of traumatic memories from the "normal" stories we tell about the past: instead of a rational, clear and chronological story that can be integrated into one's autobiography, traumatic memories are dissociated, in that the sensations entering the brain at the time of the trauma are not properly assembled into a story (as seen in the Four B's of trauma, below). This new insight is changing how we consider and innovate our methods of response to and treatment of traumatic stress.

As the evolution of trauma unfolds, all who work with trauma after war face an urgent need to look at ways of integrating our progress and professions so as to expand upon our current understanding of trauma and continue to develop our methods and approaches for addressing it. We must continue to understand trauma beyond the PTSD diagnosis and dig deeper to understand how it works, how to alleviate its symptoms and even how to heal the damage using trauma-sensitive methods (see Zelizer 2008; Hamber, Gallagher and Ventevogel 2014).

2. Debunking the myths: what trauma is and is not

A. Trauma is not something to "just get over"[2]

Many think that after war, when the peace accords have been signed and weapons are put away, people should "just get over it" and return to normal life. This myth indicates an urge and wish for a quick fix or even magical thinking – "if I don't think about it, it just might go away." Yet the wounds of war have cut through the social and political fabric on all levels of society. A refugee during the 1990s Bosnian war who later returned home to rebuild and has been working on trauma healing for the past 15 years, Amela Puljek-Shank noted:

> You can make peace on the governmental level and think that our work is over but when 2 million people are displaced and traumatized? How can you make peace when trauma healing does not take place? How can we heal conflicts if we don't have any idea how to heal traumas? To create real peace, there needs to be recognition of the trauma and time for trauma healing to take place – at the national level as well as individual level.
>
> (Good Sider 2001)

Dealing with trauma requires more than a one-time solution. Trauma healing is a journey or a process that occurs on many levels, from individual to community to country. Additionally, trauma healing is not linear. Like the stages of grief, one does not follow a tidy progression from one stage to the next. Trauma healing, like trauma itself, is messy, confusing, intense and overwhelming. People often jump back and forth between phases, from being eager to move on to not able to quiet the nightmares to shutting down to finding something hopeful, and on and on. Others experience some healing but then find themselves locked in a web of desire for revenge, wanting someone to pay for the wrongs. The pain, violation or injustice of trauma is often so great that the survivor's main impulse – which can be trapped for months or years – is to strike back, wanting someone to pay for the pain. This is entirely normal. Survivors need to find their own answers to the question "Why move on?" if they want to exit the cycle of violence (Good Sider 2006).

In the aftermath of atrocities, survivors often feel the tension of a dialectic of silence, which denies the horrible event, and the will to shout the truth from the rooftops. Herman writes that the trauma is:

> [t]oo terrible to utter aloud: this is the meaning of the word unspeakable. . . . Atrocities, however, refuse to be buried. Equally as powerful as the desire to deny atrocities is the conviction that denial does not work. Folk wisdom is filled with ghosts who refuse to rest in their graves until their stories are told. Murder will out. Remembering and telling the truth about terrible events are prerequisites both for the restoration of the social order and for the healing of individual victims.
>
> (Herman 1997, 1)

Even with decades of amnesia, the brain and the body remember and gradually find ways to tell the story, even if it is repressed (Rothschild 2000; van der Kolk 2014; Scaer 2014; Herman 1997). The body will express the wound even through unconscious behaviors.

The hope that time will heal the pain, while widely held, is not realistic. Trauma does not simply melt away with time, because trauma changes us forever. Some speak of a "new normal" as a way of indicating that when there is so much wounding and breakage, one can never return to the way things were, even though that is just what so many long for. This book repeatedly considers the reality that people who have survived a traumatic event cannot forget it. Moreover, unhealed trauma can be transferred to later generations, and the cycle of violence may continue. Trauma or pain that is not transformed will be transferred.

B. Trauma is not a mental illness

Traumatized people are not mentally ill, as they are sometimes stigmatized or labeled. Additionally, having an experience of trauma does not mean that one has PTSD.[3] Correctly put, trauma is a normal, natural response to an abnormal, overwhelming incident. Trauma elicits biological "responses of catastrophe" in the body to facilitate survival in any situation that seriously threatens our lives or safety – real or perceived (Herman 1997, 33). In her seminal text on trauma and healing, Herman describes trauma as

> events [that] overwhelm the ordinary systems of care that give people a sense of control, connection, and meaning. . . . Traumatic events are extraordinary, not because they occur rarely, but rather because they overwhelm the ordinary human adaptations to life.
>
> (Ibid.)

Trauma involves a roller coaster ride of intense emotions and biological responses. Beyond a "mental condition," the wounds of war trauma disrupt our usual functioning and have consequences in all areas of the human experience across all four

"B's": Body, Brain, Beliefs and Behavior (Good 2009; see discussion later in the chapter). Symptoms range from flashbacks to irritability and sadness, and from memory loss to dissociative states, and are a means of avoiding engaging with situations that are reminiscent of the trauma event. Symptoms can be ignited from triggers in the survivor's environment such as smells, images or sounds and can be prolonged if a sense of safety is not regained.

When these biological approaches are considered in tandem with the historical evolution of the field, trauma may be better conceptualized as a spectrum rather than a static disordered condition. As such, psychologists and trauma practitioners prefer to distinguish between traumatic stress and the diagnostic term posttraumatic stress disorder, codified in the DSM-III by Western psychiatric professionals.[4] While the term PTSD has been exported globally through humanitarian responses, peacebuilding initiatives and international security interventions, there has been little consideration of cultural and social understandings of trauma, its identification, manifestation and ways of healing it. Uniform definitions and increasing familiarity with the idea of PTSD leads many to blanketly apply the term to experiences of traumatic stress, while (self-)ascribing the diagnosis of trauma to everyday experiences of distress. British psychiatrist Derek Summerfield (1999) critiques Western mental health labeling of trauma after war and provocatively asks if PTSD is an invented Western psychological condition; he questions Western professionals who arrive in war zones and import their diagnoses and cures, ignoring cultural traditions and social practices. This corresponds to peace scholar-practitioner John Paul Lederach's (1995) urge for peacebuilders to work from an elicitive approach rather than a prescriptive one.

The simplification of traumatic stress into one blanket condition of PTSD also misses the capacity of many to find resilience and effectively cope with traumatic stress despite trauma's debilitation. While exposure to a traumatic event elicits a stress response, the reactions externally in the person's sociocultural environment, as well as her or his internal resilience, determine the extent to which that stress becomes debilitating.

C. Trauma is not solely an individual experience

In addition to individual trauma, there is also collective trauma from large-scale violence, such as the three-and-a-half-year siege of Sarajevo or the siege and then mass murder of people in Srebrenica.

> We experienced four wars in the former Yugoslavia, between 1991 and 2000, each with different traumatic events. There were concentration camps and massacres. Many people were refugees. Some lived under siege for years. People risked being shot by snipers every time they went out to shop or go to work. When the war ended. . . [t]he trauma of survival shifted from running away from guns during the war to the present situation of not having enough money to feed the family and send children to school.
>
> (Puljek-Shank 2012)

The collective dynamic of trauma can also extend to cultural and historical trauma (Alexander 2004), in which an event is contextually interpreted and becomes socially embedded into the lived experience and identity of a group. As Siniša Malešević (2016a) provocatively claimed, there is no nationalism without collective traumatic images or narratives; nationalism requires enormous energy and resources to translate micro-level solidarity or experiences of personal trauma into authentic national identities. Trauma can, in this and other ways, be passed to subsequent generations, such that the children and grandchildren, who have not experienced a trauma firsthand, are also somehow stuck in behavior patterns they learned or epigenetically received from their ancestors.

In the context of war, whole communities are exposed to the disruption of violent trauma. War trauma shifts social dynamics, with traditional gender roles often altered. For example, when men assume combat roles, they leave other roles vacant, such as the role of the family provider. Women and other traditionally excluded persons then fill those roles. As former combatants reintegrate socially after war, tensions can arise over this altered structure where women are engaging in economic and political spheres and are reluctant to return to their formerly designated spaces. Coupled with exposure to and perpetration of violence and lacking or absent economic opportunities, intimate partner violence is more prevalent. This perpetuates a cycle of violence in family and society that has been documented as correlated to later violence (e.g., Bar-Tal 2003).[5] There is a growing field of epigenetic and other biological research focused on transgenerational transmission and effects of trauma. Informed by the experiences and reflections of Holocaust survivors' children and grandchildren, indigenous peoples in North America and Black American descendants of slaves, this field examines how exposure to trauma, prolonged or episodic, impacts societies and the mental and physical health of future generations (Jasienska 2009; Yehuda and Lehrner 2018).

D. Trauma is not exclusively negative

Because trauma is far from a pleasant experience, we tend to think of it as only negative. However there is a widening scope of scholarship acknowledging the constructive side of trauma, such as the research on resilience and Post-Traumatic Growth (PTG). In that research, a perplexing paradox of trauma is explored: in the midst of the deepest suffering can be found the seeds of hope and growth (Good Sider 2003, 2006). Although the phenomenon of adversity sparking positive change is far from a new development, it was not given much scientific attention until the 1990s when positive psychology showed an interest in studying the positive aspects of the human condition, not only with a focus on disease but also with attention paid to PTG alongside PTSD. The research developed further to consider how certain people not only bounce back from adversity (resilience) but even flourish as a result of it. Psychologists Tedeschi and Calhoun (1995, 2004) coined the term Post-Traumatic Growth as they encountered victims who not only survived but thrived after their experiences of trauma. These survivors have taught us how trauma can provide strength and how for some it can even be understood as a gift. Psychiatrist Frank Ochberg expresses the sentiments of many trauma survivors who differentiate themselves from being victims in his *Survivor Psalm*, which reads, in part: "I look forward with hope rather than despair. I may never forget, but I need not constantly remember. I was a victim, I am a survivor."[6]

Decades before PTG was coined, the Austrian psychiatrist and Holocaust survivor Viktor Frankl wrote about a similar "tragic optimism," how in the face of tragedy we can turn suffering into human achievement (1992, 139–154). After three years in World War II concentration camps, Frankl wrote in detail about how the camps conspired to make prisoners lose their hold on life. What remained was "the last of human freedoms" – the ability to "choose one's attitude in a given set of circumstances" (Ibid., 9). Frankl reminds us that this choice allows for the possibility of positive growth and making meaning even in the most tragic circumstances. Frankl used tragic optimism to explain that humans can say yes to life in spite of the "tragic triad" of pain, guilt and death. This optimism in the face of great loss "presupposes the human capacity to creatively turn life's negative aspects into something positive or constructive" (Ibid., 139), which, at its best, can turn suffering into human achievement and accomplishment, even creating an incentive to take responsible action (Ibid.).

Resilience is a related term that is often used interchangeably with PTG. Resilience is the ability to successfully navigate life's challenges and changes and to bounce back from traumatic events. There are at least two important facets to resilience: sustainability and recovery. Resilience does not mean that we will be *unchanged* by the challenges of life. It means that we will be able to respond to these events in ways that do not compromise our overall ability to survive and thrive. In a previous study (Good 2013), three movements were discovered for survivors who resile: bending, bouncing and connecting. Resilience signifies the capacity to process organizational and situational stressors in a way where we *bend* with the wind that threatens to break us down, *bounce* forward or back and *connect* with others in order to find a new or renewed space where we can rebuild and thrive. New developments and research about resilience in conflict and trauma have clear implications for using intervention strategies that uncover strengths, identify coping abilities and promote growth (Sampson, Abu-Nimer and Liebler 2003).

Making meaning out of the loss and terror is one such strategy. Talking about her own meaning making process after surviving war, Amela Puljek-Shank highlighted her power of choice:

> I began to see that I had a choice to remain in the inner circle of trauma (as victim) or move to the outer circle of trauma healing: a choice to heal rather than to hate and kill; a choice to possibly become a healthy individual again; a choice to take some steps to move back home after displacement – home to my spirit, my body, my homeland.
>
> (Good Sider 2001)

Grappling to find a reason to go on after trauma is a question that many survivors ask over and over again: "What is this trauma good for?" In working with survivors, researchers are finding that it is important to pay attention to the questions that we ask; in this case, to focus on both the devastation of trauma as well as its constructive results.

While those who survive can never return to "normal" (the way things used to be), what is certain is that the trauma experience will result in change that will almost always be a mixture of positive and negative aspects. Van der Kolk is also clear that "[t]rauma really does confront you with the best and the worst. You see the horrendous things that people do to each other, but you also see resiliency, the power of love, the power of caring" (2017). The negative aspects of post-traumatic change are post-traumatic deterioration and breakdown, as already discussed. By positive aspects of post-traumatic change, we mean the PTG experience of finding strength, opportunity and meaning in the midst of and following tragedy. Interviewing women after war trauma in Bosnia and Herzegovina and Rwanda, Marie E. Berry found women choosing to network and mobilize, entering the political process at many levels with a drive to make a positive difference (2018). Many trauma and crisis practitioners see trauma as both an occurrence of injury and also a juncture in which growth and opportunity are possibilities. In fact, many researchers indicate that resilience is the rule rather than the exception for those facing traumatic events (Echterling, Presbury and McKee 2005, 11; Good 2006). This book also includes contributions exploring this new and exciting field of learning how trauma can actually be positive.[7]

E. Trauma affects not only the primary (direct) survivors

Trauma does not only impact those who are directly exposed to a traumatic event. Known as secondary traumatic stress or vicarious trauma, we now know that those who research or listen to the trauma stories or see the disturbing images – such as caregivers, researchers, journalists, counselors, peacebuilders, humanitarian staff and even community members who witness trauma events – can experience similar symptoms as the primary survivors. The concept of vicarious and secondary trauma was introduced in the 1990s as therapists and caregivers were themselves experiencing trauma symptoms as a result of observing or hearing disturbing stories from the population they were serving. Through exposure to stories of abuse and the realities of people's intentional cruelty to one another, the trauma worker is vulnerable to "cumulative and permanent" effects of vicarious trauma (McCann and Pearlman 1990; Saakvitne and Pearlman 1996). In recognition of this, the DSM-V has been updated and concludes that PTSD can also be a secondhand experience, brought on vicariously through the witnessing or viewing of disturbing images of the trauma, usually in the course of professional duties.

Being (indirectly) exposed repeatedly to traumatic stories or images can cause similar traumatic stress responses in secondary actors. As a result, those who respond or live in the aftermath of war are themselves likely in need of trauma-informed processes. "The expectation that we can be immersed in suffering and loss daily and not be touched by it is as unrealistic as expecting to be able to walk through water without getting wet" (Remen 1996, 52). Alternative medicine specialist Rachel Remen goes further and emphasizes that caregivers suffer burnout and apathy not because they don't care. Similarly, trauma expert Charles Figley's "compassion fatigue" as a concept agrees that secondary traumatic stress is an occupational hazard, even a cost of caring, such that staff who get close to traumatic material should watch out that their hearts do not become so heavy with pain that there is no space left for life (Figley 1995, 15). "Common shock" is another term for witnessing secondary trauma. Kaethe Weingarten (2003) reminds us that we are all exposed to everyday violence: we see it on television, in news reports or in the neighborhood park. For professional caregivers, humanitarian aid workers and war researchers, this secondary exposure opens us to another layer. We listen to others' stories of traumatic pain, grief and despair, in the hope that our compassion and expertise can ease their suffering; yet caregivers are rarely informed or aware of the debilitating impact on themselves.

Another term, "the silencing response" (Baranowsky 2002) is used to describe the negative effects of chronic secondary traumatic stress and is described as the inability to listen to the stories of clients, finding their experiences and stories overwhelming. In other words, when caregivers are already emotionally overwhelmed, they may find ways to silence others' painful stories so that their client's pain does not add to the helper's own trauma. This serves as an effective form of self-protection in one sense, but in another, it directs the client to material that is less distressing and keeps the caregiver from being an effective helper. In contrast to the silencing response or building up walls to trauma exposure, Laura van Dernoot Lipsky (2009) describes trauma stewardship and offers numerous strategies to helpers for offsetting a martyr complex or survivor's guilt.

Forensic anthropologist Clea Koff provides a poignant description of her own embodied secondary trauma upon flying home from exhumation and identification work on mass graves in Rwanda:

> I looked up at the film playing on the movie screen several rows ahead of me. The film was *Get Shorty*, and I had no prior knowledge of the story. I saw a man standing up against a railing at night. Another man is facing him. The second man shoots the first, who falls backward over the railing to the ground. Even with no sound and no context I actually jumped in my seat. I immediately felt a sense of outrage. I kept thinking, "This isn't right . . . they shouldn't be allowed to show that!" I looked around the plane at my fellow passengers – surely they would share my outrage – but only saw people absorbed in their glossy magazines, wanting half-and-half instead of "just milk" for their coffee. Now these innocent people were aggravating me, and I didn't know why exactly. Then I started to cry – not because the scene startled me but because my reaction to it was involuntary. I didn't like feeling as though I couldn't control my body. . . . In fear of more disjunction, I curbed my tears and sat back in my seat, avoiding the movie screen and feeling like an outsider.
>
> (Koff 2005, 77)

Employers working with trauma-affected populations have a responsibility to address issues of vicarious trauma and secondary traumatic stress in their employees. The KonTerra Group, one consultancy company that has been establishing staff care services for the humanitarian aid world, recently offered this "duty of care" statement:

> All aid organizations have a moral and legal duty of care to ensure that risks to staff are identified and managed, and that all staff receive the support, resources, information and training they need to reduce the risks to which they are exposed.
>
> (Cripe 2016)

Too often managers are more concerned with productivity and ignore the ethical responsibility to prepare staff for deployment as well as provide psychological first aid support after critical incidents. The Essential Principles of Staff Care, published by The KonTerra Group, outlines principles and practices that help humanitarian personnel to establish staff care services (Cripe 2017).[8] The DART Center for Journalism and Trauma also provides resources for secondary trauma with manuals, research and practical tips for journalists and media staff.[9]

Similarly, the academic environment needs more awareness of secondary or vicarious trauma. After four years of academic research about missing and murdered indigenous women, Annita Lucchesi wrote pointedly about the all-encompassing toll of doing academic trauma research, which is:

> [w]ork that is trauma-heavy not only because it is saturated with stories of mass death, disappearance, rape, graphic violence, and grief, but because the process of doing the work and mobilizing it requires constant navigation of and attempts to heal my trauma, the trauma of families and communities, and the impacts of ongoing colonial genocide. Even when done with the utmost care and responsibility, it is exhausting. Gray hair, hair loss, sleepless nights, night terrors, flashbacks, anger, depression, nausea, chronic stress, I have seen and experienced it all.
>
> (2019, 1)

Naming the academic environment itself as toxic, silencing and even more isolating than the traumatic research itself, Lucchesi created a set of practices that she calls "spirit-based research" as an attempt to survive academia, aid in trauma healing and practice healthy self-care practices (Lucchesi 2019).

Secondary traumatic stress or vicarious trauma remains too often unacknowledged or unknown. Instead, we who work in the field of trauma hope that it may someday not only be recognized, but understood as a sign of compassion, not of weakness.

F. Trauma is not healed by forgiving and forgetting

What does it mean to forgive and heal after violence? When the rape event is past, how do victims find life even as the assault lives on in their bodies? How does a society reconstruct when a fundamental moral offense and physical harm has occurred, such as war crime? Too often, survivors are encouraged to "forgive and forget." This suggestion ignores the reality of the offense's continued, lived presence as a physical imprint upon the survivor's brain, mind and body by suggesting doing the impossible: seeking to forget it happened. Citing writer C.S. Lewis' words: "everyone says forgiveness is a lovely idea, until they have something to forgive," Amra Delić (2019) argues instead that forgiveness should be viewed as a process which includes a personal choice and a conscious will to forgive, understood within the act of naming the harm done from such severe offenses as well as the lasting consequences. There is nothing quick or simple about this process; it requires serious consideration of the damage done, which is far from pleasant or desirable as an activity. For this very reason there is a longing to forget, thereby avoiding the task. Furthermore, Delić notes that denying the atrocities of war crimes committed against women and the wider community delays the process of healing, restorative justice and forgiveness. Her research with Children Born of War (ChiBOW) studies the so-called "invisible children" born of war and offers some avenues for hope.[10] Thus, within programs of trauma healing, reconciliation and peacebuilding, practitioners should encourage the practice of acknowledging truth and the long-lasting harms suffered by victims of war rape, including children born out of rape (2015).

This reflects a paradox: in order to forget, we need to remember. John Paul Lederach (1997, 20) discusses several paradoxes similarly with reconciliation that recognize the need to redress the wrong while also holding the space for a common, interdependent future. We need to engage within our own communities as well as between our communities comparing narratives so as not to repeat the same cycle of violence in another 40 or 50 years, as is the common expectation in Bosnia and Herzegovina after three 20th century wars following this regular cycle. Any person or group who has been horribly wronged is required to ask the question, why forgive or NOT forget; why even think about it? The pain, violation or injustice is so great that the main impulse – which can stay for months and years – is revenge, balancing scores: to make "them" suffer as we did, so they will understand our pain. However, we find that the cycle of anger, revenge and hatred restricts life and we may discover that we become like the enemy. The bitterness seems to destroy oneself more than it affects the other.

Yet how to remember and tell the trauma story so as not to re-traumatize or spark another war is a challenge. In her book *Between Vengeance and Forgiveness*, Martha Minow (1998) considers lessons learned in a study of institutional responses to collective violence, genocide, apartheid and war: what should be taught, for example, to young people growing up in a world that has known violence? Would it be better to shield young people from the facts? The conclusion was that young people are better off learning about the horrors that have occurred at the hands of adults than they are if they do not learn about such events.

To forgive and forget is not realistic; instead, trauma requires creative healing and restorative responses. We must learn how to remember so that the trauma story is healed and the conflict transformed, such that moving on is a possibility.

The mission is to open up safe spaces to hear the trauma story, revise it and receive a fuller picture of the truth(s) of the trauma (listening to narratives "from us and them") so that we begin to hold these narratives differently and are thereby enabled to live into another story for the future.

G. *Trauma is not an isolated field but requires integration into building peace*

Trauma has thus far been described in its breadth of effect upon individuals and communities. In the past decade, a growing consensus is surfacing in two arenas: (1) that the healing of trauma cannot be done isolated in a therapy office and (2) trauma healing cannot be left out, unnamed and excluded from the peacebuilding table, which is the focus of this section. It is increasingly recognized that healing the wounds of war trauma requires a multifaceted, integrative, holistic approach over time to not only stop the violence but also establish sustainable peace and justice processes on many levels.

Already in the mid-1990s, the Center for Justice and Peacebuilding (CJP) at Eastern Mennonite University began integrating trauma studies with peacebuilding. After September 11, 2001, CJP developed the Strategies for Trauma Awareness and Resilience (STAR).[11] The basis for the trauma course from the outset used a trauma healing model, initially designed by Botcharova (2001), that showed the need for many disciplines (psychology, neuroscience, restorative justice, human rights, development, conflict transformation) to work together for healing and reconciliation to occur after war.

Lederach has, relatedly, argued that a successful peacebuilding strategy must be multilevel and integrated in order to reach all components of society and not just focus on high-level political actors. Lederach cautions against a short-term focus on crisis management, since it fails "to appreciate the multiplicity and interdependence of peacebuilding roles and activities" (1997, 73), and instead uses a pyramid of three different but related processes. The first process is top-down leadership conducted by a few representative and usually highly visible leaders. The second is bottom-up approaches (grassroots leadership) that involve the encouragement of understanding and peace at local levels according to the unique characteristics of those local settings. The third is middle-out approaches that can support the other two in unique ways and that often provide linkages vertically in the society and horizontally across the lines of conflict (Ibid., 39). Lederach also uses an integrative framework for peacebuilding which is helpful to use in order to see the various time frames and dimensions of peacebuilding (Ibid., 80; Lederach 2011).

Some peace practitioners have adopted similar models. For example, Paula Gutlove and members of the Harvard-based Balkans Peace Project undertook an integrative program of training middle-level leaders across the former Yugoslavia between 1997 and 2003. This project, called Health Bridges for Peace, used an action approach of individual healing integrated with the social healing of the community. One of Health Bridges's guiding principles states: "Trauma does not happen in a social vacuum, nor does it heal apart from ongoing social processes. Trauma healing needs to be integrated into the community" (Gutlove 2009). As such, peacebuilding processes need to incorporate holistic and integrative approaches such as restorative justice, conflict transformation, psychosocial trauma healing and development.[12]

In another case, having survived a violent shooting of 25 people, including eight of his students, Burundian David Niyonzima has come to believe that peace is not possible without trauma healing, As he was working on trauma and forgiveness, he realized that: "the seeds of tomorrow's wars grow in the soil of today's unhealed traumas; the seeds of tomorrow's peace grow in the soil of today's healing and reconciliation" (Duncan 2015). He therefore founded the Trauma Healing and Reconciliation Services (THARS) in Burundi in 1998 to take a holistic approach to building peace after violence and war in his country.

Whether you call it "trauma-sensitive peacebuilding" or "trauma awareness and transformation" or "trauma-informed peacebuilding practices," it is evident that trauma healing needs to have a primary place in building peace after war trauma (Zelizer 2008; Hamber, Gallagher and Ventevogel 2014; Bubenzer and Tankink 2015; Zehr 2009). Some assert that peacebuilding is the larger umbrella that holds all these fields together (Schirch 2004) and many agree that these fields need to have more dialogue (Zehr 2008, 2009). Prompted by a series of papers that questioned how mental-health professionals focused on the individual and neglected the wounds of the larger society, it became clear that dialogue and debate were needed for healing on all levels of society (Hamber, Gallagher and Ventevogel 2014; Hamber and Gallagher 2015). Following up on this challenge, the War Trauma Foundation and the Institute for Justice and Reconciliation have initiated several conferences that examine programs integrating mental-health and psychosocial support and peacebuilding (Bubenzer and Tankink 2015, 2017). Similarly, the TPO Foundation's conference of 2016 sought to find the links between these too-often separate endeavours. The task remains one for both scholars and practitioners to understand and implement well.

3. Understanding trauma holistically

As the trauma field developed in the 1990s, many trauma practitioners discussed how the body and the mind were injured and negatively affected by trauma, so the body and brain aspects are well studied. Trauma's imprint on the body can be seen in the impairment of physical health, correlated with symptoms such as heart disease, addiction, obesity, diabetes and autoimmune issues. In the brain, trauma impairs memory, concentration and the ability to learn new things; it disrupts our ability to discern what is safe and unsafe and limits our ability to regulate emotions. However, understanding the more holistic impact of trauma – including on an individual's beliefs and behavior – has received less attention. In my earlier work (Good 2009), I developed the Four B Model to capture how trauma deeply affects individuals and communities spiritually and socially as well as physically and mentally:

Body (physical)	**Brain (mental/emotional)**
Headaches/somatic pain	Hyperactive/numbed out/emotional imbalance
Tense muscles; exhaustion	Confusion; poor concentration/ruminating
Panic attacks; eating disturbed	Flashbacks/nightmares/intrusive thoughts
Behavior (social)	**Beliefs (spiritual)**
Isolated/cut off	Apathy/hopelessness/helpless
Blaming others narrative	Cynicism/sarcasm
Us/them; projection	Doubting your sense of meaning and what is safe

In addition to trauma's impact on our bodies and brains, trauma profoundly shapes the spiritual sphere of beliefs; it affects our ability to hope, our values and our beliefs about ourselves (e.g., self-confidence) and others. And in the social realm of behavior, trauma damages our ability to trust, to form strong relationships and communicate well. The Four B Model reinforces the idea that trauma is more than a disease or mental breakdown phenomenon. Van der Kolk's psychiatric and neurological research proved that trauma is more than a past event, but rather "the imprint left by that experience on the mind, brain, and body . . . with ongoing consequences for how the human organism manages to survive in the present" (2014, 21).

Body: We know from personal experience the somatic aspect of traumatic stress, such as how one's stomach can be tied in knots, the feeling of gut-wrench, a lump in one's throat or heartbreak. This is not merely figurative language but reflects where and how one experiences the situation in the physique. In the situation of severe threat, the brain and body react from the most basic instincts, releasing stress hormones into the body so it can defend itself against the danger. However, the situation may lead to trauma when the body is overwhelmed and incapable of responding as it wishes, such as when it is immobilized in a state of fear and cannot physically complete the act required for survival – to rid itself of that danger and the connected fear. This incomplete cycle, psychologist Peter Levine (1997, 2010) says, is why the stress hormones remain active even after the danger has passed and the body remains in freeze mode, unable to return to its normal state of rest. Even when we work hard to not show the pain externally or we numb the pain somehow, the body still carries the unprocessed, "frozen" memories. Levine talks about the somatic (bodily) experience of trauma; the fight–flight–freeze response is the body protecting itself by defending (fight), running away (flight) or being scared stiff/laying still (freeze) (Levine 1997).

Brain: The most recent research in the area of neuroscience is currently exploring how trauma physically changes the brain's function as well as structure (see van der Kolk 2014). When trauma occurs, the "emotional brain" – the brainstem and limbic system – is active while our "rational brain" shuts down and goes offline. Only the most essential functions are engaged so as to allow the body to more effectively respond to the threat. Biologically, the body enters into an emergency response state, releasing hormones to prepare the body for fight or flight. The emotional brain functions to keep us alive and well, sensing danger and opportunity and responding with hormones that act on our bodies without our rational brain's engagement. In a situation of threat, the limbic system provides the helpful fight-or-flight response that keeps us alive, while the brainstem, the most fundamental part of our brains, produces the "freeze" response if the previous survival response is inadequate.

The rational brain, on the other hand, in the prefrontal neocortex – the center of language, intellect, meaning, imagination, decision-making and creativity – is inactive, cut off in such a situation. This makes speaking about and making meaning out of a truly traumatic event nearly impossible, as it is not remembered in these parts of the brain. However, if the survivor is able to speak of the trauma, her or his brain may move from being overwhelmed into a constructive process of making some sense out of what happened. In so doing, the survivor may ideally engage the full brain by reactivating and reconnecting the rational meaning-making neocortex, rather than only the reactive limbic brain. This allows the brain to consider how to rebuild, restore, re-engage and focus on the present and future rather than being trapped or frozen in the past.

Beliefs: Broken trust, bruised hope and fractured purpose for living are examples of beliefs dramatically devastated by trauma. Since devastated beliefs, such as trust, are an example of the deep invisible wounds of war, it is important to give examples of how these hidden wounds show themselves and to remember that even invisible wounds need healing. Psychologist Marta Cullberg Weston observed that "existential crisis and a loss of trust in humanity" was observed in Bosnian women as they told stories of wartime betrayal by former neighbors and friends (Cullberg Weston 2001, 6):

> The people with whom one had watched soccer games, the people who had been guests in one's house, were suddenly burning your house, shooting at you, or serving as your camp guards. People they never dreamed would turn on them did.
>
> (Ibid.)

Psychiatrist Weine (1999) interviewed many survivors in Bosnia and Herzegovina, trying to piece together memories of what had been a multiethnic society but turned into a "living nightmare." During the war, people were individually and collectively insulted and humiliated, which one of Weine's informants claimed as violence to one's dignity and worth, something that seems to remain. Weine explains, "The ethnic cleansing struck them at the heart of who they were, individually and as a people" (Ibid., 74). Another of Weine's informants asserted "I feel like I have no value compared to what I had before. Like I'm not worth anything . . . like now I am nothing" (Ibid.).

Behavior: The last of the Four B's shows up in our social relationships with others as well as ourselves where trust is broken and social interactions are disrupted.

The Peacebuilding Initiative reminds us that "societies caught up in long-term violent conflict can also undergo serious changes as a result of long-term exposure to violence."[13] Such changes have been noted by residents of Bosnia and Herzegovina after the war – an increase in violent behavior in the home, in schools, and in youth in general (who themselves did not experience the war firsthand). The war's reinforcement of group identities and victimization as a result of ethnically targeted violence also produced visible markers of nationalism in the form of dress, social practices and language. Funk's (2012) research on this theme in Bosnia and Herzegovina highlighted the ubiquitous splitting of time into "before" and "after" the war in common speech and reference, as if these were different lives and realities.

Since trauma affects our bodies, brains, beliefs and behaviors, it requires a holistic approach for transformation. This approach should be individual as well as communal; it should encompass a range of modalities that all aim to dislodge the traumatic response that can become embedded in our entire lives.

4. Conclusion

The scars of postwar trauma can be deep. In Bosnia and Herzegovina they are related not only to the loss of life and trust in neighbors and friends but also to the feeling of helplessness, hunger, lack of motivation for change, the strengthening of nationalism, a permanent threat of renewed armed conflict and all variety of exploitation by political elites to consolidate their positions and serve their interests. In order to heal this trauma and address the symptoms, practitioners and policymakers must abandon antiquated notions that trauma is a mental illness or an individual experience only and instead build peace processes that wholly integrate trauma-informed approaches at all levels of society. This requires a holistic approach about this phenomenon, which considers the multiple dimensions in which trauma survivors' experiences impact persons, brains and behavior and survivors' needs for healthy beliefs of restored safety and a trustworthy environment, in addition to empowered behavior that can even be cooperative.

We know that pain and loss are experienced on all sides of armed conflicts and require recognition and treatment. However, transferring suffering into an identity of victimization on behalf of the group can also be an obstacle to collective healing and can enhance the risk of further conflict. In order to open a process of "recovery" or "de-traumatization" toward a more just, peaceful and stable society, the society must first recognize the presence of its trauma. A social environment is needed that positively confirms the authenticity of individual victims' trauma(s) as well as the credibility of the traumatic narratives of groups, known as collective trauma. This book advances our understanding of how to promote such social environments in Bosnia and Herzegovina and beyond, from art-based interventions to symbolic forms of transitional justice. As is evidenced throughout this book, putting trauma-informed peacebuilding at the heart of our work to rebuild and recover can lead to more sustainable and holistic transformations.

Notes

1 Although updated editions follow, the 1980 Diagnostic and Statistical Manual III was the first DSM to include PTSD in its lexicon of psychiatric disorders (American Psychiatric Association. 1980. *Diagnostic and Statistical Manual of Mental Disorders* [*DSM*]. 3rd ed. Washington, DC: American Psychiatric Association).
2 Alma Jeftić discusses in her chapter the way that memory and retelling of narratives related to conflict and traumatic experiences differ within cultures and ethnic groups, particularly related to the role the group played – aggressor or victim – within the event.
3 In his chapter in this volume, Barry Hart expands upon the effects of traumatic stress contrasted with PTSD.
4 The DSM is the clinical resource produced by the American Psychiatric Association and utilized by all mental health professionals in the United States to make diagnoses.
5 Kristina Hook discusses the social effects of trauma and its transmission across generations in her chapter in this volume.
6 Ochbery, Frank, The Survivor Psalm, www.journey-through-grief.com/survivor-psalm.html. See also Spahić Šiljak's chapter in this volume.
7 See the chapters in this volume by Spahić Šiljak, Berry and Smith.
8 The KonTerra Group, InsideNGO, DisasterReady.org 2017.
9 dartcenter.org.
10 See the research of Children Born of War (CHiBOW) at https://www.chibow.org/research; also one platform, "In the Name of the Father" which shows some CHiBOW stories, breaking the silence in a documentary/theater/dance production.
11 See STAR as discussed in Mansfield's chapter in this volume.
12 See Hook's and Hart's chapters in this volume as well as the STAR model in Mansfield's chapter.
13 Peacebuilding Initiative. 2009. "Trauma, Mental Health and Psycho-social Well-being: Psycho-social Well-being & Peacebuilding Processes," International Association for Humanitarian Policy and Conflict Resolution, www.peacebuildinginitiative.org/index4a66.html?pageId=2045.

References

Alexander, Jeffrey C. 2004. "Toward a Theory of Cultural Trauma." In *Cultural Trauma and Collective Identity*, edited by Jeffrey C. Alexander, Ron Eyerman, Bernard Giesen, Neil J. Smelser, and Piotr Sztompka, 1–30. Berkeley: University of California Press.

Baranowsky, Anna. 2002. "The Silencing Response in Clinical Practice: On the Road to Dialogue." In *Treating Compassion Fatigue*, edited by Charles R. Figley, 155–170. New York: Brunner-Routledge.

Bar-Tal, Daniel. 2003. "Collective Memory of Physical Violence: Its Contribution to the Culture of Violence." In *The Role of Memory in Ethnic Conflict*, edited by Ed Cairns and Mícheál D. Roe, 77–93. London: Palgrave MacMillan.

Berry, Marie E. 2018. *War, Women, & Power: From Violence to Mobilization in Rwanda and Bosnia-Herzegovina*. New York, Cambridge University Press.

Botcharova, Olga. 2001. "Implementation of Track Two Diplomacy: Developing a Model of Forgiveness." In *Forgiveness and Reconciliation*, edited by Raymond G. Helmick and Rodney L. Petersen, 278–304. Philadelphia: Templeton Foundation Press.

Bubenzer, Frederike, and Marian Tankink. 2015. "Healing Communities, Transforming Society: Exploring the Interconnectedness Between Psychosocial Needs, Practice and Peacebuilding." www.ijr.org.za/home/wp-content/uploads/2016/11/IJR-Healing-communities-conference-WEB.pdf.

Bubenzer, Friederike, and Marian Tankink. 2017. "Introduction to Special Issue: Linking Mental Health and Psychosocial Support to Peacebuilding in an Integrated Way." *Intervention* 15.3: 192–198.

Cripe, Lynne. 2016. "Risk, Duty of Care, and the NGO Mission." The KonTerra Group. www.konterragroup.net/risk-duty-care-ngo-mission/.

Cripe, Lynne. 2017. "The Essential Principles of Staff Care." The KonTerra Group, InsideNGO, DisasterReady.org. www.konterragroup.net/essential-principles-of-staff-care-new-resource/.

Cullberg Weston, Marta. 2001. *A Psycho Social Model of Healing from the Traumas of Ethnic Cleansing: The Case of Bosnia*. Stockholm: The Kvinna till Kvinna Foundation.

Delić, Amra. 2019. "The Long-Term Experiences and Psychosocial Wellbeing of Children Born of War in Bosnia and Herzegovina." Doctoral dissertation, University of Greifswald, Germany.

Delić, Amra, and Esmina Avdibegović. 2015. "Shame and Silence in the Aftermath of War Rape in Bosnia and Herzegovina: 22 Years Later." In *Interdisciplinary Perspectives on Children Born of War – From World War II to Current Conflict Settings*, edited by Heide Glaesmer, Sabine Lee, and Philipp Kuwert. http://medpsy.uniklinikum-leipzig.de/medpsych.site,postext,rueckblick,a_id,1412.html.

Duncan, Ella. 2015. "How Might We Heal Trauma Healing? Lessons from Burundi." Search for Common Ground. www.techchange.org/2015/11/25/measure-trauma-healing-burundi/.

Echterling, Lennis G., Jack H. Presbury, and J. Edson McKee. 2005. *Crisis Intervention: Promoting Resilience and Resolution in Troubled Times*. Upper Saddle River, NJ: Pearson Prentice Hall.

Figley, Charles. 1995. *Compassion Fatigue: Coping with Secondary Traumatic Stress Disorder in Those Who Treat the Traumatized*. Florence, KY: Brunner/Mazel Psychosocial Stress Series.

Frankl, Viktor. 1992. *Man's Search for Meaning: An Introduction to Logotherapy*. Boston: Beacon Press.

Funk Deckard, Julianne. 2012. "'Invisible' Believers for Peace: Religion and Peacebuilding in Postwar Bosnia & Herzegovina." Doctoral dissertation, KU Leuven, Belgium.

Good, Nancy. 2009. "The 4 Bs in Traumatic Stress and Resilience: Body, Brain, Beliefs, Behavior." Workshop material used in traumatic stress workshops, The KonTerra Group, Washington, DC.

Good, Nancy. 2013. "Trauma, What Is It Good for?" The Knowledge Library, The KonTerra Group. www.konterragroup.net/trauma-what-is-it-good-for/.

Good Sider, Nancy. 2001. "At the Fork in the Road: Trauma Healing." *Conciliation Quarterly*, Spring. www.journeytowardforgiveness.com/mapping/article1.asp.

Good Sider, Nancy. 2003. "Transcendence: Discovering Resources for Posttraumatic Healing and Growth." In *Positive Approaches to Peacebuilding: A Resource for Innovators*, edited by Cynthia Sampson, Mohammed Abu-Nimer, and Claudia Liebler. Chagrin Falls, OH: Pact Publications.

Good Sider, Nancy. 2006. "Peacebuilders Healing Trauma: The Journey from Victim to Survivor to Provider." Doctoral dissertation, The Union Institute and University, Cincinnati, OH.

Gutlove, Paula. 2009. "Health Bridges for Peace: The Medical Network for Social Reconstruction in the Former Yugoslavia." In *Building Peace: Practical Reflections from the Field*, edited by Craig Zelizer and Robert A. Rubinstein. Sterling, VA: Kumarian Press.

Hamber, Brandon, and Elizabeth Gallagher, eds. 2015. *Psychosocial Perspectives on Peacebuilding*. New York: Springer.

Hamber, Brandon, Elizabeth Gallagher, and Peter Ventevogel. 2014. "Narrowing the Gap Between Psychosocial Practice, Peacebuilding and Wider Social Change." *Intervention* 12.1: 7–15.

Herman, Judith. 1997. *Trauma and Recovery: The Aftermath of Violence – From Domestic Abuse to Political Terror*. New York: Basic Books.

Jasienska, Grazyna. 2009. "Low Birth Weight of Contemporary African Americans: An Intergenerational Effect of Slavery?" *American Journal of Human Biology: The Official Journal of the Human Biology Council* 21: 16–24.

Koff, Clea. 2005. *The Bone Woman*. New York: Random House Trade Paperbacks.

Lederach, John Paul. 1995. *Preparing for Peace: Conflict Transformation Across Cultures*. New York: Syracuse University Press.

Lederach, John Paul. 1997. *Building Peace: Sustainable Reconciliation in Divided Societies*. Washington, DC: U.S. Institute of Peace.

Lederach, John Paul, Reina Neufeldt, and Hal Culbertson. 2011. *Reflective Peacebuilding: A Planning, Monitoring, and Evaluation Learning Toolkit*. Baltimore: Catholic Relief Services.

Levine, Peter A. 2010. *In an Unspoken Voice: How the Body Releases Trauma and Restores Goodness*. Berkeley: North Atlantic Books.

Levine, Peter A., and Ann Frederick. 1997. *Waking the Tiger – Healing Trauma: The Innate Capacity to Transform Overwhelming Experiences*. Berkeley: North Atlantic Books.

Lucchesi, Annita Hetoevėhotohke'e. 2019. "Spirit-Based Research: A Tactic for Surviving Trauma in Decolonizing Research." *Journal of Indigenous Research* 7.1. https://digitalcommons.usu.edu/kicjir/vol7/iss1/4.

Malešević, Siniša. 2016a. "Nationalism, Collective Trauma and Historical Sociology." Keynote Speech Given at the Conference Trauma, Memory and Healing in the Balkans and Beyond, Sarajevo, 12–14 July.

Malešević, Siniša. 2016b. "Ethnic Conflict and War Crimes in the Balkans: The Narratives of Denial in Post-Conflict Serbia." *Nationalities Papers* 44.1: 185–187.

McCann, Lisa, and Laurie A. Pearlman. 1990. "Vicarious Traumatization: A Framework for Understanding the Psychological Effects of Working with Victims." *Journal of Traumatic Stress* 3.1: 131–149.

Minow, Martha. 1998. *Between Vengeance and Forgiveness: Facing History After Genocide and Mass Violence*. Boston: Beacon Press.

Puljek-Shank, Amela. 2012. "Healing and Resiliency in a Post-War Setting." *Peacebuilder*, 30 May. http://emu.edu/now/peacebuilder/2012/05/healing-and-resiliency-in-a-post-war-setting/.

Remen, Rachel Naomi. 1996. *Kitchen Table Wisdom: Stories That Heal*. New York: Penguin.

Rothschild, Babette. 2000. *The Body Remembers: The Psychophysiology of Trauma and Trauma Treatment*. New York: W.W. Norton & Company.

Saakvitne, Karen, and Laurie Anne Pearlman. 1996. *Transforming the Pain: A Workbook on Vicarious Traumatization*. New York: W.W. Norton & Company.

Sampson, Cynthia, Mohammed Abu-Nimer, and Claudia Liebler, eds. 2003. *Positive Approaches to Peacebuilding: A Resource for Innovators*. Chagrin Falls, OH: Pact Publications, 287–313.

Scaer, Robert. 2014. *The Body Bears the Burden: Trauma, Dissociation, and Disease*. 3rd ed. New York: Routledge.

Schirch, Lisa. 2004. *The Little Book of Strategic Peacebuilding*. Intercourse, PA: Good Books.

Summerfield, Derek. 1999. "A Critique of Seven Assumptions Behind Psychological Trauma Programmes in War-Affected Areas." *Social Science & Medicine* 48: 1449–1462.

Tedeschi, Richard G., and Lawrence G. Calhoun. 1995. *Trauma and Transformation: Growing in the Aftermath of Suffering*. Thousand Oaks, CA: Sage.

Tedeschi, Richard G., and Lawrence G. Calhoun. 2004. "Posttraumatic Growth: Conceptual Foundations and Empirical Evidence." *Psychological Inquiry* 15.1: 1–18.

Trimble, M.D. 1985. "Post-Traumatic Stress Disorder: History of a Concept." In *Trauma and Its Wake: The Study and Treatment of Post-Traumatic Stress Disorder*, edited by Charles Figley, 5–14. New York: Brunner/Mazel.

van der Kolk, Bessel. 2014. *The Body Keeps the Score: Mind, Brain and Body in the Healing of Trauma*. New York: Penguin.

van der Kolk, Bessel. 2017. "Bessel van der Kolk: How Trauma Lodges in the Body." On Being with Krista Tippett Podcast. www.onbeing.org/programs/bessel-van-der-kolk-how-trauma-lodges-in-the-body/.

Van Dernoot Lipsky, Laura. 2009. *Trauma Stewardship: An Everyday Guide to Caring for Self While Caring for Others*. San Francisco: Berrett-Koehler.

Weine, Stevan. 1999. *When History Is a Nightmare: Lives and Memories of Ethnic Cleansing in Bosnia-Herzegovina*. Piscataway, NJ: Rutgers University Press.

Weingarten, Kaethe. 2003. *Common Shock: Witnessing Violence Every Day – How We Are Harmed, How We Can Heal*. New York: Dutton Adult.

Yehuda, Rachel, and Amy Lehrner. 2018. "Intergenerational Transmission of Trauma Effects: Putative Role of Epigenetic Mechanisms." *World Psychiatry* 17: 243–257.

Zehr, Howard. 2008. "Doing Justice, Healing Trauma – The Role of Restorative Justice in Peacebuilding Peace Prints." *South Asian Journal of Peacebuilding* 1.1. www.academia.edu/2335779/Doing_Justice_Healing_Trauma_The_Role_of_Restorative_Justice_in_Peacebuilding.

Zehr, Howard. 2009. "Intersection of Restorative Justice with Trauma Healing, Conflict Transformation and Peacebuilding." *Journal for Peace and Justice Studies* 18.1–2: 20–30.

Zelizer, Craig. 2008. "Trauma Sensitive Peace-Building: Lessons for Theory and Practice." *Africa Peace and Conflict Journal* 1.1: 81–94.

3 Holistic healing

A case for integrating trauma recovery and peacebuilding

Kristina Hook

Introduction

In the aftermath of large-scale disasters, either human-made (e.g., war, genocide) or natural (e.g., earthquakes, tsunamis), a growing cadre of clinicians, practitioners and scholars from diverse disciplinary backgrounds increasingly gather around the central shared topic of *trauma*. While definitions and professional goals remain disparate, points of agreement have emerged as these actors have attempted to understand how extreme events fracture societies and individuals. With specific reference to scholarly research on violence, recognition appears to be growing (even across disciplinary spheres) that violence impacts both bodies *and* minds and that it leaves ineffable scars after degrees of healing occur (Kirmayer, Lemelson and Barad 2007). Unfortunately, complex humanitarian emergencies, wars and armed conflicts also usher in a myriad of societal rebuilding challenges, often pushing individual and collective trauma issues to the margins of policy priorities. This chapter combines principles from the field of peace and conflict studies with anthropological perspectives to illustrate the dangers of doing so.

First, this chapter frames a holistic view of trauma by discussing established literature, with a particular focus on integrative approaches to the study of this phenomenon. As the number of integrated investigations – i.e., those drawing on and combining interdisciplinary approaches – into traumatology has increased, a multifaceted portrait is emerging of trauma experiences and expressions. This chapter focuses on sociocultural and biological anthropological findings, which jointly establish the societal and physical effects of trauma over multiple generations. Drawing from this body of research, this chapter notes the far-reaching impacts of large-scale trauma in the wake of mass violence, including biological, mental and social ramifications. This combination of consequences indicates that holistic efforts that target minds, bodies and spirits and that promote effective healing practices are essential.

Integrated trauma recovery programs that utilize holistic approaches prove challenging to establish, particularly in overburdened humanitarian contexts. I establish the justification for such an argument by incorporating cross-cultural conflict recovery and recurrence research, thus framing trauma healing issues in Bosnia and Herzegovina within broader conversations of the subject. In turn,

I discuss the impact of unaddressed trauma on three key areas that are important for long-term societal stability: (1) economic spending and decision-making; (2) conflict and violence recurrence; and (3) political and institutional vulnerabilities. Taken as a whole, this chapter aims to expand justifications for and to stress the urgency of trauma interventions in peacebuilding contexts by establishing how these efforts enable populations to move forward toward a spectrum of physical and mental well-being, how trauma has intergenerational societal and physical impacts and how trauma interventions may ultimately mitigate future conflict risks. Ultimately, this chapter underscores the urgency of linking trauma healing and peacebuilding efforts in the Western Balkans and beyond.

Toward a holistic view of trauma

A snapshot of existing integrative research on trauma

Partnerships across academic disciplines and across scholarly and practitioner divides appear to be increasing around the subject of trauma. Describing the full richness of this emerging interdisciplinary literature is beyond the scope of this chapter, but a few particularly illustrative examples are worth presenting here. In grasping the breadth of academic analyses on trauma and related subjects, Figley's sweeping *Encyclopedia of Trauma: An Interdisciplinary Guide* demonstrates the results of greater multidisciplinary participation on a topic that began as a narrow specialty associated with emergency medical practices (2012). This work also exemplifies the explosive growth in interest on a variety of trauma-related subtopics, listed literally from *A* (agriculture) to *Z* (Zen) in Figley's volume. By drawing together such a diverse array of trauma-related subtopics, Figley's edited volume is intended to push for a more holistic view of *traumatology* (i.e., the study of trauma, its impacts and intervention efforts) that considers the phenomenon from all possible angles. Figley's encyclopedia draws heavily from the work of psychiatrist Paul Valent, a child of Holocaust survivors (see also Valent 1998), to distinguish between trauma as *cause* and stress as a *response*. Valent's foundational work provides several important conceptual parameters for understanding trauma, which structure Figley's approach. Valent notes that *trauma* should metaphorically be understood as distinct from *stress* in the same way that injuries like strains are distinct from bone fractures. He explains that while stressors can be resolved and prior equilibriums can be restored, trauma irretrievably disrupts life-enhancing balances. In other words, mechanisms that a person previously relied on for coping become irreversibly interrupted. In Valent's conception, trauma is therefore "the area between where attempts to restore life-enhancing equilibria have failed, and death. It is the area of struggle, compromise, and creation of ways of finding new balances and healing" (Figley 2012, xxvii). However, given the prior interruption and the metamorphosis in coping strategies that occurs, these new dynamics take place in entirely different contexts and narratives.

Scientific breakthroughs in biological research and closely related fields help explain the growth of interest in trauma and related research clusters, such as posttraumatic stress disorders and mental health in humanitarian crises. In the 1970s, Ader and Cohen pushed forward earlier ideas of psychoimmunology (see Solomon and Moos 1964) to coin the term "psychoneuroimmunology," an interdisciplinary approach that examines the interaction between the body's immune and nervous systems as they interact with psychological processes (Ader and Cohen 1975; see also Segerstrom 2012). This research, which draws from fields including neuroscience, immunology, psychology, psychiatry, behavioral medicine, genetics and other closely related disciplines, has produced a variety of experimental ways to measure the complexity of the relationship between stress and illness, such as biomarker diagnostic tools that rely on relatively easy tools such as saliva tests. Increased attention to the biophysical ramifications of stress marks a shift in the study of a topic once confined primarily to the realm of the mind. A myriad of disciplines, including psychology, anthropology (particularly biological and medical anthropology) and the medical fields are now actively exploring trauma-related research questions, indicating a growing sense of research promise. Figley and Nash similarly note a contemporary emphasis on psychopathology and on topics of "growth" and "resiliency" as formalized diagnoses of posttraumatic stress disorder (PTSD) increased (2007).

Broadly speaking, attempts to weave together disparate biological, clinical, sociocultural and historical research on trauma appear to be multiplying, particularly over the last decade and a half. For example, Kirmayer et al.'s (2007) recent edited volume incorporates research on trauma from biological, clinical and cultural experts, with topics including neurobiological perspectives on fear, best practices for PTSD cognitive behavioral treatments and cross-cultural and evolutionary perspectives on adaptation. Psychiatrist Devon Hinton and anthropologist Alexander Hinton also have collaborated on an edited volume (2014) that explores the traumas of genocide and mass killing from their respective disciplinary lenses. Meanwhile, Golden and Bergo's edited volume (2009) approaches trauma through clinical, anthropological, historical, psychoanalytic and philosophical approaches, while also seeking to include foundational ideas from well-known academic thinkers like Foucault, Heidegger and Freud. A variety of additional interdisciplinary efforts have tackled specific contexts, such as Mengel, Borzaga and Orantes's (2010) collection of interviews (with contributors ranging from academics to psychologists to novelists) on South African trauma and memory 20 years after apartheid. Such holistic efforts are important markers in interdisciplinary approaches to trauma. They additionally form the basis for the integrated approaches to post-violence trauma for which this chapter develops a case.

Toward an integrated view of trauma experiences and expressions

Before developing such a case, however, a final body of literature to note is that which seeks to position trauma experiences and expressions at the intersection of biology and culture. Part of this research appears to be a natural outcome of the interdisciplinary approaches surveyed earlier. This approach also benefits from parallel research trends in fields that have heavily studied trauma-related topics, particularly anthropology. Recognizing the interplay and the "centrality of distinctive, physiological, social, semiotic, and cognitive processes," anthropologists like Fuentes (2015, 302) advocate for integrative anthropological approaches to topics historically consigned to biological anthropology. Applying similar, systems-based thinking to the study of trauma may likewise be beneficial, although the challenge of coordinating and comparing varying methodologies across academic disciplines will have to be carefully managed. The wide array of subtopics studied under the umbrella of trauma research highlight the artificiality of researching solely biologically based impacts of this phenomenon – or, conversely, of studying the cultural impact of trauma without careful consideration of its biological impacts as well. Rather, research that seeks to bridge this divide by looking at the intersections of "nature" and "nurture" may provide the most detailed sketch of the complexity of trauma. This biocultural approach has been used to reframe similar topics, such as interdependence between caregivers and infants, as biologically based and contextually nurtured (see Hinton 1999). Such a biocultural framework is ripe for continued application on various aspects of trauma research.

One possibility for applying a biocultural trauma framework may include immediate post-violence trauma assessments, as bodies, minds and social systems are impacted in a continuing, potentially reinforcing cycle. To guide such an approach, the work of biological anthropologists who study the evolutionary interactions between human populations and their environments is ripe for application. Biological anthropologists have approached human evolutionary adaptation through understandings of *niche construction*, defining a niche as the "structural, temporal, and social context in which as species exists" (Fuentes 2015, 32). Niche construction explores the "modification of both living and non-living components in environments through the metabolic, physiological, and behavioral activities of organisms, as well as through their choices" in ways that have evolutionary or ecological consequences (Flynn et al. 2013, 296). Niche construction theory explores deep time and evolutionary change and thus cannot be directly applied to the relatively short time frames of armed conflict. However, some researchers have begun to utilize niche construction theory outside strictly evolutionary contexts (Lansing 2011; Ellis 2015; O'Brien and Bentley 2015). Therefore, a key principle of this approach, namely, that humans concurrently shape their environments even as they shape them, may push the study of trauma forward by reconstituting the factors that should be considered when discussing cycles of violence and trauma. This research approach is related to other social scientific approaches, such as *social norm theory*, first proposed by Perkins and Berkowitz to analyze the impact of interpersonal and environmental factors in patterns of student alcohol consumption (1986a, 1986b). However, niche construction approaches more explicitly address and incorporate the influence of biological modifications in ways that can guide similar biocultural approaches to trauma and trauma-impacted populations.

Folding ecological and biological impact themes into conversations of trauma is also critical for designing robust investigations of the long-term impact of trauma. Although tentative and under-explored at present, some research is suggesting that ecological and biological inheritances of violence, conflict and genocide may present especially fruitful research avenues. Studies of transgenerational transmission of trauma among Holocaust survivors to their children are most prominently represented in the secondary trauma literature, as Kellerman's meta-analysis of relevant research summarizes (2001). In one example of how these studies are structured, Yehuda et al. (2016) studied a population of Nazi Holocaust survivors and their children born after the conclusion of World War II. Their findings show that both the Holocaust survivors and their children had lower cortisol (a hormone associated with the human ability to cope with stress) levels than other Jewish families who did not live in Europe during the war and the genocide. Lower cortisol levels flagged the attention of the researchers, as such levels can be associated with social anxiety, depression, emotional hypersensitivity and other negative mental-health indicators. Other research on the September 11, 2001, terrorist attack survivors and their immediate offspring (Chemtob et al. 2010), on combat veterans (Yehuda et al. 2010), on U.S. Japanese internment survivors (Nagata 1991) and on displaced Native American populations (Brave Heart and DeBruyn 1998) has yielded parallel results. While single-generational and even second-generational epigenetic effects from severe trauma are therefore becoming more established in scientific findings, scholars debate whether such negative impacts can also be found in third-generation offspring (or further), raising important questions for long-term societal recovery. While possible, these findings are more difficult to establish and complicated by questions about designating a control group for the third generation and beyond (Lev-Wiesel 2007). It is also important to stress here that trauma is not inherited *in* DNA but rather in the mechanisms that impact DNA activity and regulation (Friedman and McEwen 2004). With sociocultural impacts of trauma well established in the social science literature (Šuber 2006; Hinton and Hinton 2014), this developing body of epigenetic literature on trauma transmission (Nugent, Goldberg and Uddin 2016; Yehuda, Lehrner and Bierer 2018) is an important step toward an integrated sociocultural and biological approach.

In addition to informing both scholarly research on trauma and practitioner approaches to healing and recovery, biological and ecological ramifications of trauma over time add to a growing list of reasons to justify immediate post-violence trauma intervention efforts, which will be further explored in the following section. Before we move to this next section, however, a few notes on how trauma is preserved not only in bodies but also within broader sociocultural contexts are helpful here in pulling these research themes together. Hinton and Hinton's (2014) previously mentioned edited volume explores the aftermath of genocides and mass killings through the lens of memory, symptom and recovery. Taken as a collective whole, the volume presents the aftermath of severely traumatic violence-caused events as containing culturally specific individual and collective remembrance mechanisms, such as ritualized commemoration ceremonies or symbolic motifs that frame survivor accounts or symptom presentations. The work also touches upon an area of research to which this paper will return, as it presents a variety of viewpoints regarding idioms of distress, cultural syndromes and locally contextualized methods for coping and recovery, exemplified through accounts of widely held beliefs in evil spirit attacks in Sierra Leone (Henry 2014) and high rates of sleep paralysis in Cambodian refugee populations (Hinton, Hinton and Eng 2014; see also Hinton et al. 2005). Varying across geographic locations, these case studies emphasize that even somewhat similar types of violence may be reconstructed by different groups through differing meaning-making filters. This key point guards against one-dimensional attempts to either diagnose or to "fix" trauma in different contexts or within different sub-segments of a certain population. These findings also offer caution to what is perhaps an overemphasis on one-size-fits-all PTSD diagnostic frameworks, as does well-known research that points out that much (particularly survey-based and quantitative) psychological research draws from undergraduates in Westernized contexts[1] (Summerfield 2008; Henrich, Heine and Norenzayan 2010). While difficult to design and implement, this research indicates that the most effective trauma interventions will be grounded in overarching biological and psychological principles but adapted and recontextualized for specific cultural contexts.

The case for implementing integrative trauma interventions

The concurrent impact of trauma on minds, bodies, environments and societies is linked to another important reality: the array of factors that precipitated large-scale violence in the first place may continue to affect populations even after the crescendo of violence has passed. Accordingly, complex, destabilizing crises like genocides and mass killings present a myriad of humanitarian needs. In such a context, the case for implementing holistic trauma interventions ultimately rests upon establishing the urgency of these specific needs. A brief sketch of the negative consequences of unaddressed trauma is a helpful first step in establishing such a case. As these harmful consequences are discussed, this section aims to equip trauma intervention advocates to articulate the urgency of prevention *and* recovery programs.

The impact of unaddressed trauma on economic spending and decision-making

When considering the costs of unaddressed trauma in post-violence societies, the human costs certainly carry the most moral weight. As the various chapters in this book capture, the human cost of violence is not limited to the number of people killed or wounded; violence also generates a series of societal traumas that disrupt the sense of normalcy and daily rhythms for those who survive it. Moreover, differing expressions of violence can reverberate after armed conflicts, as a growing body of evidence describes an uptick in intimate partner violence, likely impacted by postwar societal shifts (Ray and Heller 2009; Lwambo 2013; Slegh et al. 2013). Additional social tolls can include increased child and adult mortality rates, reduced life expectancies, continuing physical and mental-health problems and the destruction of the health and educational facilities that would enable societies to cope with these issues (Hoeffler and Reynal-Querol 2003; Hook 2013).

Beyond the moral imperative to assist such populations in any ways possible (see Van Arsdale and Nockerts 2008), these disruptions also complicate rebuilding efforts in already fragile contexts (see Hook 2013; Salehyan and Gleditsch 2006). Many medical and psychological studies, including those surveyed in the first section of this chapter, have rigorously covered the range of negative health and well-being consequences of trauma (e.g., Schnurr and Green 2004). With the goal of justifying the linkage between trauma healing programs and peacebuilding, this chapter considers not only the health impacts of trauma but also the health costs of unaddressed trauma. Priebe et al. (2009) tracked long-term mental-health outcomes in 264 former Yugoslavian residents (now residing in Croatia, Serbia, Germany and the United Kingdom) who had all suffered from PTSD and yet had not received treatment for this diagnosis. This research team presented results showing that 83.7 percent of participants were diagnosed as still having PTSD nearly a decade after the violent conflict (as measured on the Clinician Administered PTSD Scale for Diagnostic and Statistical Manual of Mental Health Disorders-IV, aka DSM-IV). Low scores were also reported on subjective quality of life (SQOL) assessments. Additionally, those suffering from unresolved trauma generated significant care costs even a decade after the violence, with the average care costs in the three months prior to this 2009 assessment exceeding 1,110 Euros.

Considered in this light, the economic costs of violent conflict therefore appear to have a cascading impact over time, strengthening the argument that the earlier introduction of mental-health programs may actually save direct financial costs over time, while also supporting survivors who in turn are able to contribute to their own social and economic outcomes. This research should also be considered in tandem with works that discuss the perhaps even more crippling impacts of trauma on children, such as long-term cognitive emotional effects that can lead to substance abuse or other harmful life choices which similarly translate into higher health care costs and decreased economic productivity (Perry and Szalavitz 2007). Taken together, these findings support new ways of viewing post-violence trauma interventions as in fact *preventive*: while these interventions are typically in response to past events, these treatment options can also be viewed as preventing the accumulation of future economic and social suffering at individual and societal levels. It is estimated that a civil war lasting five years decreases a nation's annual GDP growth rate by two percent – and of course many wars last much longer (Hoeffler and Reynal-Querol 2003). These economic costs are compounded in a variety of ways, including through the destruction of infrastructure, the diversion of funds toward non-productive (and even violent) ends, a loss of private assets and investments and capital flight. Improved mental health through post-violence trauma interventions alone will certainly not reduce these economic challenges. However, a case can be made that supporting constructive meaning-making and coping in the wake of traumatic events can result in civil societies with lower long-term costs of care and with higher levels of social engagement in productive activities that aid economic reconstruction, such as by heightening perceptions of societal consequences for corrupt behavior (see Bolongaita 2005).

The impact of unaddressed trauma on potential conflict recurrence

Beyond human flourishing, a strong case can be made that untreated traumas may feed into negative feedback loops that increase the risk of future outbreaks of violence. Post-conflict societies face extremely high probabilities of conflict recurrence, which is well documented in conflict literature (Collier et al. 2003; Collier and Hoeffler 2004; Hegre, Nygard and Ræder 2017). To explore potential causal mechanisms, Call (2012) employs multi-method analysis (including a quantitative analysis of Uppsala Conflict Data Program data, an in-depth case study of Liberia and shorter comparative case studies) to examine violence recurrence following civil wars. The author notes the fragility of a "post-conflict" status by tracing destructive relapses into armed conflict and violence even after achieving apparent peace, such as "Lebanon in 1975, Nicaragua in the early 1980s, Russia in Chechnya in 1999, Burundi in 1993, the Central African Republic in 2001, Haiti in 2004, and East Timor in 2006" (Ibid., 1). Call shies away from one-size-fits-all solutions to the issue of civil war recurrence in the diverse contexts he explores. Nevertheless, he highlights the broad category of *political exclusion*, defined as "perceived or actual deprivation of an expected opportunity for former warring parties, or the social groups associated with them, to participate in state administration, through either appointed posts or elective office," as playing the decisive role in the majority of civil war recurrence cases (Ibid., 37). Importantly, for this study on trauma, Call explicitly conceptualizes the risk of exclusion as a *process*, not a specific policy or programmatic outcome. Meanwhile, *political inclusion*, i.e., processes that do not prohibit either former parties to warfare or the groups associated with them from access to future state and societal positions, is highly correlated with peace consolidation or making widespread nonviolence "stick." Here again, Call clearly distinguishes that processes of inclusion are more important than specific programmatic or policy outcomes, providing examples such as controlling even a small portion of a country's mayorships or local districts or managing the profits and production of valuable natural resources, even when said groups lack parliamentary or other national representation. Drawing from Mark Suchman's work, Call posits that these processes of encouraging inclusion and mitigating feelings of exclusion create widely shared perceptions of *legitimacy*, which Suchman defines as a "generalized perception or assumption that the actions of an entity are desirable, proper, or appropriate within some socially constructed system of norms, values, beliefs, and definitions" (1995, 574). Complementing Call's focus on *political* exclusion, other researchers have focused on the consequences of basic goods and services deprivation, particularly when such deprivation is prolonged and/or repeated (Herman 1992; Klasen et al. 2013). These consequences can elicit similar traumatic stress responses, called simple or "little t" trauma, as seen with acute, catastrophic events, and can pave the way for rebel movement participation and recruitment (Ibid.).

The emphasis on considering negative factors (exclusion) and positive factors (inclusion and legitimacy) as processes is a significant finding for both trauma scholars and clinicians in post-violence settings. As some of the psychological research presented here suggests (see Priebe et al. 2009), untreated trauma indicators, including shock, confusion, difficulty concentrating, anger, anxiety, self-blame, guilt, withdrawal from individuals or society, feelings of helplessness or powerlessness, may result in societal members struggling to engage in emerging civil society efforts that would create the sense of legitimacy and inclusion that Call (2012) and Suchman (1995) address as critical to achieving long-term peace. As subjective quality-of-life indicators may worsen over time if trauma-related disorders are untreated (Priebe et al. 2009), and as biological ramifications may compound individuals' physical abilities to cope with stressors (Yehuda et al. 2016), these seemingly unrelated factors may be playing into the construction of negative feedback loops that increase the likelihood of armed conflict recurrence. Further, with negative biological factors apparent in survivors' children (Chemtob et al. 2010), and as children may disproportionately struggle to cope with experienced trauma (Perry and Szalavitz 2007), future generations of civil society leaders who could continue through their actions to mitigate conflict recurrence risk factors may be physically and mentally impacted not to do so. Such a premise is consistent with psychoanalytic assessments of large-scale violence employed by some South American governments, including mass incarcerations and systemized torture of prisoners (Ulriksen de Viñar 2012). In a finding that again echoes Valent's definition of *trauma*, Ulriksen de Viñar (2012) explores next-generational transmission of trauma specifically in the area of healthy personality development and next-generational political participation, finding each constrained by prior family trauma. Metaphorically referring to trauma as inscribed in families' lives as Auschwitz tattoos were imprinted on skin, Ulriksen de Viñar presents a view of embodied trauma based upon defense mechanisms intended to ensure psychic survival. Such findings are again highlighted to establish how programmatic failures to ensure some level of continued trauma recovery may create negative environmental, societal and individual biocultural reinforcing conditions that heighten risks of conflict recurrence.

The impact of unaddressed trauma on political vulnerabilities

Finally, even short discussions of the negative impacts of trauma like this one would be inadequate without acknowledging additional political risks of unaddressed traumas, including heightened susceptibility to political narrative co-optation. These themes have permeated discussions of two major events in the 1990s that are frequently framed as genocidal: the Rwandan and former Yugoslavian killings. In Rwanda, for example, medical anthropologist Christopher Taylor (1999) explored how historical practices of violence structured threat perception of Tutsi "invaders" and specific killing behaviors in Rwanda. Such a finding is supported by Straus's seminal work (2006), which situates the 1994 killings as linked to the dynamics of prior violence in 1957–1962, in 1963–1964 and in 1973.

Des Forges's (1999) analysis of the ideological speeches that justified the killing, such as those delivered by Leon Mugesera, again returns to the theme of historical grievances allowing victim groups to be framed as invading foreigners who should be expelled to their so-called real home in Ethiopia.

Analyses of Southeast Europe have theorized along parallel paths. Vamik Volkan's (1990) work underscores the importance of perceived collective identity, pivotal historical events and trauma through the conceptual contributions of "chosen traumas" and "chosen glories." In describing the development of chosen trauma narratives, Volkan highlights the Ottoman defeat of the Serbs at Kosovo Polje in 1389 as providing the narrative flagpole around which Serb national identity was constructed (1990, 1996). Mack's related contribution of the "Egoism of victims" (1990) has also undergirded the work of Puljek-Shank and Puljek-Shank in Southeast Europe, as they noted that victim-centered identities permeate the self-conceptions of many regional groups and reduce "the ability to critically look at the participation of their own group in the various regional wars or the possibility of becoming perpetrators in future acts of large-scale violence" (2008, 159). These authors also note the roles of chosen traumas in heightening the nationalist sentiment attached to various memorializing events in Bosnia and Herzegovina. While memorial activities can be an important part of meaning-making in the midst of tragedy and an important healing activity, Puljek-Shank and Puljek-Shank provocatively question if the investment of this type of nationalist energy in memorial ceremonies and in anniversaries of key events instead deepens divisions in this postwar context.

While political elites co-opting historical senses of grievances and culturally specific motifs are extremely common in conflict contexts, it is worth injecting this literature into our conversation on the value of trauma healing activities as we explore the unclear boundaries between yesterday's victims and tomorrow's perpetrators, or vice versa (see Redekop 2008). Šuber's research on the consequences of mythical narratives and collective trauma on the Serbian population in the mid-1980s contends that "Serbia's particular cultural-historically inherited frame of perception provided a fertile seedbed for Milošević to successfully launch a policy of re-traumatization and thus establish widespread consent to his war policy among the population" (2006, 1). Anthropological efforts to trace re-traumatization processes in Balkan societies have also focused on how new exclusionary cultural norms may be generated in these contexts. Povrzanivic (2001) links the existence of cultural collective traumas to the phenomenon of "cultural fear" in the Balkans, referencing themes of historical expulsion and exclusion as helping to justify in-group/out-group othering.

In addition to creating favorable conditions for large-scale violence against dehumanized others, the role of cultural fear and re-traumatization may help to explain the incredible rates of direct participation in large-scale violence. In Rwanda's case, approximately 200,000 citizens with no prior history of homicidal violence joined in the killings, a factor which helps to explain how approximately 800,000 victims were claimed over a short three-month period with relatively rudimentary weapons like machetes (UHRC 2009). Looking back several decades in

Rwandan history, particularly episodes of violence following the transition from Belgian colonial rule in which conservative estimates place the death toll at hundreds of thousands, (Lemarchand 1970), it is worth revisiting the question, using a trauma-specific lens, of how such high numbers of "ordinary citizens" were persuaded to participate (see also Fujii 2008, 2009; Browning 1992). Other scholars have raised a parallel question in the Yugoslavia context, namely, whether policies to ignore suffering and loss in the World War II and post-World War II period contributed to later conflict dynamics. When considering the former Yugoslavia and Rwanda in tandem, a haunting question remains: would holistic, effective trauma interventions that sought to address historical grievances have reduced the number of citizens who participated or who responded to calls from leaders to participate in violence? As researchers continue to study Rwanda and the former Yugoslavia, answering such questions is urgent. Simultaneous research on both locations may also allow for any emerging and generalizable trends or theories to be explored. Drawing from the integrative approaches discussed here may also allow for more tailored treatments to be designed that support (and not unintentionally undermine) local practices of meaning-making in the midst of trauma recovery.

A call to link trauma healing and peacebuilding efforts

In summary, integrative approaches can prove helpful in both the study of violence-caused trauma as well as in establishing the value of holistic, carefully contextualized interventions at the earliest possible stages. While this volume focuses on the Western Balkans, the findings and principles covered here extend to other active conflict and post-conflict contexts, such as Northern Ireland, Israel and the Palestinian Territories, Cyprus, Burma, Chechnya, eastern Ukraine, the Democratic Republic of Congo, Burundi and many others. Echoing ongoing interdisciplinary approaches to traumatology (see Kirmayer, Lemelson and Barad 2007; Figley 2012), additional insights into the expressions and experiences of trauma may be gleaned through a steady focus on the intersections of biological and cultural factors. As researchers consider the variety of social, biological and environmental impacts of trauma, it will be essential to explore the impact of trauma across multiple generations. Established conflict data, including data on conflict consequences and recurrence risks, portray social, economic and political stressors as potentially accumulating over time (Herman 1992; Collier et al. 2003; Collier and Hoeffler 2004; Call 2012; Klasen et al. 2013; Hegre, Nygard and Ræder 2017). Therefore, trauma-specific interventions can present not only a positive ethical choice but a wise political and economic prioritization as well, provided they are carefully and thoughtfully designed to support and not undermine local perspectives, responses and needs. Although history is dotted with conflicts and violence, the same can be said for resilient responses and meaning-making in the midst of intense and prolonged suffering. While holistic approaches to the study of trauma and the designing of trauma interventions are critical, tailoring these responses to cultural contexts remains the lynchpin in ensuring sustainable progress, as disrupting beneficial local coping practices could potentially usher in re-traumatization processes of their own. The challenge of not simply doing trauma interventions but doing them *well* remains substantial. The integrative approaches that mark many ongoing efforts offer clear signs of promise as dedicated clinicians, survivors and scholars work together to support populations along spectrums of recovery and flourishing.

Note

1 Or in Henrich et al.'s memorable acronym, W.E.I.R.D.: Western Educated Industrialized Rich Democratic societies (2010)

References

Ader, Robert, and Nicholas Cohen. 1975. "Behaviorally Conditioned Immunosuppression." *Psychosomatic Medicine* 37.4: 333–340.

Berkowitz, Alan D., and H. Wesley Perkins. 1986a. "Problem Drinking Among College Students: A Review of Recent Research." *Journal of American College Health* 35: 21–28.

Berkowitz, Alan D., and H. Wesley Perkins. 1986b. "Resident Advisors as Role Models: A Comparison of Drinking Patterns of Resident Advisors and Their Peers." *Journal of College Student Personnel* 27.2: 146–153.

Bolongaita, Emil. 2005. "Controlling Corruption in Post-Conflict Countries." Kroc Institute Occasional Papers #26. Joan B. Kroc Institute for International Peace Studies, University of Notre Dame, Notre Dame.

Brave Heart, Maria Yellow Horse, and Lemyra DeBryn. 1998. "The American Indian Holocaust: Healing Historical Unresolved Grief." *American Indian and Alaska Native Mental Health Research* 8.2: 60–82.

Browning, Christopher. 1992. *Ordinary Men: Reserve Police Battalion 101 and the Final Solution in Poland.* New York: HarperCollins Publishers.

Call, Charles. 2012. *Why Peace Fails: The Causes and Prevention of Civil War Recurrence.* Washington, DC: Georgetown University Press.

Chemtob, Claude, Yoko Nomura, Khushmand Rajendran, Rachel Yehuda, Deena Schwartz, and Robert Abramovitz. 2010. "Impact of Maternal Posttraumatic Stress Disorder and Depression Following Exposure to the September 11 Attacks on Preschool Children's Behavior." *Child Development* 81.4: 1129–1141.

Collier, Paul, V.L. Elliot, Havard Hegre, Anke Hoeffler, Marta Reynal-Querol, and Nicholas Sambanis. 2003. *Breaking the Conflict Trap: Civil War and Development Policy.* Oxford: World Bank and Oxford University Press.

Collier, Paul, and Anke Hoeffler. 2004. "Greed and Grievance in Civil War." *Oxford Economic Papers* 56.4: 563–595.

Des Forges, Alison. 1999. *Leave None to Tell the Story: Genocide in Rwanda.* New York: Human Rights Watch.

Ellis, Erle. 2015. "Ecology in an Anthropogenic Biosphere." *Ecology Monographs* 85.3: 287–331.

Figley, Charles, ed. 2012. *Encyclopedia of Trauma: An Interdisciplinary Guide.* Thousand Oaks, CA: Sage.

Figley, Charles, and William Nash. 2007. *Combat Stress Injury: Theory, Research, and Management.* New York: Routledge.

Flynn, Emma, Kevin Laland, Rachel Kendal, and Jeremy Kendal. 2013. "Developmental Niche Construction." *Developmental Science* 16.2: 296–313.

Friedman, Matthew, and Bruce McEwen. 2004. "Posttraumatic Stress Disorder, Allostatic Load, and Medical Illness." In *Trauma and Health: Physical Health Consequences of Exposure to Extreme Stress*, edited by Paula Schnurr and Bonnie Green. Washington, DC: American Psychological Association.

Fuentes, Agustin. 2015. "Integrative Anthropology and the Human Niche: Toward a Contemporary Approach to Human Evolution." *American Anthropologist* 117.2: 302–315.

Fujii, Lee Ann. 2008. "The Power of Local Ties: Popular Participation in the Rwandan Genocide." *Security Studies* 17.3: 568–597.

Fujii, Lee Ann. 2009. *Killing Neighbors: Webs of Violence in Rwanda*. Ithaca: Cornell University Press.

Golden, Kristen, and Bettina Bergo. 2009. *The Trauma Controversy: Philosophical and Interdisciplinary Dialogues*. Albany: State University of New York Press.

Hegre, Harvad, Havard Mokleiv Nygard, and Ranveig Flaten Ræder. 2017. "Evaluating the Scope and Intensity of the Conflict Trap: A Dynamic Simulation Approach." *Journal of Peace Research* 54.2: 243–261.

Henrich, Joseph, Steven Heine, and Ara Norenzayan. 2010. "The Weirdest People in the World?" *Behavioral and Brain Sciences* 33.2–3: 61–83.

Henry, Doug. 2014. "Attack of the Grotesque." In *Genocide and Mass Violence: Memory, Symptom, and Recovery*, edited by Devon Hinton and Alexander Hinton, 242–260. Cambridge: Cambridge University Press.

Herman, Judith Lewis. 1992. "Complex PTSD: A Syndrome in Survivors of Prolonged and Repeated Trauma." *Journal of Traumatic Stress* 5.3: 377–391.

Hinton, Alexander. 1999. *Biocultural Approaches to the Emotions*. Cambridge: Cambridge University Press.

Hinton, Devon, and Alexander Hinton, eds. 2014. *Genocide and Mass Violence: Memory, Symptom, and Recovery*. Cambridge: Cambridge University Press.

Hinton, Devon, Alexander Hinton, and Kok-Thay Eng. 2014. "Key Idioms of Distress and PTSD among Rural Cambodians." In *Genocide and Mass Violence: Memory, Symptom, and Recovery*, edited by Devon Hinton and Alexander Hinton, 212–241. Cambridge: Cambridge University Press.

Hinton, Devon, Vuth Pich, Dara Chhean, Mark Pollack, and Richard McNally. 2005. "Sleep Paralysis Among Cambodian Refugees: Association With PTSD Diagnosis and Severity." *Depression and Anxiety* 22.2: 47–51.

Hoeffler, Anke, and Martha Reynal-Querol. 2003. *Measuring the Cost of Conflict*. Oxford: Oxford University. Unpublished Manuscript, Centre for the Study of African Economies.

Hook, Kristina. 2013. "The Cost of Conflict: Understanding the Ramifications of Internal Warfare." In *Beyond Intractability*, edited by Guy Burgess and Heidi Burgess. Boulder: Conflict Information Consortium, University of Colorado.

Kellerman, Natan. 2001. "Psychopathology in Children of Holocaust Survivors: A Review of the Research Literature." *The Israel Journal of Psychiatry and Related Sciences* 38.1: 36–46.

Kirmayer, Laurence, Robert Lemelson, and Mark Barad, eds. 2007. *Understanding Trauma: Integrating Biological, Clinical, and Cultural Perspectives*. Cambridge: Cambridge University Press.

Klasen, Fionna, Johanna Gehrke, Franka Metzner, Monica Blotevogel, and James Okello. 2013. "Complex Trauma Symptoms in Former Ugandan Child Soldiers." *Journal of Aggression, Maltreatment, and Trauma* 22.7: 698–713.

Lansing, Stephan. 2011. "Niche Construction on Bali: The Gods of the Countryside." *Philosophical Transactions of the Royal Society* 366.1566: 927–934.

Lemarchand, Rene. 1970. *Rwanda and Burundi*. New York: Praeger Publishers.

Lev-Wiesel, Rachel. 2007. "Intergenerational Transmission of Trauma Across Three Generations: A Preliminary Study." *Qualitative Social Work* 6.1: 75–94.

Lwambo, Desiree. 2013. " 'Before the War, I Was a Man': Men and Masculinities in the Eastern Democratic Republic of Congo." *Gender and Development* 21.1: 47–66.

Mack, John. 1990. "The Enemy System." In *The Psychodynamics of International Relationships: Concepts and Theories*, edited by Vamik Volkan, Demetrios Julius, and Joseph Montville. Lanham, MD: Lexington Books.

Mengel, Ewald, Michela Borzaga, and Karin Orantes. 2010. *Trauma, Memory, and Narrative in South Africa Interviews*. New York: Rodopi.

Nagata, Donna. 1991. "Transgenerational Impact of the Japanese-American Internment: Clinical Issues in Working with Children of Former Internees." *Psychotherapy: Theory, Research, Practice, Training* 28.1: 121–128.

Nugent, Nicole, Amy Goldberg, and Monica Uddin. 2016. "Topical Review: The Emerging Field of Epigenetics: Informing Models of Pediatric Trauma and Physical Health." *Journal of Pediatric Psychology* 41.1: 55–64.

O'Brien, Michael, and Alexander Bentley. 2015. "The Role of Food Storage in Human Niche Construction: An Example from Neolithic Europe." *Environmental Archaeology* 20.4: 364–378.

Perry, Bruce, and Maria Szalavitz. 2007. *The Boy Who Was Raised as a Dog and Other Stories from a Child Psychiatrist's Notebook: What Traumatized Children Can Teach Us About Love, Loss, and Healing*. New York: Basic Books.

Povrzanivic, Maja. 2001. "Kultur und Angst: Über den Kriegsalltag." In *Kroatische Volkskunde/Ethnologie in den Neunzigern*, edited by Jasna Čapo Žmegac, Reinhard Johler, Sanja Kalapos, and Herbert Nikitsch, 291–315. Vienna: Verlag des Instituts für Europäische Ethnologie.

Priebe, Stefan, Aleksandra Matanov, Jelena Janković Gavrilović, Paul Mccrone, Damir Ljubotina, Goran Knezević, Abdulah Kucukalić, Tanja Francisković, and Matthias Schützwohl. 2009. "Consequences of Untreated Posttraumatic Stress Disorder Following War in Former Yugoslavia: Morbidity, Subjective Quality of Life, and Care Costs." *Croatian Medical Journal* 50.5: 465–475.

Puljek-Shank, Amela, and Randall Puljek-Shank. 2008. "The Contribution of Trauma Healing to Peacebuilding in Southeast Europe." In *Peacebuilding in Traumatized Societies*, edited by Barry Hart. Lanham, MD: University Press of America.

Ray, Sam, and Lauren Heller. 2009. *Peril or Protection: The Link Between Livelihoods and Gender-Based Violence in Displacement Settings*. New York: Women's Refugee Commission.

Redekop, Vern Neufeld. 2008. "A Post-Genocidal Justice of Blessing as an Alternative to a Justice of Violence: The Case of Rwanda." In *Peacebuilding in Traumatized Societies*, edited by Barry Hart. Lanham, MD: University Press of America.

Salehyan, Idean, and Kristian Skrede Gleditsch. 2006. "Refugees and the Spread of Civil War." *International Organization* 60: 335–366.

Schnurr, Paula, and Bonnie Green. 2004. *Trauma and Health: Physical Health Consequences of Exposure to Extreme Stress*. Washington, DC: American Psychological Association.

Segerstrom, Suzanne C. 2012. *The Oxford Handbook of Psychoneuroimmunology*. New York: Oxford University Press.

Slegh, Henry, Gary Barker, Augustin Kimonyo, Prudence Ndolimana, and Matt Bannerman. 2013. "'I Can Do Women's Work': Reflections on Engaging Men as Allies in Women's Economic Empowerment in Rwanda." *Gender and Development* 21.1: 15–30.

Solomon, George F., and Rudolf H. Moos. 1964. "Emotions, Immunity, and Disease: A Speculative Theoretical Integration." *Archives of General Psychiatry* 11.6: 657–674.

Straus, Scott. 2006. *The Order of Genocide: Race, Power, and War in Rwanda*. Ithaca: Cornell University Press.

Šuber, Daniel. 2006. "Myth, Collective Trauma, and War in Serbia: A Cultural-Hermeneutical Appraisal." *Anthropology Matters* 8.1: 1–15.

Suchman, Mark. 1995. "Managing Legitimacy: Strategic and Institutional Approaches." *Academy of Management Review* 20.3: 571–603.

Summerfield, Derek. 2008. "How Scientifically Valid Is the Knowledge Base of Global Mental Health?" *British Medical Journal* 336.7651: 992–995.

Taylor, Christopher. 1999. *Sacrifice as Terror: The Rwandan Genocide of 1994*. New York: Berg.

Ulriksen de Viñar, Maren. 2012. "Political Violence: Transgenerational Inscription and Trauma." *International Journal of Applied Psychoanalytic Studies* 9.2: 95–108.

United Human Rights Council (UHRC). 2009. "Genocide in Rwanda." Accessed 27 December 2016. www.unitedhumanrights.org/2009/05/the-genocide-in-rwanda.

Valent, Paul. 1998. *Trauma and Fulfillment Therapy: A Wholist Framework*. Philadelphia: Taylor and Francis.

Van Arsdale, Peter, and Regina Nockerts. 2008. "A Theory of Obligation." *Journal of Humanitarian Assistance*, 12 May: 1–14.

Volkan, Vamik. 1990. "An Overview of Psychological Concepts Pertinent to Interethnic and/or International Relationships." In *The Psychodynamics of International Relationships: Concepts and Theories*, edited by Vamik Volkan, Demetrios Julius, and Joseph Montville. Lanham, MD: Lexington Books.

Volkan, Vamik. 1996. "Bosnia-Herzegovina: Ancient Fuel of a Modern Inferno." *Mind and Human Interaction* 7: 110–127.

Yehuda, Rachel, Linda Bierer, Laura Pratchett, and Michelle Pelcovitz. 2010. "Using Biological Markers to Inform a Clinically Meaningful Treatment Response." *Annals of the New York Academy of Sciences* 1208, October: 158–163.

Yehuda, Rachel, Nikolaos P. Daskalakis, Linda M. Bierer, Heather N. Bader, Torsten Klengel, Florian Holsboer, and Elisabeth B. Binder. 2016. "Holocaust Exposure Induced Intergenerational Effects on FKBP5 Methylation." *Biological Psychiatry* 80.5: 372–380.

Yehuda, Rachel, Amy Lehrner, and Linda Bierer. 2018. "The Public Reception of Putative Epigenetic Mechanisms in the Transgenerational Effects of Trauma." *Environmental Epigenetics* 4.2: dvy018.

4 Building peace in complex contexts of psychosocial trauma

An integrated framework

Barry Hart

Introduction

This chapter addresses the challenges and issues of integrating psychosocial trauma and related support structures into peacebuilding processes. It discusses a comprehensive peacebuilding framework as a means of linking psychosocial support to a comprehensive peace plan. The framework is clear about the need for psychosocial support in the trauma awareness and recovery process of individuals and groups – after their experiences of complex violence and related ongoing circumstances. I present a model for building peace in the Peacebuilding Wheel (Figure 4.1). Peacebuilding as understood in this model requires many actors and skill sets working together to allow the wheel to move forward. The integration of these elements and operationalization of this theoretical model has its roots in peacebuilding and humanitarian and development work that has been put in place over the past several decades (Lederach 1997; Schirch 2004; Wessells 2008; Zelizer 2013); it is suggested here that there is a need for imaginative thinking to revitalize and further develop this integrative process.

Of course, such an approach to change requires the willingness of numerous actors and organizations, as well as donors, to work out the means toward a more comprehensive and dynamic peace process. When this is done in regard to post-war and other complex violent conflicts, improved mental health and individual and collective resilience and well-being can be more fully realized.

It is therefore important to first engage in a discussion about what peacebuilding is, its evolution, current status and what it is moving toward. Within this larger discussion, this chapter focuses on psychosocial change processes and their relationship to peacebuilding now and possibilities for the future. I present several examples specific to Bosnia and Herzegovina that reflect this relationship, ones that demonstrate the high relevance of psychosocial trauma awareness, recovery and well-being as part of the larger process of building peace with justice.

Peacebuilding

According to Johan Galtung, a founder of the field of peace studies, peacebuilding, "focuses on transforming relationships and structures in society to decrease

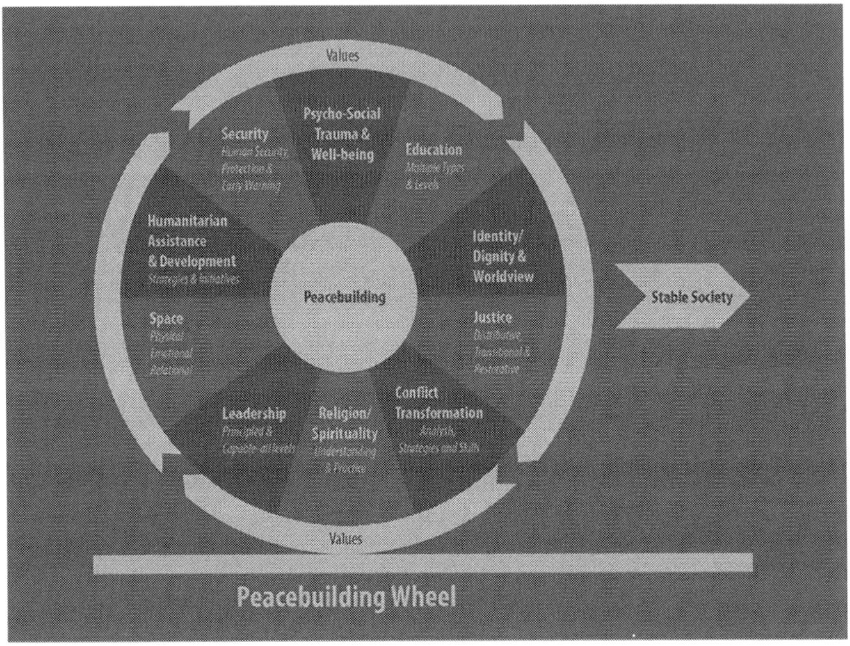

Figure 4.1 The Peacebuilding Wheel (Hart 2008, ix)

the likelihood of future conflicts" (Zelizer 2013, 7). Other scholars also emphasize the necessity of both relationships and structures, and the need to engage all levels of society in building peace after war and other major acts of violence (Lederach 2003; Schirch 2004).

Lisa Schirch notes that peacebuilding has two broad meanings, which refer "to the *direct* work that intentionally focuses on the factors driving and mitigating conflict. . . [and] to the *efforts* to coordinate or set up channels for communication to develop a comprehensive multilevel, multi-sectoral strategy" (2013, 7). These include, but are not limited to governance, justice, education, psychosocial trauma awareness and recovery processes, education, and humanitarian assistance and development. Peacebuilding is therefore "an overarching concept useful for describing a range of interrelated efforts" (Ibid., 8).

For the purposes of this chapter, the focus will be on *strategic* peacebuilding that involves the following characteristics:

- Works at all levels of society and is rooted in different cultures around the world.
- Dependent on deep and sensitive analysis of conflict, determining the causes and trajectory of the violence.

- Promotes just and sustainable social, economic and political structures and relationships, with attention paid to culture, race, gender, religion, ability and environmental factors.
- Concerned about short-term responses to complex and violent conflicts *and* long-term responses to build the capacity of societies and not allow them to drift back into similar violent situations (conflict prevention).
- Uses conflict analysis and transformation, mediation, negotiation, dialogue and psychosocial trauma and well-being theory and practice, promoting the integration of these processes for transformative purposes.
- Not limited to postwar or post-violent situations. Peacebuilding processes have an important role to play *during* war in order to stop it, and are used to strengthen societies after war.

Moreover, strategic peacebuilding is sensitive to and engages both *tangible* and *intangible* issues (Hart 2008). The tangible issues are objectively measurable, such as a cease-fire or peace accord, the rebuilding of community or state infrastructure after war and the restructuring of political, economic and judicial structures related to power sharing, legal frameworks such as "rule of law" and equitable resource distribution. The other part of the peacebuilding equation refers to the intangible factors that are hard to objectively measure but nevertheless are *real* to those who have experienced the devastating impact of large-scale violence and war. They include identity and worldview – how people view their worlds under new and difficult postwar/post-violence circumstances; self/group identity and dignity issues, as well as issues of trust, hope and moral and spiritual injury.

> The "moral and spiritual worlds" of individuals and groups of people have been fractured by the violence of war and need to be restored.[1]

It should also be noted that the transforming of conflict through a peacebuilding process is, as Kevin Clements notes, "as much about unmasking the powerful, and equalizing relationships as it is about solving problems. . . [since] it puts the emphasis on justice and fairness rather than on preserving harmony and political order" (cited by Schirch 2005, 6). Yet it is also about political harmony and order (contextually constructed and practiced) that provides the space and means to meet the needs of all members of society. Therefore, the positive power of peacebuilding, in contrast to the use of negative power that disrupts, abuses, alienates, manipulates and destroys, helps transform relationships and allows for the construction of political and social systems and structures that support these relationships.

To effectively aid this process of change, peacebuilding uses conflict-sensitive and systems analysis that allow for the development of context-specific theories of change. These theories of change explain how transformation can take place and become the link to a holistic and strategically focused intervention plan. In this regard, the theories *address* the importance of reducing violence, allowing for healthy intragroup and intergroup relationships; and speak clearly to the need for "stable/reliable social institutions that guarantee democracy, equity, justice, and fair allocations of resources" (Woodrow and Chigas cited by Burgess 2016). Ongoing monitoring and evaluation mechanisms provide additional means for these intervention strategies to remain dynamic in order for a peaceful, just and stable society to emerge out of a complex and violent conflict.

The Peacebuilding Wheel

The Peacebuilding Wheel was developed in 2006, emerging from peacebuilding and psychosocial trauma work I did in Northern Ireland, Liberia and the Balkans. The wheel is intended as a model and tool to be used by practitioners in NGOs and INGOs whose focus is conflict transformation, trauma awareness and psychosocial support, transitional justice and development in postwar contexts. It also has utility for all practitioners represented in each section of the wheel. The further intent of the model is to assist practitioners in seeing the larger and interrelated elements of peacebuilding, and as a visual tool to help them and their organizations enhance their understanding that peacebuilding happens (the wheel moves forward) when there is a multidisciplinary and intersectoral approach to transformational change. The Wheel can also be used as a teaching aid in academia, and my hope is that more peacebuilding scholars will see its relevance as they develop and write about theories of change and strategic planning and intervention strategies.

There were other models available at the time the Peacebuilding Wheel was developed but rather complex ones that did not provide easy *entrance* into an admittedly complex field. Now, as then, the Peacebuilding Wheel (Figure 4.1) provides access to the field to the individual interacting with it. Its different sections show the multiple factors necessary for peacebuilding, and the wheel or circle represents an archetypal symbol readily identifiable through human experience. What follows briefly explains what makes up the Wheel and the values that undergird its function.

- Culture and context (social, political, economic and environmental) *always* inform this model – as does ongoing violence and emergent issues. *Tangible* and *Intangible* variables must be considered in every Peacebuilding process.
- The values that "inflate" the tire come from all sections of the wheel. These values are related to human security in the form of human needs, rights and dignity as well as beliefs. Reconciliation can also be seen as an underlying value, as part of the peacebuilding process and/or a potential outcome of this process.
- The Peacebuilding Wheel can be used as a "template" for complex conflicts in order to see what is required to build peace. As a template, the Wheel shows peacebuilders with a particular focus, such as psychosocial trauma and well-being, transitional justice, education or leadership, who their potential partners are, so that together they might build peace with justice.

- Each section is a potential entry point to peacebuilding. One or more of the sections may be the starting point(s) for this process – but peacebuilding toward a more stable society requires the eventual (inter)action of *all* sections of the Wheel.
- Societal stability, the result or output of the wheel's action, refers to safety, adequate health care, economic and social justice, good governance and the ability to build and constructively maintain relationships and supportive social systems.

The Peacebuilding Wheel[2] can also be considered a type of *lens* through which to view the high relevance of an integrated approach to change, one that is focused on the people it is meant to serve, the local and possibly national and international partners it is meant to work with for the purpose of relieving suffering after complex violence. The Wheel is designed to help build stable economic, political and judicial structures that promote peace and the dignity, freedom and equality of all persons, as enshrined in the Universal Declaration of Human Rights.

Trauma and violence

The Peacebuilding Wheel can be used to address the results of multiple kinds of violence and the subsequent trauma it produces. For our purposes, trauma of an individual is understood as the response to violence determined by the

> interaction between environmental forces and an individual's skills, experience and characteristics. When resources and support are insufficient, an overwhelming traumatic experience can disrupt a person's self-image as well as the person's entire identity. Whether a person becomes traumatized is thus connected with the context in which the event occurs and is experienced.
>
> (Bubenzer and Tankink 2016, 4)

Violence, in the form of physical and/or psychological abuse of individuals by other individuals, groups or structures, is that which can and very often does produce these overwhelming, painful and disruptive experiences. How these experiences differ at the collective level is related to the fact that there is a social crisis involving communities and often tens of thousands of people who make up a social system. According to Jeffery Alexander (2004), the impact of trauma at the collective level means that this social crisis has become a cultural crisis:

> [E]vents are one thing, representations of these events quite another. Trauma is not the result of a group experiencing pain. It is the result of this acute discomfort entering into the core of the collectivity's sense of its own identity. Collective actors "decide" to represent social pain as a fundamental threat to their sense of who they are, where they come from and where they want to go.
>
> (Alexander 2004, 10)

Though quite different in assessment and response, both individual and collective trauma impact identity and worldview and are context-focused. Violent events and their psychological, social, spiritual, cultural, political and economic influences also deeply impact an individual's or group's sense of safety and hope and make decision-making difficult. The emphasis here is on the *response* to these violent events – at the individual level or in the case of major traumatic events, the collective one. The responses to the event are based on individual personalities, social and political environment, culture, group solidarity, religious beliefs, community and social assets, as well as leadership and structures that facilitate or hinder these responses.

When the focus is on collective trauma, a peacebuilding process assesses the level of violence that has occurred and whether it results from revenge, religion or ethnic division, unjust structures or a combination of these and other factors. It is through this assessment process that a clearer understanding of *why* the violence occurred emerges. This assessment also helps determine *what* intervention strategies should be considered to address the trauma and *how* they might be applied in a specific context.

Psychosocial trauma and well-being

A critical element in the Peacebuilding Wheel is psychosocial trauma and well-being. In order to build peace with justice in relationships and systems, trauma-informed practitioners need to analyze and address the emotional and psychological factors that result from individual and group responses to violence. It is being highly aware of and engaging with these *intangible* issues of the peacebuilding process that aids in the trauma integration/recovery methods used for individuals, communities and potentially entire societies. The emphasis should not solely be on individual harm or woundedness as a result of experiencing and reacting to a traumatic event; collective harm/injury that has the potential for destroying the social fabric also needs to be emphasized (Blanco, Blanco and Diaz 2016).

Psychosocial trauma sensitivity and related recovery methods, along with further sensitivity to sociocultural practices that may enhance (or hinder) recovery practices, are essential for helping improve society members' emotional ability and willingness to begin dialogues and reconciliation processes. Also, it is necessary to encourage society members to develop livelihood and education programs and to rebuild infrastructures that lead to feelings of security and a sense of normalcy. As a general term, "psychosocial well-being" involves people's relationships, psychological state and their development within a specific social context (Baingana, Bannon and Thomas 2005).

Moreover, psychosocial well-being, "indicates the interaction between the emotional, mental, spiritual, attitudinal and behavioral to the relational, traditional and cultural spheres or environments of being" (Dandaura Suma 2013, 1). The concept of *psychosocial trauma and well-being* used in this chapter fully encompasses these definitions, with its focus on trauma. When this concept is *operationalized* through related skill sets and actions, individual and collective trauma awareness and recovery are possible; further, related well-being has a greater possibility of taking place. This in turn should substantially strengthen persons and help them develop the emotional ability and courage to protect and develop the social fabric of their communities and societies in healthy and helpful ways.

Traumatic stress: breaking the human bond

Along with the devastating psychological and sociocultural impact natural disasters have on people, humanity experiences the overwhelming psychological and emotional pain brought on by "onerous and egregious acts such as wars, genocide, forced displacement, terrorism, ethnic and social cleansing" (Blanco, Blanco and Diaz 2016, 188). These are the acts that *fracture the moral and spiritual worlds* of individuals and groups of people. It is a moral (and often spiritual) injury that occurs when the human bond between people is broken by physical and/or psychological acts of violence.

The "woundedness" of this break is deep and disturbing to the human psyche, since neuroscience now confirms what philosophers throughout history have told us: "[W]e are born to bond" (Siegel 2011). This bonding is part of what humans need to strengthen who they are; along with autonomy and meaning, bonding completes the core human needs cycle required to experience life fully (Clark 2002). Fracturing this bond through violence leads to emotional, cognitive, behavioral, physical and spiritual reactions, as well as less than positive societal effects and responses (STAR 2002).

Therefore, a psychosocial trauma-sensitive and well-being approach to suffering caused by others in the human community helps address this suffering and related *brokenness* by taking into consideration these specific needs, which fit John Burton's (1990) broader categorization of *universal human* needs. By definition, this psychosocial approach, which deals with suffering of the individual and large groups of people within a social environment, differs significantly from one that focuses solely on an individual's psychological trauma, where the diagnosis is usually framed as posttraumatic stress disorder (PTSD). To address PTSD, a clinical diagnostic method is used, but it is not generally one that is socially and culturally sensitive.

Figure 4.2 shows the differences between two models and makes the important distinction between PTSD and post-traumatic stress (PTS), indicating that the majority of people experience the latter as a result of the high impact of violence. Where PTSD causes clinically significant distress or impairment in an individual's social interaction, capacity to work or other important areas of function (DSM IV of the American Psychiatric Association 2013) and has long-term symptomology, PTS has similar initial symptoms as PTSD but is more often short term and "won't [or may not] cause any prolonged meaningful interference in [one's] life" (Bender 2013).

In Figure 4.2, Model B clearly points out the complexity of the psychosocial trauma framework and how it considers the whole person and group in context. This includes people's social and historical contexts and their risk and level of

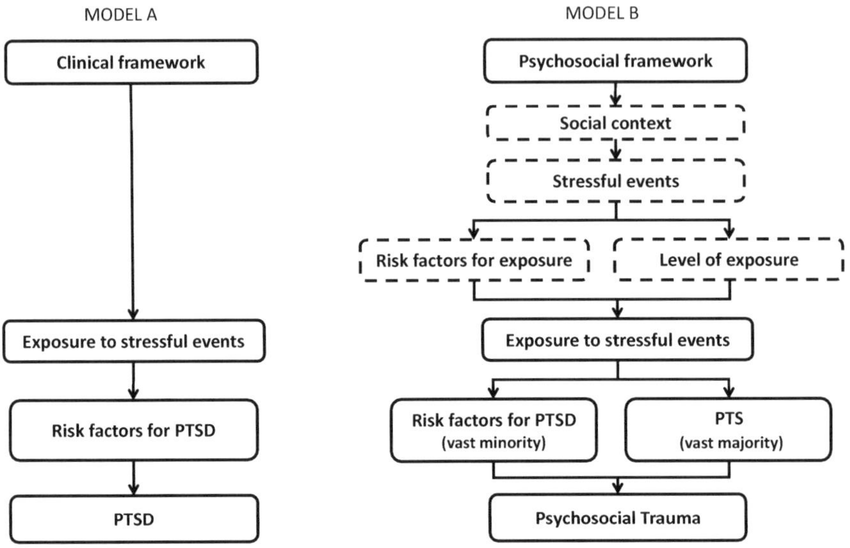

Figure 4.2 Clinical and Psychosocial Frameworks (Blanco, Blanco and Diaz 2016, 190)

exposure to violence. Also implied here is how psychosocial trauma must be addressed. It is evident that a clinical approach to individual transformation (Model A) has its place in the trauma recovery process, where specialized cases related to traumatic experiences occur (Inter-Agency Standing Committee 2007). In complex violent circumstances, however, the healing of individuals and large groups is better facilitated and sustained when a systems approach is taken.

This systems approach addresses social, economic, political, cultural as well as relational dynamics and their roles in both allowing violence to emerge, which results in a high number of traumatized people, and finding the best means to creatively and constructively engage this collective trauma. Ultimately, such an approach allows interventions to address the structures and their leaders who perpetrated and/or allowed the traumatic events to take place.

Integrating peacebuilding and psychosocial trauma/well-being

The myriad of social, cultural, political, economic and other variables that lead to war, and allow various types of violent conflict to take place, indicates the need for a multidimensional and strategic approach to peacebuilding in order to radically reimagine and transform conflict and address post-violence conditions. I argue here that one important change factor that should always be considered in this multidimensional approach is a psychosocial trauma analysis and intervention plan. In order to help in the emotional and psychological recovery of often tens of thousands of people who have experienced high stress and trauma – from rape, mass killings/genocide, displacement, loss of property, related domestic abuse and so forth – it is essential that individuals and communities, and other large groups of people, find ways to restore their sense of safety, identity, dignity and trust in themselves and others. Under the same rubric, these people will also need to find ways to restore meaning in their lives and rediscover a sense of hope for a better future.

The importance of integrating peacebuilding and psychosocial trauma and well-being understanding and practices in postwar situations has been recognized for some time (Fuertes 2004; Zelizer 2008; Pouligny 2010). In this regard, the International Association for Humanitarian Policy and Conflict Research states,

> [B]ringing the concepts of psycho-social recovery to the peace-building field is an attempt to broaden that perspective and describe a process of coming to terms with the wide range of emotionally, socially and culturally traumatic events, losses, isolation, destruction of social norms and codes of behavior most individuals and communities face in a conflict and post-conflict situations. It is also a way to emphasize the magnitude of the transformations experienced by the communities and societies concerned.
>
> (cited in Suma 2013, 3)

Although the need for psychosocial trauma/well-being processes is critical to peacebuilding, "[T]here are only a few studies that focus explicitly on the relationship between psychosocial work and peacebuilding" (Hamber, Gallagher and Ventevogel 2014, 8). A seminal study of this nexus was done by Wessells (2008), who provides insights into the relationship between peacebuilding and psychosocial trauma and well-being in the African context, factoring in the importance of *development* in the process of transforming communities and societies after destructive conflicts. For Wessells, the interrelationship of these issues in the aftermath of political trauma speaks to their importance in the healing and recovery process from "the collective issues of polarization, social division, hatred and fear, and the issues of structural violence that underlie them" (2008, 22).

Two examples of this healing and recovery process come from the postwar realities of Bosnia and Herzegovina (BiH). The first is from the mid-1990s, when CARE International started a psychosocial and peacebuilding-related project in the city of Žepče in central Bosnia and Herzegovina (BiH). The case demonstrates how psychosocial trauma awareness and recovery are integral to peacebuilding, as indicated in the Peacebuilding Wheel (Figure 4.1).

The Žepče case highlights the difficulties of ethnicity and fears of the Croat community, which was caught up in the larger war context as a minority group among the majority population of Bosniaks. Croats in Žepče felt the need to strike quickly and hard against their Bosniak neighbors, and did so through killing, raping, incarcerating and eventually expelling them from Žepče. CARE was asked by women in Žepče in late 1996, a year after the war ended and when Bosniaks were returning to the city, to engage both ethnic groups through the psychosocial and peacebuilding arm of its Welcome and Information Program (WICP).

WICP's focus was on the women of Žepče. A mixed group of men and women would have been preferable, but it was the women of the city who asked WICP to address their trauma, relational and livelihood needs. Excerpted below are the key elements of their story (adapted from Hart and Čolo 2014).

> *The director of the Žepče health clinic, whose main clientele were Bosnian Croat women, made the initial contact with CARE's WIC Project. The director indicated that her staff needed support in dealing with stress and trauma issues related to the war and current family, school and community problems. She asked local WICP staff members and an international trauma and peacebuilding expert to lead a series of workshops with her staff and other Bosnian Croat women from Žepče in order to begin to address these issues. A week later, a Bosniak women's group made a similar request to WICP. They identified their need to address issues of war, rape, incarceration and being driven from Žepče by their Croat neighbors, as well as psychosocial factors concerning their group's return to Žepče after nearly six years of being either internally displaced or refugees in other countries.*
>
> *The next step for WICP staff was to create safe spaces in order to address these needs in* <u>*intra*</u>*group settings. It was in these sessions that women's narratives were shared, emotions released and information examined about traumatic stress and everyday problem solving processes. Cultural symbols and metaphors were used to further enhance safety and sharing of stories – past experiences about the war and current stories related to economic, physical and emotional health issues. Ongoing traumatic stressors, or aspects of continuous trauma (Fischer and Petrovic-Ziemer 2013), were a result of everyday life experiences with the postwar context. Both Bosniak and Croat women of Žepče knew these realities all too well and sought ways to address them in the intragroup workshops. [This was done to benefit themselves as well as their families, whom they represented.]*
>
> *Content of specific workshops focused on the impact of trauma on the physical and emotional well-being of the individuals and groups, with discussion about symptoms and possible responses to stress- and trauma-related issues. Problem solving techniques were also discussed for many types of everyday issues experienced within a postwar context, such as education of children and jobs. WICP's involvement was an attempt to empower both groups of women by helping them identify their needs, find ways to fulfill them and build on what they were already doing to increase individual and community well-being. This intragroup process had been going for three months when a special request came to a local WICP staff member – the groups wanted to meet each other.*

The two groups of women did meet and began both a reconciliation process for themselves and their families, laying the groundwork for a joint business venture. WICP contacted an INGO that provided 3,000 chickens to help the women start a poultry business, which began to provide income for their families. They also began developing a legal entity, the Women of Žepče, to enhance their power to negotiate joint needs and interests.

A second project in BiH was developed by Catholic Relief Services (CRS) and called "Choosing Peace Together" (CPT). This project began 18 years after the end of the wars in the region and extended the psychosocial trauma recovery and peacebuilding process to numerous communities throughout BiH. CRS brought victim groups together from Croat, Serb and Bosniak communities into safe, well-structured environments. Here they told their stories of pain, fear and anger in front of their own or mixed ethnic group communities (see the contribution in this volume by Čolo Zahirović). One example is CRS's work in Potoci.

Potoci is a small town near Mostar, in the southwestern Herzegovina part of BiH. It is located in a valley and divided in two by the river Neretva. Before the war, all three majority ethnic groups (Bosniaks, Croats and Serbs) lived there. At the beginning of the conflict in 1992, coalitions of Bosniaks and Croats fought against Serbs, who were forced from the region and resettled in the east of BiH.

In 1993, the coalition between Bosniak and Croats ended, and armed conflict between these two groups started. Two war camps were established. One on the right side of river Neretva was a war camp for captured soldiers and civilian Croats, and on the left side was a war camp for captured soldiers and civilian Bosniaks.

Horrible war crimes took place during this period, which resulted in a great number of victims and people who, even today, suffer severe health or psychological problems.

Years after the war, people very reluctantly returned to the town. Through international support, houses were eventually rebuilt and people slowly rebuilt their community. However, for many years Bosniaks lived on the left side of river Neretva, and Croats lived on the right (members of the Serbian community have not returned to Potoci). Hostility and hatred between these two groups remained, or became more intense. Even today, Potoci is faced with these ethnic problems.

Five Croats from Potoci (former war camp prisoners) participated in the CPT project by attending multiethnic, psychosocial workshops organised throughout different parts of BiH. The Bosniak association of victims from Potoci was not willing to participate in these workshops. At the beginning, even Croat cooperation was limited. However, with time, and the opening of a safe place for dialogue, the Croat participants were able to share their narratives and needs and began to build constructive relationships with other members who participated in the workshops. Over time, attitudes. . . [about] reconciliation became more and more positive for all participants of the workshops.

For one of the participants from Potoci, a former war camp prisoner, a cognitive and behavioural shift started to take place, which resulted in a request to CPT to help him organise a "Peace Walk in Potoci" with a group of young people from different ethnicities and religions of the town. The aim of the event was to raise awareness of the need for embracing reconciliation processes and to show that people who were heavily affected by the war could be agents of change and builders of peace.

This person believed that reconciliation was possible and that people of different ethnic and religious backgrounds could and should visit each other. The "Peace Walk" involved walking through Potoci, visiting both the Croat and Bosniak sides of the town, and having coffee in cafés on both sides.

(The walk was organised during the "Peace Camp for Youth, 2011" by "S.K." (Former war camp prisoner) and proud leader of the Peace Walk in Potoci.)

(Hart and Čolo 2014, 84)

The Peace Walk in Potoci is just one of many examples of movement from individual cognitive change to social behavioral transformation that a number of CPT project participants experienced. Participation and storytelling was also a motivator for a number of joint peacebuilding activities in BiH, such as the commemoration of International Peace Day (September 21, 2012), which was led by two associations of former war camp prisoners, one Bosniak and the other Croat. Furthermore, a number of associations of members from different ethnic backgrounds (Bosniaks, Croats and Serbs) united their efforts and created a coalition with the aim of pressuring the BiH government to create and adopt a law for victims of torture.

These, and other local CRS-sponsored peacebuilding activities, indicate that providing safe spaces for reflection and dialogue, even within and among the most vulnerable groups in BiH, leads to positive change and helps form new behaviors that promote and support healing and reconciliation. Discussion and/or workshops that took place using psychosocial, trauma-informed peacebuilding theory and practice allowed for a certain level of healing and trust-building to begin. The shared stories and exchanges were reported to be encouraging, "because empowerment happens by acknowledging the suffering individuals and groups have experienced. When creatively included in transformational change process narratives, they help build peace" (Hart and Čolo 2014, 84; See also Čolo Zahirović's chapter in this volume.)

Both the CARE and CRS examples demonstrate the importance of such projects to create intragroup and intergroup safe spaces where individual and collective stories of traumatic events and related pain and anger are shared. In both cases, safety was created for people who sought to share narratives related to their response to complex traumatic events and allowed individuals to begin to experience the "other" in a more constructive manner. Physical, emotional and relational space, as noted on the Peacebuilding Wheel, are necessary for this change process to start. It is in these spaces that the beginning of healing and relational change processes takes place, in addition to the addressing of educational, legal and livelihood issues, also reflected on the Wheel. In regard to education, multiple types were used, from workshops to joint gatherings and public forums where narratives from former enemies were shared. Leadership was also an essential factor, since it had to be principled and capable at many levels to encourage participation and guide various processes of change. In reality, multiple elements of the Wheel needed to be put in play for each of these projects to function as well as they did.

In both cases, a psychosocial framework (Figure 4.2) was used which emphasized a cultural and identity-sensitive analysis and approach to change. Also, in each case, the entry points for engaging local actors were through the psychosocial trauma/well-being and identity sections of the Peacebuilding Wheel (Figure 4.1). In both Žepče and Potici, the peacebuilding process would have been enhanced if a more robust link had been made between these and other elements or sections represented in the Peacebuilding Wheel, an important recommendation for anyone using this model. A further recommendation for its use is that it can be altered to replace or add sections of the Wheel that better reflect the analysis done of conflict in a particular context and culture. It may even be changed in this way as new elements emerge in the conflict to which it was first applied.

Expanding the vision

In order to transform systems and structures of oppression that involve corruption, social exclusion, economic and gender inequalities, sectarianism and a range of other factors that divide and categorize people, oppressive and destructive psychological, emotional and related social issues must themselves be transformed. As this happens, specifically because a larger peacebuilding dynamic is in place, psychosocial well-being emerges and becomes an important means in bringing about further systems and mental-health change. There is no hierarchy when it comes to understanding and activating this perspective – it is informed and shaped by *interconnectivity*, where everything impacts everything else. In planning intervention strategies that are transformative at all levels, it is critical to take this whole person/whole system approach to change.

Intervention beyond "Doing No Harm"

Psychosocial trauma and well-being intervention strategies and related plans should seek to ensure that no further traumatization or psychological harm is done through the intervention process (Zelizer 2008). It is therefore necessary to do a rigorous analysis, develop related theories of change and undergird the work with a set of values that honor the human needs, rights and dignity of the people and culture where the intervention is taking place. Such intervention plans must also fully consider the strengths and resilience of the individuals and communities involved, along with their intersecting identities that grant them various levels of power in a particular context, and must recognize that any forward movement toward healing and peace with justice starts with and remains grounded in the people themselves. It is *their* intervention, and if outside help is asked for, the goal is to establish a "true partnership" grounded in dignity, where effort has been made to forge the best possible working relationship.

In this same vein, those who intervene in settings where violence has occurred must avoid categorizing or labeling people as traumatized only because they have been through traumatic events. Anytime interventions are carried out in a post-violence context, it is essential to understand and recognize that individuals, communities and even entire societies respond to severe and violent events within specific political and social contexts in different ways (Papadopoulos 2005). Moreover, a trauma-sensitive approach to peacebuilding developed by International Alert (Lange and Quinn 2003) assumes that an organization or individual involved in peacebuilding will understand the potential negative or positive interactions of the intervention on the psychological well-being of individuals and the larger community.

Additionally, those who intervene should be clear about the ethical guidelines of their work and where appropriate engage in cross-discipline and multi-sector approaches in order to find the best means of bringing about change (see Figure 4.1). To emphasize this concept, it is important to note that when psychosocial trauma/well-being interventions come together with justice, education and development interventions, as well as those focused on the economic, political or religious elements of conflict, the work must first benefit those directly impacted by the violence but also be of mutual benefit to members from each discipline and sector.

The premise outlined here indicates that a collective approach to transformational change will enhance the overall process of healing and building peace with justice in specific contexts. As difficult as this might be to conceptualize and put into practice, failure to take seriously this interdisciplinary/interactive intervention approach to change may prevent the development of sustainable peace and lay the groundwork for future conflict (Volkan 2004).

Toward a comprehensive interdisciplinary approach

In the peacebuilding field, on-the-ground examples of interdisciplinary approaches to change are rare, especially those that include a psychosocial trauma and well-being component. More research and action steps have taken place in the public health sector, as noted in a 2012 report of the Health Foundation (Evidence Centre 2012). An example of such an interdisciplinary "whole systems approach" took place in Sweden in the 1980s concerning health safety issues. The Swedish government set up a cross-sector advisory group that focused on developing "cross sector initiatives to improve safety awareness and to measure and report on performance" (Evidence Centre 2012, 9). When this successful program was transferred to another government agency in the 1990s, it was ultimately shut down since the agency did not hold a parallel cross-sector work orientation.

Another example from the Health Foundation Report is from the United States, where a center in Pennsylvania was set up to prepare and plan for crisis situations. Nine teams were drawn from "public health, emergency medicine, emergency management, hospitals and public safety agencies" (Evidence Centre 2012, 9) According to this plan, "[E]ach team works on a strategic issue for one year to build capacity within the region." Though successful, the initiative experienced some barriers that included "different organizational cultures and issues with jurisdiction" (Ibid., 9).

In a somewhat more positive vein, there is the example of a Canadian program called "The Pan Canadian Joint Consortium for School Health," a joint action of organizations that functioned well and was more sustainable. The organizers of this program, located on Prince Edward Island, Canada, set up cross-sector collaboration to "coordinate policy and funding from the health and education sector." In this case, government departments, "worked together to reduce duplication and minimize gaps in policies and practices" (Ibid., 10).

Multidisciplinary, cross-sector programs, having been put in place throughout the world and though rare, are nevertheless on the radar of many individuals and organizations. Professor Joop de Jong, psychiatrist and professor emeritus of the Vrije University Amsterdam, for example, established *public mental-health* programs in Burundi and Cambodia and explored this issue in several countries in South America. He promotes a public mental-health program that align well with the peacebuilding-psychosocial trauma/well-being integration paradigm emphasized in this chapter. De Jong consistently argues for an interdisciplinary approach to public mental-health issues, "drawing upon fields of anthropology, community psychology, clinical psychology, psychotherapy, psychiatry and epidemiology" (de Jong 2009, 24).

This multidisciplinary or "multi-modality" theory and practice is not meant to just address mental-health issues – although that is a central focus – but speaks to physical well-being of individuals and their communities. This is due to public mental-health practitioners' holistic body-mind awareness of the persons they serve and a deep analysis of the context and culture in which they live. Psychological and physical health, as well as social well-being, go hand in hand. The World Health Organization (WHO) reports on this triad of health factors, stating:

> Mental health is an integral and essential component of health. The WHO constitution states: "Health is a state of complete physical, mental and social well-being and not merely the absence of disease or infirmity." . . . Mental health is a state of well-being in which an individual realizes his or her own abilities, can cope with the normal stresses of life, can work productively and is able to make a contribution to his or her community.
>
> (World Health Organization 2016)

The extreme psychological, physical and social systems violation that occurs in war and other complex and violent situations requires addressing interrelated issues in an analytical and coordinated manner. Various actors and/or organizations and their unique disciplines should be engaged from the outset in partnership with each other and also in partnership with, and honoring the wisdom and skills of, the people they serve. This is not easy, since complicating and competing factors are always at play. That being the case, it is necessary to find creative and sensitive ways to facilitate these multidisciplinary, cross-sector and partnership approaches to change.

From a peacebuilding perspective, a relevant integrated cross-sector programming model is found in the Catholic Relief Services' "HIP" criteria for Peacebuilding Integration. In this model, the approach taken is "Holistic, Intentional and Professional" (Rogers, Chassy and Bamat 2010). These three criteria speak to the importance of comprehensively addressing human needs, giving full attention to micro-level community issues while also strategically engaging meso- and macro-level actors, being intentional about weaving peacebuilding into all programming and finally, requiring high-level skills training for staff (done together across sectors where possible).

Recommendations for a way forward

Multidisciplinary and cross-sector applications of peacebuilding that are sensitive to and engaging of all sectors in the complex process of building peace will first require leaders who understand the benefits of this method of change. Their visions and values need to be reasonably matched, and they need to support an informed, well-trained and cared for work force. These leaders also will understand the importance of encouraging donors to be both supportive and flexible. Such leaders are emerging and need to be affirmed as they attempt to further understand and take steps toward realizing cross-sector cooperation for change.

There is also a need to enhance the education of those who hold various forms of political power in order to bring their influence into the peacebuilding process. To ensure this happens effectively, an expansion of the just noted recommendations is required, offering political actors access (or at minimum, exposure to) research data, salient narratives of cooperation between psychosocial mental health and related trauma recovery work within peacebuilding processes as well as coherent explanations of how all disciplines are part of a holistic peacebuilding framework.

It is also essential that *champions* for cross-sector practices imaginatively and constructively explain the importance of this information to these power brokers. They need to point out that multidisciplinary, cross-sector peacebuilding is the best way, after violent and complex conflict, to lift individuals, communities and even entire societies to new levels of physical and psychological health. Assuming this is important to those in power positions, it can further be explained to them that this multidisciplinary and cross- sector approach to change is an important means of strengthening and sustaining social, economic and political systems and structures that stabilize societies and allow them to expand in positive ways.

Conclusion

When psychosocial trauma and well-being are fully factored into the peacebuilding analysis, design and intervention plan, constructive outcomes are more comprehensive, creative and durable. This is because such an approach shifts focus to the whole person within their community and emphasizes that respect for the dignity of all persons is of paramount importance. Undergirded by these values, this approach to change enhances the development of trust and sets up the conditions for overall human security to be more fully realized.

Over time, a comprehensive interdisciplinary and cross-sector peacebuilding plan should be established by INGOs and national, regional and community-based NGOs, specifically those organizations and practitioners noted earlier in the fields of peacebuilding, psychosocial mental health and trauma awareness, development, and restorative justice. The same is true for organizations and practitioners in transitional justice, education and public health. This plan will prove to be the most effective means of providing the foundation for the prevention of conditions that lead to future and violent conflicts. It will also go a long way in helping individuals and groups of people within a social context experience bonding, autonomy and meaning – essential criteria for peace and relational justice leading to social, political and economic stability.

Notes

1 This statement was developed from the author's peacebuilding and psychosocial trauma work in the Balkans and West Africa as well as in response to a MSF special report about trauma assessment in Sierra Leone (de Jong, Mulham and van der Kam 2000). It captures the force and speaks to the importance of addressing intangible factors as part of the peacebuilding process.

2 For another wheel that presents multiple and integrated approaches necessary for a career in peacebuilding, see Lederach and Mansfield's (2010) "Strategic Peacebuilding Pathways."

References

Alexander, Jeffery. 2004. "Toward a Theory of Cultural Trauma." In *Cultural Trauma and Collective Identity*, edited by Jeffrey C. Alexander, Ron Eyerman, Bernard Giesen, Neil J. Smelser, and Piotr Sztompka, 1–30. Berkeley: University of California Press.

American Psychiatric Association, ed. 2013. *Diagnostic and Statistical Manual of Mental Disorders*. 5th ed. (DSM-V). Arlington: American Psychiatric Association Publishing.

Baingana, Florence, Ian Bannon, and Rachel Thomas. 2005. "Mental Health and Conflicts: Conceptual Framework and Approaches." Health, Nutrition and Population Discussion Paper. The International Bank for Reconstruction and Development/The World Bank, Washington, DC.

Bender, James. 2017. "What Are the Differences Between PTS and PTSD?" Accessed 9 January. www.brainlinemilitary.org/content/2013/12/what-are-the-difference-between-pts-and-ptsd.html.
Blanco, Amalio, Rubén Blanco, and Dario Diaz. 2016. "Social (Dis)Order and Psychosocial Trauma, Look Outside and Look Beyond the Persons." *American Psychologist* 71.3: 187–198.
Bubenzer, Friederike, and Marian Tankink. 2016. "Towards an Integrated Framework: Narrowing the Gap Between Psycho-Social Needs, Practice and Peacebuilding." Paper presented at the Conference 'Trauma, Memory and Healing in the Balkans and Beyond,' Bosnia & Herzegovina, Sarajevo, 12–14 July.
Burgess, Heidi. 2016. "Limiting Violence and Intimidation for Educators and Trainers." Accessed 14 May. www.beyondintractability.org/userguide/limitviolence-educators.
Burton, John. 1990. *Conflict: Human Needs Theory*. New York: Palgrave Macmillan.
Clark, Mary E. 2002. *In Search of Human Nature*. London: Routledge.
Dandaura Suma, Maiwa'azi. 2013. "Psychosocial Trauma Support Consultancy Strategies." nebula.wsimg.com/5213352dd3c2329b02463ae8cf448ef1?AccessKeyId=FD950DBF5959381B5267&disposition=0.
de Jong, Joop. 2009. "Public Mental Health." In *Trauma, Development and Peacebuilding: Toward an Integrated Psychosocial Approach*, INCORE, 24–25. New Delhi: International Development Research Centre.
de Jong, Kaz, Maureen Mulham, and Saskia van der Kam. 2000. "Assessing Trauma in Sierra Leone." Medicins Sans Frontieres, 11 January. www.doctorswithoutborders.org/news-stories/special-report/assessing-trauma-sierra-leone.
The Evidence Centre. 2012. "Evidence Scan: Cross Sector Working to Support Large-scale Change." The Health Foundation. www.health.org.uk/publication/cross-sector-working-support-large-scale-change.
Fischer, M., and L. Petrocic-Ziemer. 2013. Initiatives for Peacebuilding and Transitional Justice in Bossnia-Herzegovina, Serbia and Croatia. Berghof Foundation Report, no. 18.
Fuertes, Al B. 2004. "In Their Own Words: Contextualizing the Discourse of (War) Trauma and Healing." *Conflict Resolution Quarterly* 21.4: 491–501.
Hamber, Brandon, Elizabeth Gallagher, and Peter Ventevogel. 2014. "Narrowing the Gap Between Psychosocial Practice, Peacebuilding and Wider Social Change." *Intervention: Journal of Mental Health and Psychosocial Support in Conflict Affected Areas* 12.1: 7–15.
Hart, Barry, ed. 2008. *Peacebuilding in Traumatized Societies*. Lanham, MD: University Press of America.
Hart, Barry, and Edita Čolo. 2014. "Psychosocial Peacebuilding in Bosnia and Herzegovina: Approaches to Relational and Social Change." *Intervention: Journal of Mental Health and Psychosocial Support in Conflict Affected Areas* 12.1: 76–87.
Inter-Agency Standing Committee [IASC]. 2007. *Guidelines on Mental Health and Psychosocial Support in Emergency Settings*. Geneva: IASC.
Lange, Maria, and Mick Quinn. 2003. *Conflict, Humanitarian Assistance and Peacebuilding: Meeting the Challenges*. London: International Alert. http://pdf2.hegoa.efaber.net/entry/content/650/5_Conflict__Humanitarian_Assistance.pdf.
Lederach, John Paul. 1997. *Building Peace: Sustainable Reconciliation in Divided Societies*. Washington, DC: United States Institute of Peace.
Lederach, John Paul. 2003. *The Little Book of Conflict Transformation*. Intercourse, PA: Good Books.

Lederach, John Paul, and Katherine Mansfield. 2010. "Career Paths in Strategic Peacebuilding." Kroc Institute for International Peace Studies. http://kroc.nd.edu/strategic-peacebuilding-pathways.

Papadopoulos, Renos K. 2005. "Political Violence, Trauma and Mental Health Interventions." In *Art Therapy and Political Violence, with Art, Without Illusion*, edited by Debra Kalmonowitz and Bobby Lloyd, 35–59. New York: Routledge.

Pouligny, Béatrice. 2010. "Resilience, Trauma and Violence." Background paper to the report 'Societal Dynamics and Fragility: Engaging Societies in Responding to Fragile Situations,' World Bank, Washington, DC. doi:10.1596/978-0-8213-9656-8.

Rogers, Mark, Aaron Chassy, and Tom Bamat. 2010. *Integrating Peacebuilding into Humanitarian and Development Programming*. Baltimore: Catholic Relief Services. www.crs.org/sites/default/files/tools-research/integrating-peacebuilding-into-humanitarian-and-development-programming.pdf.

Schirch, Lisa. 2004. *The Little Book of Strategic Peacebuilding*. Intercourse, PA: Good Books.

Schirch, Lisa. 2005. "Strategic Peacebuilding: State of the Field." wiscomp.org/pubn/wiscomp-peace-prints/2-1/Lisa%20Schirch.pdf.

Schirch, Lisa. 2013. *Conflict Assessment and Peacebuilding Planning: Toward a Participatory Approach to Human Security*. Boulder: Kumarian Press.

Siegel, Daniel. 2011. "Mindsight, Mindfulness and the Journey from Me to We." Presentation at the Attachment Conference, Eastern Mennonite University, 31 March–2 April. emu.edu/now/attachment/2011/dan-siegel/.

Strategies for Trauma Awareness and Resilience (STAR). 2002. Level 1 Participant Training Manual. Development by the Faculty and Staff of the Center for Justice and Peacebuilding, Eastern Mennonite University.

Volkan, Vamik. 2004. *Blind Trust: Large Groups and Their Leaders in Times of Crisis and Terror*. Charlottesville: Pitchstone Publishing.

Wessells, M. 2008. "Trauma, Peacebuilding and Development: An Africa Region Perspective." A paper presented at the Trauma, Development and Peacebuilding Conference, New Delhi, India, September 9–11.

World Health Organization. 2016. "Mental Health: Strengthening Our Response." Media Centre Fact Sheet. www.who.int/mediacentre/factsheets/fs220/en/.

Zelizer, Craig. 2008. "Trauma-Sensitive Peace-Building: Lessons for Theory and Practice." *Africa Peace and Conflict Journal* 1.1: 81–94.

Zelizer, Craig, ed. 2013. *Integrated Peacebuilding: Innovative Approaches to Transforming Conflict*. Boulder: Westview Press.

Part II

How to remember and tell stories of trauma

5 "I can(not) remember"

The creation of collective narratives in postwar Bosnia and Herzegovina

Alma Jeftić

Introduction

The purpose of this chapter is to analyze the ways through which collective narratives have been created out of difficult memories that currently exist in postwar Bosnia and Herzegovina (BiH). In order to do so, I present an original model with the phases of a conflict narrative's development as a schematic blueprint for its creation, maintenance and further transmission. I analyze this model within the example of history teaching in divided postwar Bosnia and Herzegovina and discuss the problems related to the different teaching curricula that have existed since the late 1990s. It is important to notice that the period of 1992 to 1995 is not represented in two out of three history textbooks, which highly influences the important process of recognition of responsibility and crimes of one's own group.

The Conflict Narrative Development Model presented in this chapter is based on Bar Tal's (2013) rules of the formation of conflicting narratives, the divisions of memory errors given by Schacter (2001), Kraft's (2004) division of episodic memory and existing theories about unconscious bias. The study is based on qualitative approach that includes literature review and an analysis of three different history textbooks applied in three highschool teaching curricula in Bosnia and Herzegovina. These data serve as examples of divergent contemporary narratives of the past that may lead to further social divisions and influence the transmission of difficult memories (especially those related to the dissolution of Yugoslavia and the 1992–1995 wars). The chapter takes into consideration the way people often rely on familiarity and can be guided by implicit prejudice and stereotypes when filling in the content of difficult memories, especially in situations where their in-group committed wrongdoing. The vast powers of the human mind can be revealed not only through memory studies and cognitive science but also through the failure to recall and recollect certain information.

Social cognition research contributes to the understanding that prejudice and stereotypes affect the way people remember and report on the same events. It is believed that old-fashioned prejudice has given way to a modern bias that is implicit, subtle and often unintended (Goff et al. 2008). However, implicit prejudice can easily become an integral part of both individual and collective memory and is therefore transmitted to the following generations. The Conflict Narrative

Development Model formulated in this chapter seeks to shed some light on the processes and factors underlying and contributing to the creation of narratives out of difficult and/or traumatic memories as well as provide a basic understanding of memory's distortions, its maintenance and further transmission. The Model is analyzed within the context of history teaching in contemporary BiH, and the main implications and suggestions for teachers are proposed. The elements of the proposed Model are provided and implications for its further application are discussed.

Memory and remembrance in conflict

Memory and remembrance in conflict have been commonly studied within their contribution to the creation and maintenance of commemoration ceremonies, public events and culture in certain societies (Igartua and Paez 1997; Ross 2001; Hewer and Roberts 2012). Common culture, rituals, ceremonies and commemorations constitute a society's past, which is brought into the present and shaped according to the characteristics of that society. Connerton (1989) says that societies become more connected and unified through collective memory. The past becomes present for a group only through symbolic interactions, narratives and discourses. While studying cultural trauma of the Spanish civil war, Igartua and Paez (1997) came up with four factors of generational cycles of remembrance: the existence of the necessary psychological distance, an accumulation of the social resources aiming to cope with commemoration activities, progressive aging and the selective memories of those involved and the consequences of aging on socio-political repression. This is how memory becomes part of culture and is transferred cyclically through generations, adjusting to the context and needs of each cycle. Culture itself plays a role in this process by subtracting or adding content and by being changed for the generations that follow.

According to Halbwach's (1992) view, members of groups differ in the way they remember a common past. It is not unusual that members remember the past in ways that would put their group in a more favorable position, or at least in a way that provides explanations and justifications for in-group wrongdoing. Social groups remember the same past events in varying ways depending on the needs of the present and the *zeitgeist*(e.g., spirit or mood of a particular time in history described through beliefs or ideas) to which they belong. Liu (1999) found that the events in the history of New Zealand were remembered differently and described with different words by the indigenous and Anglo populations in the country, while Gaskell and Wright (1997) found differences between lower- and upper-class British residents in the quality of memory (as measured by the clarity and importance of and the emotional reaction to the memory) around Margaret Thatcher's resignation. Cairns and Roe (2003) discovered significant variation in the memories of British- and Irish-identified people of Northern Ireland about recent social and political events. Devine-Wright and Lyons (1997) found that different social groups (traditional vs. non-traditional in terms of political party preference) in Ireland associate different values and feelings with historical landmarks because they remember the history of these places differently. Therefore, Trinity

College, the oldest university in Ireland, which did not open its doors to Roman Catholics until the 1960s, was associated with feelings of shame, confusion and anger by traditionalists, whereas the same place revealed hope, pride and fascination for the non-traditionalists. Different memories for the same events lead to different stories that can be transmitted through generations and therefore enable groups to create their own deeply rooted interpretations and beliefs.

Ross (2001, 159) introduced the concept of psychocultural interpretations, which he defined as "shared, deeply held worldviews that help groups make sense of daily life and provide psychologically meaningful accounts of a group's relationship with other groups, their actions and motives." Group narratives contain important information about "the deep fears and threats to identity that drive ethnic conflict" (Ibid., 165) along with how the community explains conflict and what kind of motives they attribute to others' behaviors in the conflict.

Having in mind that people very likely attribute their own success to internal factors and failure to external factors, one can expect to find similar "errors" when analyzing the relationship between two groups in conflict. In their research, Doosje and Branscombe (2003) looked at the types of attributions Dutch people made for their colonization of Indonesia and the German invasion of the Netherlands (the Dutch were the aggressors in the former case and the victims in the latter). When the Dutch were the victims, they were more likely to make internal/character attributions for the negative behavior of Germans (e.g., Germans are aggressive by nature), while when they were the aggressors in Indonesia, they made more external/contextual attributions (e.g., "it is important to consider the acts of the Dutch in a historical context") (Doosje and Branscombe 2003). This pattern was emphasized by the strength of national identification; in other words, the stronger one's Dutch identity, the more internal attributions for the out-group's negative historical behavior and the more external attributions for the in-group's negative historical behavior.

In other research, Branscombe and colleagues have provided strong evidence for the relationship between categorization, identification, understanding history and feelings for one's in-and out-group (Branscombe and Miron 2004; Branscombe and Doosje 2004). They have shown that members of high status groups are more likely to feel collective guilt when inequality between groups is framed as in-group privilege (e.g., white privilege), as opposed to out-group disadvantage (e.g., black disadvantage) (Powell, Branscombe and Schmitt 2005), and that categorizing groups at more inclusive levels (e.g., humans vs. North American Jews and Native/First Nations Canadians) resulted in more forgiving attitudes toward the members of groups that had done harm in the past (e.g., Germans and White Canadians) (Wohl and Branscombe 2005).

Difficult memories in Bosnia and Herzegovina: elements of the conflict narrative development model

The formation of collective memories depends on both remembering and forgetting. Memory is fallible and our remembrance of things past is imperfect (Lehrer 2012, 82). Therefore, cognitive psychologists study both oral testimony and narratives to learn about the memory of atrocities, its aftermath and distortions. It is important to analyze the formation of conflict narratives at the individual level first, together with all the important factors that contribute to their formation and further development as collective memories and rooted narratives of conflict.

Both collective memories and formed narratives have important meaning for members of one society or social group. However, it is impossible to treat a collective memory as simply a set of shared individual memories due to its role in shaping identity.[1] Collective memories are in most cases shaped by conversations that can serve as both supportive and decisive mnemonic resources for spreading memories across a group or even nation (Mehl and Pennebacker 2003). Conversations can have an almost equal role in the formation of collective memories and narratives as textbooks, memorials or commemorations do. In a naturalistic context that is neither manipulated nor changed by the observer, members of a conversational dyad (the smallest possible social group of two persons engaged in conversation) can shape one another's memory of material they each viewed (Wright, Self and Justice 2000). When people remember the past in a social context, what they remember within the conversation has the potential to influence an individual's subsequent memories and thus increase the cohesiveness of these initially disparate memories (Coman, Brown and Koppel 2009, 135).

One mechanism that underlies the formation of collective memories through forgetting is retrieval-induced forgetting (RIF), a memory phenomenon that can reliably be found when a person retrieves information in a selective manner (Coman, Brown and Koppel 2009, 136). In such a way, the person can inhibit competing memories and thus have difficulty recalling them later. Cuc, Koppel and Hirst (2007) modified the RIF paradigm to investigate how it works in a social context, especially in free-flowing conversations. Based on the research findings, they concluded that listening to a speaker not only enhances the listener's memory of the information introduced by the speaker but also leads to increased probability of forgetting information related to what the speaker mentions (Coman, Brown and Koppel 2009, 136)[2] They named this phenomenon socially shared retrieval-induced forgetting (SS-RIF).

SS-RIF is important for explaining the construction of difficult narratives of conflict, as such selective narratives are mainly formed (and transmitted further) through communication between members of the same ethnic and/or religious group. During conversation, some parts of the stories are changed, some silenced and some emphasized. Therefore, in order to explain the process of conflict narrative formation, it is important to mention that our memories of specific events have been formed primarily through communication between our group members and further transmitted to other members of our group. However, communication is not the only factor that can modify our memories of the difficult past. The Conflict Narrative Development Model is a blueprint for the formation of difficult narratives in postwar conflict. As such, it is based on the following theories: Kraft's (2004) theory on core and narrative memory, Schacter's (2001) "sins of memory" (faults or mistakes due to bias) and Bar-Tal's (2013) themes of conflict formation (justification of conflict, delegitimization of the opponent, glorification and victimhood of the in-group, the in-group's need for patriotism and unity, and in-group's aspirations for peace). I describe group glorification and group belongingness factors together with the implicit stereotypes and prejudice that can heavily influence our attitudes toward the out-group.

The model (Figure 5.1) can be used to analyze how narratives of conflict are formed. Here I use the postwar context of Bosnia and Herzegovina, where different historical truths have led to the formation of more than three mnemonic communities. The model seeks to clarify the processes that contribute to the formation of individual memory and the processes that influence further grouping, transmission and maintenance of such memories.

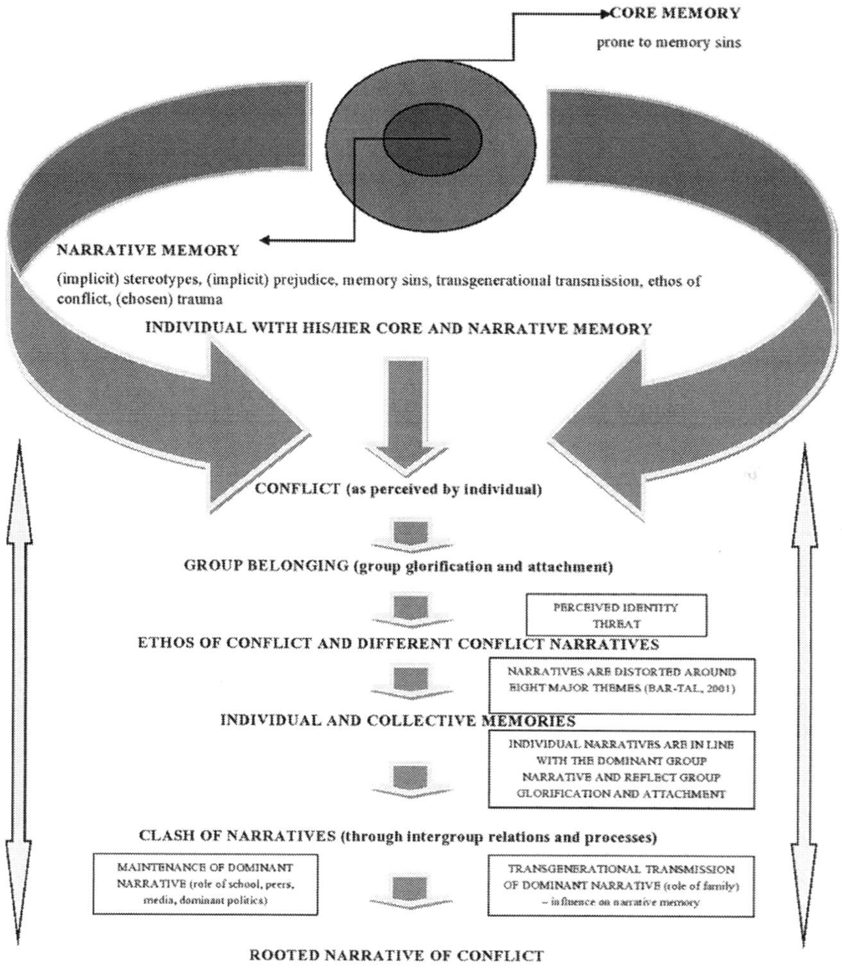

Figure 5.1 Conflict Narrative Development Model

The first part of the schema includes two circles corresponding to Kraft's description of episodic and narrative memory. The elements of episodic memory and the episodes themselves constitute two separate levels of memorial representation: core memory and narrative memory (Kraft 2006). Core memory is the representation of the original phenomenal experience in the form of perceptual, emotional and physiological experience such as visual images, sounds, smells, tastes, emotions and bodily sensations and can be both explicit and implicit. Representations of imagery and emotion that can be consciously experienced during extended recall, as well as implicit representations of emotional, physiological and bodily responses triggered by external events, are part of core memory as well (Kraft 2004). Core memories are then integrated and constructed into episodic narratives, creating memory's second level (Kraft 2006).

Narrative memory is constructed from the images in core memory, shaped in accordance with narrative conventions and conveyed primarily in language (Kraft 2006). The term narrative explains how one structures episodes in personal memory for the purpose of thinking about oneself in silent remembering and in communicating with others to tell the events of the past (Sarbin 1986). Core memory is prone to memory "sins" as described by Schacter[3] (2001), while narrative memory consists of and reveals (implicit) stereotypes, (implicit) prejudice, memory sins, transgenerational transmission, the ethos of a conflict and (chosen) trauma all together.

When an individual is faced with conflict, the way they perceive and understand it is highly influenced by memories they already possess. The sense of group belonging, glorification and attachment as a second part of this model influences the way threats to identity are or are not perceived. Glorification corresponds to beliefs of in-group superiority and deference to group norms and symbols (related to nationalism), whereas attachment refers to cognitive and emotional attachment to the in-group, such as self-definition as a group member or commitment to the group (Bilali 2012). The ethos of the conflict and of (different and difficult) conflict narratives are formed based on an individual's perception of conflict as a threat to themselves and in line with eight themes of conflict narratives given by Bar-Tal and presented as the last (third part) of the Conflict Narrative Development Model. Individual narratives correspond to the dominant group narrative and reflect the sense of group glorification and attachment. Even though the Model can be applied to the different context of intergroup relations, here I analyze it within the current schoolsystem in BiH.

Further intergroup relations in schools and classrooms lead to the clash of different and difficult narratives and therefore contribute to even stronger expressions of in-group superiority. Dominant narratives will be maintained through transgenerational transmission in the family and through external factors in society such as schools and the educational system (particularly history classes), peers, the media, dominant politics and the general *zeitgeist*. These narratives will be again stored within a core memory reservoir and reflected in the narrative memory of both individuals and groups. Therefore, there is a circular line between the individual's core and narrative memory, collective memory, the ethos of the conflict and the rooted narrative of conflict. Those subjects should be analyzed in one perpetual, circular stage, in which they mainly hinder reconciliation processes and contribute to the selective remembering of in-group wrongdoing, denial and different historical truths.

When applied to a divided history teaching situation, the model yields the following scenario: Each student and professor enters the class with their core and narrative memory, which is formed through the mechanisms just explained. When a certain historical narrative is presented in the class, depending on its significance for both group attachment and group belongingness, students and professor will either perceive it as a threat, a historical truth or a neutral description of an "unimportant" event. However, if either student(s) or professor perceive(s) it as a threat to their identity, a personal explanation or collective narrative will emerge. This narrative will be in line with individual memory (which could be a memory of survival or a transmitted memory) for a described event, which is aligned with one or more themes of the conflict narrative described by Bar-Tal (2013). In that sense the story contains all forms of the conflict ethos, which is in line with the dominant group narrative as well as with the perceived level of threat to group identity. This is very common among peers, such as high school students in BiH who did not experience the recent war but possess information from their in-group members about it. Since multiperspectivity – or the presentation of different narratives without emphasizing which is "historical truth" or a selective/distorted story (e.g., allowing students to present their own narratives) – does not exist in the Bosnian and Herzegovinian education system, both students and professors are faced with the fact that they are somehow allowed to present the dominant narrative of their group and to neglect all the other narratives that could be perceived as a threat to the dominant majority in one particular classroom. Therefore, that narrative becomes a rooted narrative of conflict in the sense that it is widely accepted by the majority in the classroom or neighborhood or work organization, maintained through school, intergroup relations, media and dominant politics and also transmitted to the generations that follow.

The beliefs expressed through conflict narratives feed the continuation of the conflict, which means there is a need to change these beliefs in order to move towardconflict resolution. The necessary change of scope can only begin with the intersection of individual and collective memory, and with special emphasis on the difference between core and narrative memory. It is especially important to analyze the ways through which the eight themes of conflict narratives occur (especially within the family and school) in order to mediate changes of belief related to the justness of conflict goals, delegitimization of the opponent, feelings of victimhood and notions of peace. Specifically, beliefs about contradictory goals have to change in order to remove the epistemic foundations of the conflict (Bar-Tal 2000). Reconciliation would require developing new goals that are achievable even in the absence of conflict that justify the resolution of the conflict and the sustaining of peace (Ibid.). Legitimization and personalization of the past rival/enemy should be achieved.

The new beliefs should also recognize the "contribution" of one's own group to the outbreak of the conflict and its extension, and the misdeeds of one's own group in the course of the conflict. This includes taking responsibility for atrocities committed (Bar-Tal 2013). The changes should reduce the monopolization of victimhood feelings, which characterize groups in intractable conflict. In the case of Bosnia and Herzegovina, a major emphasis should be given to school systems, including both primary and secondary school education, since different approaches to history, literature and art necessarily lead to deeper division from the younger generations upward. This second generation has also experienced problems of transmission of both difficult memories and trauma on the following levels: ethnic and religious identity, interethnic relations, the position of "others," the consolidation of traumatic memories and readiness for reconciliation. Therefore, multiperspectivity in education and the possibility to talk and discuss what their parents have survived can be beneficial for youth on different levels. However, strong emphasis should be given to history teachers and the way they organize their classes.

Teaching history means understanding its cognitive and affective dimensions (Rafferty 2013). History should be presented in a way that humanizes both victims and perpetrators and provides dialogue based on source evidence that can be further explored and questioned. It should neither excuse harmful actions nor fall into moral relativity (Rafferty 2013). Also, it is important not to forget the local context in which teaching takes place. History teachers should be trained on how to learn the basic elements of experiential learning (Kolb 1984), which integrates cognition, perception, behavior, experience and reflection in a holistic learning process. In that sense, in-class activities will be combined with field trips to museums and memorial sites, workshops and discussions on different perspectives in order to help students develop empathy and ability to understand different opinions on the same issues.

Multiperspectivity should also be integrated outside the school system in terms of more summer schools and non-formal seminars/workshops through which students have the chance to meet their peers from other regions, discuss different narratives and learn about the narratives' formation. It is important to evolve new beliefs about the nature of peace, which on the one hand, realistically describe the meaning of living in peace, and on the other hand, present the concrete conditions necessary for achieving and living in peace (Bar-Tal 2013). At this point, the first attempts to practice multiperspectivity in primary and secondary school history teaching in BiH are being initiated by the Association of History Teachers in Bosnia and Herzegovina in the form of workshops, education in terms of field trips and site visits and plans for new history textbooks. One of the first steps taken by this group was an initiative to educate history teachers about the meaning, importance and applicability of multiperspectivity in BiH. To date, they have completed several workshops related to this matter as well as projects on capacity-building among history teachers, the uses and abuses of history in the classroom and "history for the future."

History teaching in contemporary Bosnia and Herzegovina: a challenge to the conflict narrative development model

Although Bosnia and Herzegovina is an internationally recognized and independent state, the country's three constitutive people have not yet agreed on a unified history curriculum for elementary and secondary schools. Instead, three different curricula persist: those of the two entities (the Federation of BiH and Republika Srpska) and parts of BiH where teaching follows the Croatian curriculum (Jeftić 2013). At the beginning of 2008, the Office of Security and Cooperation in Europe (OSCE) Mission to BiH and the Georg Eckert Institute for International Textbook Research conducted a survey among 184 history teachers from across the country in order to determine the most commonly used textbooks and teachers' opinions on topics dealing with the war period of 1992–1995. About 53 percent of the examined teachers expressed that the war should be included in history textbooks as a special teaching unit since they found the themes "the consequences of war" and "the destruction of cultural and historical monuments" very interesting and as such necessary for inclusion in history textbooks (Ibid.).

Since the late 1990s, the recent war has not been included in the official curriculum in most parts of BiH, which is in line with the Council of Europe's recommendations to temporarily suspend teaching about the war years. This hiatus, which remains to this day, has contributed to the way in which these three different narratives have been transmitted to future generations.

The transgenerational transmission of narratives requires understanding the formation of generational communities within a society and their relationships to the past. A generation is an ambiguous term because, on the one hand, it indicates the continuity of life, and the other, marks a new beginning (Kuljić 2009). Living in the past can be very dangerous, because it prevents progress and creation of a vision of future. However, without knowing the past, a vision for the future does not exist (Ibid.). Different generational communities form various community memories and their relationships to the past define their system of values (including knowledge, attitudes and beliefs shaped by a group's prevailing memories).

The revision of history flows in several directions (Ibid.): contents in historical narratives may be omitted or complemented, the meanings of facts can be variously interpreted, the relationship between relevant historical facts may been changed or the interpretation of historical facts modified. History and history textbooks have always been trapped between the way a nation perceives itself and the (distorted) image of the "other," namely, those who represent a minority and therefore do not fit within the idealized picture of that nation (Cole and Barsalou 2006). This is usually the case in postwar divided communities such as Bosnia and Herzegovina.

BiH is a country where history teaching suffers more because of the political situation and attempts to establish peace than because of the applied pedagogical methods. The Parliamentary Assembly of the Council of Europe proposed guidelines for teaching about the war in its 2000 recommendation (Recommendation

1454) for historians from all ethnic groups to collaborate with international experts in developing a common approach (Karge and Batarilo 2008).[4] The Parliamentary Assembly of the Council of Europe intervened in the case of BiH's curriculum by establishing a committee and proposing guidelines; however, these approaches contributed more to the formation of an intellectual vacuum and the omission of 1992–1995 events from history textbooks than they did to the creation of a common narrative. A commission composed of representatives from BiH's three constituent peoples, supervised by the international experts, analyzed the history textbooks used in BiH primary and secondary schools in order to eliminate "inappropriate" and "offensive" material that could be considered discriminatory from any of the three positions and also according to the International Convention on Human Rights (Pingel 2008). Textbook publishers were obliged to change textbooks in accordance with the agreement reached by this commission established by the Parliamentary Assembly of the Council of Europe. The Council subsequently sent representatives from UNESCO with the task of monitoring history teaching in schools, which generated protests and also provoked students to read "prohibited" sources. The Parliamentary Assembly of the Council of Europe cooperated with the BiH Ministry of Education, which aimed to organize the review and verification of textbook manuscripts prior to printing. Although the work of this committee largely "offset" language and excluded extreme interpretations within the textbooks, it did not change the opinions of experts from the three constituent peoples and did not result in a unified history textbook to be used by all (Ibid.). The process did not encourage anyone to be critical about their own community's conflict narrative.

The committee's next step was writing new history textbooks for four grades of high school. However, in 2003, guidelines for writing history and geography textbooks were adopted as the basis for developing a balanced, comparative and multi-perspective narrative (Ibid.). These Guidelines for the Evaluation of History Textbooks for Primary and Secondary Schools in BiH were forwarded to the ministries of education in both entities (Ibid.). Three years later those guidelines were officially signed and accepted for printing (Ibid.). The guidelines define: the quantity of information related to the political history that should be reduced; how history textbooks should be written, since the modern textbook is expected not only to educate, but also to encourage, guide and lead the development of students; and how history textbooks should look, from format to content (Jeftić and Joksimović 2014). However, recognizing responsibility and crimes of one's own group is still a key problem faced by the authors of history textbooks, and certainly this is one of the reasons why the period of 1992 to 1995 is not mentioned in two out of three history textbooks used in BiH today (Ibid.). It is clear that textbook authors and experts in the field of education refuse to use material from international courts and tribunals located outside the borders of their state "since the courts are considered biased" (Corkalo et al. 2004, 147). In order to overcome bias and to give the opportunity for other stories to be heard, multiperspectivity could therefore be introduced into history teaching.

Although the guidelines for drafting the textbooks exist, the results of our content analysis reveal that none of the three current textbooks[5] follow them fully

(Jeftić and Joksimović 2014). This is especially true of the textbook used in the areas of BiH applying a Croatian curriculum, within which the war years in BiH (as well as in Croatia) are described in full (Jeftić 2013, 44). The inconsistencies of the three curricula are visible in their descriptions of the dissolution of Yugoslavia, especially when it comes to highlighting the role of neighboring countries and the frequency of mentioning these countries (Jeftić 2013, 44). The textbook used in the Republic of Srpska, for example, mostly mentions Serbia and its role in the breakup of Yugoslavia, and the textbook used according to the Croatian curriculum in BiH emphasizes Croatia and its role, as well as the subsequent events during the Croatian "Homeland War" of 1991–1995 (Jeftić 2013; Jeftić and Joksimović 2014).

Although the contents of textbooks used in the Federation of BiH do not mention the war in BiH, the topic is mentioned in the preface:

> This textbook deals with world, European and Bosnian history of the late nineteenth and the entire twentieth century. . . . It is particularly important to note that in this period, an independent state of BiH was established, after a long and terrible war, which was led against it by all means.
>
> (Hadžiabdić et al. 2007, 5)

A textbook used in the Republic of Srpska contains very interesting and specific instructions for students/readers at the end of the chapter "Yugoslavia after World War II":

> You can be informed of the events of our most recent past (after 1991) on the basis of interviews with contemporaries (teachers, parents, participants in events) as well as from other sources (newspapers, documents, photographs, documentaries, etc.). [This] information can be discussed during history class and tutorials.
>
> (Živković and Stanojlović 2012, 163)

These examples imply that, while not described in the book, the controversial events of the 1990s can be discussed during history classes, which is not in accordance with the Guidelines. If we analyze this in terms of the Conflict Narrative Development Model, we realize that without a narrative of the war formalized in history textbooks, the dominant in-group narrative can be given priority during history classes. Therefore, topics which are not in line with that narrative will be silenced and thus excluded.[6]

Differences in approaches to the historical record can greatly influence adolescents' identity development, which is further influenced by the transmission of narratives of the difficult past. That leads to different interpretations of the same historical events and different, usually negative attitudes toward the ethnic and religious "other." Two outcomes from this process seem possible: the construction of a common narrative that could be widely accepted, or the formation of conflicting narratives. In postwar divided societies, the creation of a shared narrative presents the safest way to prevent further conflict, as it can promote unity and cohesion. However, the persistence of multiple narratives could open a space for intergroup discussion as well as for grouping and selecting *our* and *their* narratives. Therefore, the level of in-group glorification and belongingness determines the extent atrocities committed by one's own group are silenced and how much one's own group's victimization is emphasized.

This is in line with Bar-Tal's (2013) themes of narrative formation. In the case of history teaching, both students and professors will also be more likely to accept narratives that correspond to the positive sides of their in-group, to discuss those narratives more, and to find excuses and reasons for the atrocities committed by their in-group, which is again in line with Bar-Tal's theory. Hence, memory bias, as one of the memory sins described by Schacter (2001), is the main mechanism that governs the formation of difficult narratives, especially in situations when we are faced with two opposite and conflicting interpretations of the same event: the higher the level of group glorification and group belongingness we possess, the higher our bias and tendency to defend our own group will be. Moreover, we will be more inclined to further transmit narratives that support views dominant in our group, as well as to silence those narratives that can harm the group image.

Because of this, it is essential to apply multiperspectivity in history teaching. However, multiperspectivity cannot be applied in BiH and neighboring countries without agreement on a common terminology.[7] It is of great importance to leave empty space between the three narratives, to give students and teachers room for discussion (and possible selection of a new narrative). That is also in line with the dialogical method based on biographical storytelling invented by Bar-On (1995). The method emphasizes the importance of telling one's life stories in order to distract attention from the prevailing political climate (Pingel 2017, 235). Experimental social psychological research has also highlighted the potential positive effects of empathy and perspective-taking, with the aim of biographical storytelling to ready oneself for what Pettigrew has defined as "self-closure": to open oneself to others (Pettigrew 1998). Thus, the stories' coherence and the sincerity of narration and the narrator create confidence and allow the listeners to relate themselves to the experiences of the "other" (Pingel 2017, 236). In this way, both students and teachers could freely and openly discuss all issues as long as they ensure no offense to the dignity of the "other."

Conclusion

To conclude, the formation of difficult narratives of conflict include several factors:

- A core memory that is prone to memory errors;
- narrative memory that includes (implicit) stereotypes, (implicit) prejudice, memory sins, transgenerational transmission, an ethos of the conflict, (chosen) trauma;
- group belonging (group glorification and attachment).

However, difficult narratives are maintained through the following mechanisms:

- socially shared retrieval-induced forgetting, which includes both communication between family members and larger groups as well as silencing the difficult past;
- the existing*zeitgeist*, which includes school, peers, the media and dominant politics.

These three elements and two mechanisms contribute to the formation of rooted narratives of conflict, which further develop in society and through the repetition of those mechanisms. In order to change difficult narratives of the past in postwar societies such as Bosnia and Herzegovina, it is important to promote changes in primary and secondary education. Multiperspectivity should be introduced during extra classes, summer schools and/or workshops in which students and teachers have an opportunity to discuss their core and narrative memories and to understand the mechanisms of their formation (the eight themes of conflict narratives, memory sins, implicit prejudice and stereotypes). Also, history teachers should become aware of the necessity to develop empathy instead of teaching facts only. The ability to take the perspective of the "other" and to listen to different narratives are two main preconditions for multiperspectivity in history teaching. Also, both in-class activities and field trips and seminars contribute to the experiential learning that contributes to the important fact that students learn through reflection, application and understanding of examples from everyday life. "*Remembrance for peace*" cannot be introduced without a clear understanding of the processes through which difficult (and different) narratives of the past are formed and transmitted through generations. Once revealed, these mechanisms will help highlight the whole range of problems and misunderstandings, as well as paths to their possible solutions – or at least methods to overcome the most rooted ones.

Notes

1 For instance, we can say that all Bosnians and Herzegovinians know the alphabet of their native language; however, knowing the alphabet is not something that shapes their identity. On the contrary, knowing the exact year when the last war started (1992) is something that shapes their identity (regardless of different approaches and interpretations of the same date).

2 For instance, Coman, Brown and Koppel (2009) found out that listening to somebody remembering how she/he experienced 9/11 induces one to forget their own personal memories in a manner consistent with the speaker's forgetting. Also, Cuc, Koppel and Hirst (2007) found that listening to a speaker remember selectively can induce forgetting of related information in the listener.

3 These are transience, absent-mindedness, blocking, misattribution, suggestibility, bias and persistence. The first three are described as sins of omission, since the result is a failure to recall an idea, fact or event; the last four are described as sins of commission.

4 Until March 2017, no mutual agreement had been reached regarding the representation of the 1992–1995 war in history textbooks in BiH. In December 2016 the Governor of Canton Sarajevo announced the establishment of the Working Group for Drafting

History Textbooks, whose main task is to include events from the 1992–1995 war in history textbooks in the Federation of BiH so that students could start learning about it. As of July 2018, there is no further information regarding the progress of this group, nor is there any information that the same or similar activities have begun in the Republic of Srpska or areas in Herzegovina where the Croatian curriculum has been applied since the 1990s.

5 Hadžija Hadžiabdić, Edis Dervišagić, Alen Mulić and Vahidin Mehić, 2007, *Historija-Istorija-Povijest* (Tuzla: Bosanska Knjiga); Hrvoje Matković, Franko Mirošević, Božo Goluža and Ivica Šarac, 2003, *Povijest 4 – Udžbenik za četvrti razred gimnazije* (Mostar: Školska naklada and Zagreb: Školska knjiga); Dušan Živković and Borislav Stanojlović, 2012, *Istorija za treći razred gimnazije prirodno-matematičkog i za četvrti razred gimnazije opšteg i društveno-jezičkog smjera* (East Sarajevo: Zavod za udžbenike i nastavna sredstva).

6 BiH as a state is referred to 18 times in "The Dissolution of Yugoslavia" chapter of the Federation of BiH textbook and 16 times in the Croatian curriculum textbook, whereas the Republic of Srpska's textbook does not mention BiH within that chapter (Croatia is mentioned once and Serbia six times). Two curricula used in BiH devote more attention to the events in the neighboring countries of Serbia and Croatia than to the events in BiH when relating Yugoslavia's disintegration.

7 There are different interpretations of the same war events in contemporary Bosnia and Herzegovina. For instance, what is considered to be genocide or a massacre for one group never happened or included too few victims to be described as either genocide or a massacre, according to another group.

References

Ajduković, Dean, and Dinka Čorkalo. 2004. "Trust and Betrayal in War." In *My Neighbor, My Enemy: Justice and Community in the Aftermath of Mass Atrocity*, edited by Eric Stover and Harvey Weinstein, 287–302. Cambridge: Cambridge University Press.

Bar-On, Daniel. 1995. "Encounters Between Descendants of Nazi Perpetrators and Descendants of Holocaust Survivors." *Psychiatry* 58.3: 225–245.

Bar-Tal, Daniel.2000. *Shared Beliefs in a Society: Social Psychological Analysis*. Thousand Oaks, CA: Sage.

Bar-Tal, Daniel. 2013. *Intractable Conflicts: Socio-Psychological Foundations and Dynamics*. Cambridge: Cambridge University Press.

Bilali, Rezarta. 2012. "Identity Centrality and In-Group Superiority Differentially Predict Relations to Historical Victimization and Harm Doing." *International Journal of Conflict and Violence* 6.2: 322–338.

Branscombe, Nyla R., and Bertjan Doosje. 2004. *Collective Guilt: International Perspectives*. Cambridge: Cambridge University Press.

Branscombe, Nyla R., and Anca Miron. 2004. "Interpreting the Ingroup's Negative Actions Toward Another Group: Emotional Reactions to Appraised Harm." In *The Social Life of Emotions*, edited by Larissa Z. Tiedens and Colin Wayne Leach, 314–355. New York: Cambridge University Press.

Cairns, Ed, and Michael Roe. 2003. *The Role of Memory in Ethnic Conflict*. New York: Palgrave MacMillan.

Cole, Elizabeth A., and Judy J. Barsalou. 2006. *Special Report: Unite or Divide? The Challenges of Teaching History in Societies Emerging from Conflict*. Washington, DC: United States Institute of Peace.

Coman, Alin, Adam Brown, and Jonathan D. Koppel. 2009."Collective Memory from a Psychological Perspective." *International Journal of Politics, Culture and Sociology* 22: 125–141.

Connerton, Paul. 1989. *How Societies Remember*. Cambridge: Cambridge University Press.

Cuc, Alexandru, Jonathan Koppel, and William Hirst. 2007."Silence Is Not Golden: A Case for Socially-Shared Retrieval-Induced Forgetting." *Psychological Science* 18: 727–737.

Devine-Wright, Patricia, and Evanthia Lyons. 1997. "Remembering Pasts and Representing Places: The Construction of National Identities in Ireland." *Journal of Environmental Psychology* 17.1: 33–45.

Doosje, Bertjan, and Nyla Branscombe. 2003."Attributions for the Negative Historical Actions of a Group." *European Journal of Social Psychology* 33: 235–248.

Gaskell, George, and Daniel B. Wright.1997. "Group Differences in Memory for a Political Event." In *Collective Memory of Political Events: Social Psychological Perspectives*, edited by James W. Pennebaker, Dario Paez, and Bernard Rim, 175–191. Mahwah, NJ: Lawrence Erlbaum Associates.

Goff, Phillip A., Jeniffer L. Eberhardt, Melissa J. Williams, and Matthew C. Jackson. 2008. "Not Yet Human: Implicit Knowledge, Historical Dehumanization, and Contemporary Consequences." *Journal of Personality and Social Psychology* 94.2: 292–306.

Hadžiabdić, Hadžija, Edis Dervišagić, Alen Mulić, and Vahidin Mehić. 2007. *Historija-Istorija-Povijest*. Tuzla: Bosanska Knjiga.

Halbwachs, Maurice. 1992. *On Collective Memory*. Chicago: The University of Chicago Press.

Hewer, Chris J., and Ron Roberts. 2012. "History, Culture and Cognition: Towards a Dynamic Model of Social Memory." *Culture Psychology* 18.2: 167–183.

Igartua, Jaunjo, and Dario Paez. 1997. "Art and Remembering Collective Events." In *Collective Memory of Political Events: Social Psychological Perspectives*, edited by James W. Pennebaker, Dario Paez, and Bernard Rim, 79–101. Mahwah, NJ: Lawrence Erlbaum Associates.

Jeftić, Alma. 2013. "Social Discourse in History Teaching: A Case of Bosnia-Herzegovina." In *Economic Crisis and European Union*, edited by Ali Gosku and Merdzana Obralic, 84–98. Sarajevo: International Burch University.

Jeftić, Alma, and Jelena Joksimović. 2014. "Divided Presentations in History Textbooks in Three Ex Yugoslav States: Discussing Implications for Identity Development." In *Official Conference Proceedings: The European Conference on Psychology and Behavioral Sciences*, 47–60. Japan: International Academic Forum (IAFOR).

Karge, Heike, and Katarina Batarilo. 2008. *Reforma nastave historije u BiH. Modernizacija udžbenika historije u BiH: od uklanjanja uvredljivog sadržaja iz udžbenika u toku 1999. godine do nove generacije udžbenika u školskoj 2007/2008. godini*. Braunschweig: Georg Eckert Institute for International Textbook Research.

Kolb, David A. 1984. *Experiential Learning: Experience as the Source of Learning and Development*. Vol. 1. Englewood Cliffs, NJ: Prentice-Hall.

Kraft, Robert N. 2004. "Emotional Memory in Survivors of the Holocaust: A Qualitative Study of Oral Testimony." In *Memory and Emotion*, edited by Daniel Reisberg and Paula Hertel, 347–389. New York: Oxford University Press.

Kraft, Robert N. 2006. "Archival Memory: Representations of the Holocaust in Oral Testimony." *Poetics Today* 27.2: 311–330.

Kuljić, Todor. 2009. *Sociologija generacija*. Belgrade: Čigoja.

Lehrer, Jonah. 2012. *Proust Was a Neuroscientist*. London: Canongate.

Liu, James H. 1999. "Social Representations of History: Preliminary Notes on Content and Consequences Around the Pacific Rim." *International Journal of Intercultural Relations* 23.2: 215–236.

Mehl, Mathias R., and James W. Pennebacker. 2003. "The Social Dynamics of Cultural Upheaval: Social Interactions Surrounding September 11." *Psychological Science* 14: 579–585.

Pettigrew, Thomas F. 1998. "Intergroup Contact Theory." *Annual Review of Psychology* 49:65–85.

Pingel, Falk. 2008. "Can Truth Be Negotiated? History Textbook Revision as a Means to Reconciliation." *Annals of the American Academy of Political and Social Science* 617: 181–198.

Pingel, Falk. 2017. "A Clash of Communication? Intervening in Textbook Writing and Curriculum Development in Bosnia and Herzegovina After the War of 1992–1995." In *History Education and Conflict Transformation: Social Psychological Theories, History Teaching and Reconciliation*, edited by Charis Psaltis, Mario Carretero, and Sabina Cehajic-Clancy, 231–255. Basingstoke: Palgrave Macmillan.

Powell, Adam A., Nyla R. Branscombe, and Michael T. Schmitt.2005. "Inequality as In-Group Privilege or Out-Group Disadvantage: The Impact of Group Focus on Collective Guilt and Interracial Attitudes." *Personality and Social Psychology Bulletin* 31.4: 508–521.

Rafferty, Rachel. 2013."Teaching History After Violent Conflict: The State of an Emerging Field." Master's thesis, University of North Carolina at Chapel Hill.

Ross, Mark Howard. 2001."Psycho-Cultural Interpretations and Dramas: Identity Dynamics in Ethnic Conflict." *Political Psychology* 22.1: 157–178.

Sarbin, Theodore R. 1986. "The Narrative as a Root Metaphor for Psychology." In *Narrative Psychology: The Storied Nature of Human Conduct*, edited by Theodore R. Sarbin, 3–21. Westport, CT: Praeger Publishers/Greenwood Publishing Group.

Schacter, Daniel. 2001. *The Seven Sins of Memory: How the Mind Forgets and Remembers*. New York: Houghton-Mifflin.

Wohl, Michael A., and Nyla R. Branscombe. 2005. "Forgiveness and Collective Guilt Assignment to Historical Perpetrator Groups Depend on Level of Social Category Inclusiveness." *Journal of Personality and Social Psychology* 88.2: 288–303.

Wright, Daniel B., Gail Self, and Chris Justice. 2000. "Memory Conformity: Exploring the Misinformation Effects When Presented by Another Person." *British Journal of Psychology* 91: 189–202.

Živković, Dušan and Borislav Stanojlović. 2012. *Istorija za treći razred gimnazije prirodno-matematičkog i za četvrti razred gimnazije opšteg i društveno-jezičkog smjera*. East Sarajevo: Zavod za udžbenike i nastavna sredstva.

6 Creating a multidirectional memory for healing in the former Yugoslavia

Stephanie C. Edwards

Public witness is central to communal healing in post-conflict zones. In this process, "testimony records a movement from individual experience to the collective archive, from personal trauma to public memory. But when testimony located on a national stage is riven by conflicting aims among those bearing witness, such a transformation is impeded" (Miller and Tougaw 2002, 13). The International Criminal Tribunal for the former Yugoslavia (ICTY) provides a perfect example of the stilted transformation of traumatic experience. Rather than providing the peaceful resolution so many hoped for, the ICTY seems, from my perspective, incapable of promoting true reconciliation. Deeply intertwined with religious and cultural expression, many residents of the former Yugoslav region today view their former compatriots as directly complicit in past violence because of their membership in an ethno-religious group, not just for their individual actions. Conflicts over identity persist on all levels of society, from intrapersonal to governmental to religious. This prompts the question of how such embedded identities and narratives, forged in the trauma of war, can be bridged. This chapter proposes one avenue for peace through reading trauma theory in general and the work of Michael Rothberg, in particular, in the former Yugoslav context. Rothberg provides a fruitful proposition of "multidirectional memory" that seeks to overcome competing narratives of suffering by uncovering connections across experiences of trauma. This chapter explores multidirectional memory in the former Yugoslavia as a possible tool for the development of non-harmful cultural memories within shared physical and figurative spaces.

As an outsider to the region and its lived experience, I hope to offer a thematic reflection that focuses on the universal experience of "geography of self" that is deeply harmed in communal violence (Erikson 1994, 159). Three months of personal travel throughout the former Yugoslavia in 2011, particularly the people I met during that time, also inspired this project. Their willingness to share not only their experiences of the conflict but their ongoing struggles for personal and political peace form the structure behind my arguments. Finally, it should be noted that I am a theological ethicist and practicing social worker whose research is located in interdisciplinary trauma studies. As such, my methodology draws upon research from diverse fields and examines their findings in the light of trauma theory. In this chapter, I first present a very brief assessment of the former Yugoslav conflict as what anthropologist Mark Juergensmeyer terms "cosmic war." This provides context for the broader, often negative, embedded social realities that endure in the region. Second, I offer a treatment of the ICTY from international legal scholars who determine that it actually represents, at best, a lackluster attempt at peacemaking and, at worst, a direct miscarriage of justice. Following this dismal assessment of the ICTY, I then explore the possibility for multidirectional memory in the former Yugoslavia through trauma literature. This third and final discussion presents an interdisciplinary approach that aims to provide a potential reframing of the regional experience and explore theoretical ways forward through trauma theory. Authentically addressing the intricate patterns of complicity and connection that persist in the region today reveals the truly interwoven nature of its identities and communities and the potential for lasting peace.

I. The Yugoslav conflict as "cosmic" war

The dissolution of the former Yugoslavia was brutal. As theologian and Croatian native Miroslav Volf succinctly put it: "The result: a world without the other. The price: rivers of blood and tears. The gain: except for the bulging pocketbooks of warlords and war profiteers, only losses, on all sides" (2010, 57). Beginning officially with unrest in Kosovo in 1991, the wars finally ended in 1999 with an estimated 130,000–140,000 dead, up to 60,000 women raped (mostly Bosniak/Muslim), and the destruction of near countless homes, villages and historical sites.[1] Although frequently framed as an embedded ethnic war, the conflict is better understood as rooted in the desire to control material resources and political power in a climate very attuned to state control.[2] Prior to the conflict there was distinctiveness between Bosniak (Muslim), Croat (Catholic) and Serb (Orthodox) groups, but there was also general social cohesion in the daily lives of most communities. While everyone did not "get along" at all times, neither was hatred de facto (Broz 2004, xxiii). In fact, religion was *not* a defining factor in many (if not most) citizens' lives, but it became central to their identities because victims of violence were selected based on religious group, and religious "institutions, symbols, rituals, and ideologies" were the primary modes through which violence was motivated and justified. In fact, "Some survivors have remarked, for example, that they had not viewed themselves as religious or even thought about their religious identity until they were singled out for persecution because of it: they discovered they had a religious identity only in the act of its being imposed upon them" (Sells 2003, 308–309). The resulting ethnic cleansing, and indeed the term "ethnic" itself, can hide the imposed nature of religious categories in the Yugoslav conflict. These identities "are political categories that have emerged from historical struggles" (Broz 2004, xxix). Although this chapter cannot fully treat the development and time line of the conflict, it is important to draw out the true nature of ethnic identity in the region in order to explore the ongoing narratives of culture-wide complicity as well as possible healing from such trauma.

Of particular importance to any new narrative is the recognition of the history and root of current cultural scripts. Manipulations of such scripts are incredibly effective in creating what anthropologist and religion scholar Mark Juergensmeyer calls "cosmic war." The cosmic orientation posits that the existing conflict "transcend[s] human experience" (2003, 149). Religion provides the most common framework to justify the motivations that compel persons to act violently. In cosmic terms, individual "acts of violence, by implication, were merely responses to a great ongoing struggle" (Ibid., 148). In the breakdown of Yugoslavia, Serb leader Slobodan Milošević instrumentalized religious mythology to purge moderates, put nationalists in charge, and formulate secret police and death squads to carry out his vision. The institutions and symbols of Orthodox Christianity provided Milošević with "a framework from which such bloodshed made sense and was not only justified, but was an act of sacrificial redemption" (Sells 2003, 314).

One of the most powerful myths that emerged in this space was of a "Serb Jerusalem," a concept that extended sacred space into national geography. The "Serb Jerusalem" promoted a narrative of a hallowed Christian past that existed in Serbia, encouraged through the construction of new religious sites (with a claim to historical ties, even if fabricated), alongside hyperbolic claims of the destruction of Serbian holy art and architecture, mostly in modern-day Kosovo. With the cooperation of the Orthodox Church, Milošević and his allies supported these actions, and also encouraged the ritual reenactment of the death of Serbian King Lazar, who died at the Battle of Kosovo in 1389 while leading a Christian army to resist the invasion of the Ottoman empire. Lazar had sought to resurrect the Serbian empire, a task he, and the Orthodox Church, believed he was chosen by God to complete. In death, he was deemed a martyr and is now venerated as an Orthodox saint. Rituals calling back to Lazar's death fostered an attitude of constant threat, particularly from Muslims: that the powerful, sacred space of the so-called "Serb Jerusalem" is "always being destroyed by different facets of the same hostile ethnic and religious power" (Sells 2003, 313). This threat was to be understood as not only spiritual but also material. To survive, as a faith and a people, the physical spaces of the nation state must be protected at all costs. Milošević endeavored to create a climate of constant conflict through such symbols that manipulated the region toward his own power. Importantly, cosmic war need not have actions considered legitimate to groups outside the conflict but only to the involved communities themselves. Therefore, localized "moral, ideological, and organizational support necessary" for violence is created (such as "Serb Jerusalem") that then collectivizes individual actions, implicating all individuals, which leads to a fear-driven society (Juergensmeyer 2003, 11). For example, worshiping a new religious narrative that tied itself explicitly to political violence meant that even if one questioned its veracity and did not enact violence personally, one might still cooperate with groups/individuals that did pursue violence through material support or merely inaction (whether motivated by religion, safety or basic needs, see Kissell (1999) and Kutz (2000) for further discussions of complicity). In the context of "cosmic war," this moral implication, again couched in cosmic religious terms, encourages further violence.

Imposition of nationalized religious identity to create "cosmic war" defined the Yugoslav conflict. Institutional categories overrode individual roles and hid the actions of normal civilians behind the gruesome behavior of the few. In the Yugoslav wars, genocide was not done by "popular participation"; "people struggled against this radical reinterpretation of the world that was played out by power politics on their identities, bodies, and homes" instead (Broz 2004, xvi–xvii. See also Biro and Milin 2005, 135). However, complicity occurred through threats by civil authorities and the power of the religious narrative that urged even minor participation. Indeed, "help and aggression come from various quarters" (Broz 2004, xxi).[3] Still today, victims remain "faced with a world in which unspeakable crimes not only went unpunished but were rewarded with glory, profit, and power" (Ibid., xvi). Many citizens continue to cling to the narratives of power and division fostered through the conflict to retain a sense of justification for past actions, or merely ongoing hope for the future. The complex realities operating within Balkan rhetoric, such as the conflict's "cosmic" orientation, must be recognized to illuminate effective pathways toward the creation of new cultural memories.

II. The ICTY and its discontents

A crucial component of the current climate in the former Yugoslavia is the resonating impact of the ICTY. While this chapter cannot provide an exhaustive treatment of the ICTY, this summary demonstrates the failure of the ICTY to counter harmful cultural narratives and the need to look for more effective means of doing justice. The ICTY was created in a "revolution" of public international law during the early 1990s. International tribunals were initiated around the world to hold individuals criminally responsible for mass atrocities (Arzt 2006, 226). More generally, the aim of such tribunals is to consolidate democracy and ensure "the triumph of the rule of law over the instinct for revenge after prolonged periods of communal violence" (Ibid., 227). As the first such international trial court since Nuremburg, a mandatory resolution of the United Nations Security Council established the ICTY in 1993. Every country of the former Yugoslavia opposed the resolution. As the war was still raging, the court was located in The Hague. Ordered to conclude its proceedings multiple times, the ICTY finally officially closed in December 2017, nearly 25 years after it began ("ICTY Marks Official Closure" 2017).

A central problem of the ICTY for many critics is that The Hague is "physically and psychologically remote to the population" (Arzt 2006, 228). Necessary because of ongoing conflict, locating the ICTY outside the former Yugoslavia made its mission harder to accomplish. Additionally, early in its development, "ICTY personnel were focused on the tasks of institution building and did not pay much attention to the continual fanning of the flames of ethnic hatred by regional leaders and the media, who were simultaneously spewing paranoid rhetoric against the tribunal itself" (Ibid., 230; see also Spoerri and Freyberg-Inan 2008). After five years of existence, the ICTY began an outreach program to educate the citizenry about its process and purpose; however, national leadership had already colored much of the popular language regarding the court as biased, unfair and even an extension of discrimination against the region (particularly in Serbia, where it was framed as an "international conspiracy") (Arzt 2006, 234; see also Ramet 2012, 8). Additionally, the trials were used by Serbian politicians to glorify war criminals (Spoerri 2011, 1844; Clark 2008, 337–338). Despite general local disdain for the ICTY, a 2004 survey showed that 64 percent of those Serbs questioned had "little or very little" knowledge of the ICTY's purpose or progress in its mission (Arzt 2006, 232). Similar but not as stark statistics existed in Croatia (Ibid., 233). The Serbian electorate seemed to hold an "almost fatalistic resignation to the state's low standard of living. . . [and] seems to no longer believe change is possible and accepts the truism that nothing ever changes, except the political party in power" (Aleksić 2013, 196).

Most of the successes of the ICTY fall within its expansion of the power and use of international law rather than within the situation it was created to address. As many legal scholars have noted regarding international courts, it is one thing to articulate goals and another to determine if such goals are understood "on the ground" (Arzt 2006, 229, 231).[4] Although international law was upheld by the court, its method did not ensure the triumph of the rule of law within the former Yugoslavia, nor did it eliminate a drive for revenge. In fact, the four central aims of criminal trials such as the ICTY (dissipation of calls for revenge, individualization of guilt, establishment of a historical record and contribution to reconciliation) are at the very least found to be problematic in their practice and efficacy (Clark 2009a). However, multiple studies have established that through radio and televised trials, as well as the creation of a thorough website of records, some victims feel a measure of vindication. Such "proof," given publicly from a body other than a state involved in the conflict, provides some legitimation of victims' experience. It relieves pressure from the victims by confirming their experience and showing (at times) full confessions by those at fault. Yet the trials also have a perceived bias from the perspective of many citizens of the former Yugoslavia, and many victims question its overall effectiveness (Ibid., 235; Saxon 2005).[5] Even guilty pleas, often induced through plea bargains, while seen by the ICTY as a method of fostering reconciliation, have little to no impact on the broader climate of tension in the former Yugoslavia (Clark 2009b). Additionally, guilty pleas are often associated with some form of perceived (or real) impunity, which can exacerbate the fear of victims who may feel a continued threat from the group responsible for their suffering through ongoing political upheaval and traumatization (Başoğlu et al. 2005). Although the ICTY continued to prosecute persons involved in genocide and war crimes, it did little to counter the continuation of harmful cultural narratives. Indeed, "[A]ll three primary national communities in the region, the Serbs, Croats, and Muslims, views itself [sic] as a victim and not as a perpetrator of aggression and atrocities against the other parties" (Saxon 2005, 562). With such embedded narratives and experiences of victimization, fear and exclusion from the justice process, an alternative avenue toward cultural healing must be sought.

III. Reading Bosnia in Belgrade

From this footing, both reading the Yugoslav conflict as "cosmic war" and the failure of the ICTY to address violent cultural narratives, I now turn toward trauma theory. Trauma theory, in particular the work of Michael Rothberg, provides a unique lens through which to view the current moment as one of possibility for citizens to create their own "multidirectional memory." While this chapter cannot provide a full assessment of trauma theory to date, I will present here theoretical reflections that may provide support for those seeking to foster generative cultural memories in the region currently, a potential way of rereading, for example, *Bosnia in Belgrade*.

IIIa. Multidirectional memory in contested space

Rothberg's theory of multidirectional memory is rooted in the systemic location of those who suffer and focuses on the globalized nature of the world and what this global awareness means for creating a productive discourse across traditional national, ethnic or racial boundaries (Rothberg 2013, xi–xiii).[6] By expanding the vision of traumatic experience beyond particular traumatic histories, Rothberg explores how experiences of communal trauma are remembered in the public sphere. With ever-increasing access to stories of particular events around the world, it can appear that competing narratives of suffering overcome one another, again and again, as new traumas occur and survivors vie for support to pursue justice, reconciliation or aid programs. However, Rothberg posits that it is possible that public memory can be seen beyond its competition for headlines. Instead, according to him, we must view memory as "multidirectional," where the

> public sphere [is] a malleable discursive space in which groups do not simply articulate established positions but actually come into being through their dialogical interactions with others; both the subjects and spaces of the public are open to continual reconstruction."
>
> (Rothberg 2009, 5)

It is the *working through* to which we must turn our attention. In the former Yugoslav successor states, claiming what has been done *to* the space of discourse (as outlined earlier) and reclaiming it as non-competitive is a crucial move for any sort of new, generative cultural memory. The tendency and attraction to create a competitive "uniqueness discourse" remains strong, yet narratives of suffering are intertwined and interrelated across the region. In this way, "multidirectional memory posits collective memory as partially disengaged from exclusive versions of cultural identity and acknowledges how remembrance both cuts across and binds together diverse spatial, temporal, and cultural sites" (Ibid., 11). *Multidirectional memory cuts and binds*. Such a memory displaces historical fidelity as the central aim of narrative formation, which can be painful in situations of intragroup, and particularly religiously justified, conflict. In the former Yugoslavia, historical fidelity must be read via its very real manipulation by sociopolitical powers. "History" can be challenged by multidirectional memory to transcend what is presented as "fact" to allow for creation of new memory in the midst of, because of, and beyond historical fidelity.

However, this globalized notion of multidirectional memory is incredibly challenging, both theoretically and practically, when engaged within groups involved in internal conflict. As sociologist Kai T. Erikson outlines, the impact of disasters, natural or man-made, is not limited to the event itself but becomes intertwined with the physical and psychological condition of the community (1994, 230). Trauma and stress from the event itself, in this case the former Yugoslav wars, and the so-called recovery supposedly addressed within the ICTY, are eventually woven into the fabric of the community (Gill 2007, 625; Erikson 1976, 1994). Suffering can then become central to identity, creating "the real problem . . . that the inhumanity people experience comes to be seen as a natural feature of human life rather than as the bad manners of a particular corporation [or broader entity]" (Erikson 1994, 239). In this way, creating a multidirectional memory in the former Yugoslav region must attend to the recognition of the "bad manners," to put it blithely, of power-seeking politicians, and instead attempt to reach an understanding beyond what are presented as "natural" cultural divisions.

Political scientist Jenny Edkins offers a way forward in such a climate by maintaining a critical view toward traumatic memory's usurpation by political powers (2003, 7). She resists the ease with which trauma is discussed publicly, and instead highlights the production of a trauma narrative as an aspect of a complicit body politic. In fact, the attempt to force trauma into language and the public sphere is arguably impossible, as our language and expressions are so thoroughly mediated by the status quo of a given power structure that any account of suffering is immediately translated into digestible language for consumption, rather than service to the real experience of pain (see also Scarry 1985). Thus, in proceeding through attempts at communal memory, a linear, exact narrative of trauma must not be the main goal. However, translation of experience remains necessary and sought after by communities dealing with trauma. Edkins recognizes this and points toward a new way of communicating trauma, one that presents "an alternative, that of *encircling the trauma.* We cannot try to address the trauma directly without risking its gentrification. We cannot remember it as something that took place in time, because that would neutralize it" (Edkins 2003, 15).[7] Neutralizing trauma allows for the experience to be neatly packaged into a given narrative and then often manipulated by structures of power. In the former Yugoslavia, certain narratives of trauma are kept active in current memory for better or worse depending on the power structures at play. In proposing the practice of "encircling," Edkins is supporting much of Rothberg's aims of multidirectional memory, including highlighting the ongoing nature of trauma, but with a keen, suspicious, unwavering attention to the damaging political, social and cultural structures of power – all too often responsible for trauma, and all too willing to co-opt and reinscribe trauma for their purposes.

In the former Yugoslavia, a region where narrative space and identity is much contested, the restoration of neutral space is one way multidirectional memory can be fostered. Physical and metaphorical space creates a sense of individual and communal location, and "people need location almost as much as they need shelter, for a sense of place is one of the ways they connect to the larger human community" (Erikson 1994, 159). War and violence produce a devastated "geography of self" (Ibid.) that must be reclaimed. This is the potential locus of transformation not only of individual or intragroup narrative but a method that can ultimately reach across divisive regional boundaries. Creating spaces of cross-cultural access, or reviving old ones, is an essential activity to "attempt to re-knit the fragile web of inter-ethnic and inter-religious solidarity" (Spahić Šiljak 2016). Yet, as security specialist Jelena Subotić summarizes:

> the past in the Western Balkans . . . is not yet over. In fact, to paraphrase Faulkner, it is not even the past . . . the countries of the region are stuck in public narratives of the past that are mutually exclusive, contradictory, and irreconcilable.
>
> (2012, 108)

Subotić clearly outlines how state powers in the Western Balkans mediate history. Leaders attempt to establish "themselves as dominant, constituting for many an unquestioned 'common sense' and marginalizing alternative understandings" (Subotić 2013, 307, quoting Krebs and Lobasz 2007, 412–413). Therefore, a delicate combination of attention is necessary for multidirectional memory in the region. This balance must be one that binds particularity and universality, intertwines linear, historical accounting and unbound, nonlinear suffering, and seeks justice and truth alongside poetic expression, all to uncover hope for a new cultural narrative.

An illustration of multidirectional memory in another context is helpful. Rothberg offers a reflection upon W.E.B. Du Bois's 1949 visit to Poland, and Du Bois's subsequent article, "The Negro and the Warsaw Ghetto." Du Bois was distinctly moved by his time in the ghetto, reflecting on the disturbing echoes of suffering of the Jews and black Americans. On this site, he saw the production of biopolitical space that reveals racialized thinking and state violence enacted on bodies (Rothberg 2009, 115). A double vision of uniqueness as a well as similarity emerged and became central to all of Du Bois's work, balancing both the extreme particularities of a context while simultaneously recognizing commonalities. In this way, a multidirectional memory becomes the condition for authentic solidarity, not a false "unity" that only supports the political priorities of the powerful (Ibid., 12, 121). Standing in the rubble of Warsaw, Du Bois uncovered a relational view, that the "experiences of particular suffering can be brought into dialogue with each other" (Ibid., 131). Such a counter-discourse can only be found, however, if groups embrace Rothberg's proposition of non-competition. Only when "one is willing to give up exclusive claims to ultimate victimization and ownership over suffering" can new cultural, and even religious, narratives be created (Ibid., 132). It is not that metaphorical "real estate" and concrete physical space do not matter but that both can be resisted, reinterpreted and brought under the greater goal of a relational effort toward mutual understanding and peace. In recognizing connection, it is clear that all people are "implicated subjects, beneficiaries of a system that generates dispersed and uneven experiences of trauma and wellbeing simultaneously" (Rothberg 2013, xv; see also Rothberg 2009, 310). In very real ways, histories are "implicated in each other" and it is impossible to maintain a wall between them, even if desired. Perhaps someday a Bosniak will stand in in Belgrade, as Du Bois stood in Warsaw, to testify that "the only way forward is through . . . entanglement" (Rothberg 2009, 303).

IIIb. Truth, fidelity and ethics in multidirectional memory

Entanglement, however, does not necessitate an abandonment of justice. Rothberg himself points toward the ethical implications of multidirectional memory, and determines that "all articulations of memory are not equal" (Ibid., 14–15; see also Aleksić 2013, Chapter 5). When dealing with large-scale, insidious narratives such as those present in the Balkans, Rothberg ties resistance and creativity to democratic power. Citing political philosopher Nancy Fraser, he argues that post-traumatic contexts need to move toward justice through "struggles for *meta-political democracy* . . . [such that there is] no redistribution or recognition without representation" (Rothberg 2009, 20). In this mode, the quest for justice itself is enacted through speech about justice. While this turns attention from very real material needs and demands, the ethics of multidirectional memory rather focus on the concept of *fidelity* to the event, as outlined by Alain Badiou (Ibid., 22). In Badiou's construction, connections or disconnections must be explored, not assumed. Fidelity in this sense is a commitment to the truth, but one that seeks to transcend private or material concerns. Fidelity in practice uncovers truth, where "a truth is innovation *en acte*, singular in its location and occasion, but universal in its 'address' and import" (Hallward 2001, ix). Multidirectional memory turns our gaze toward the metaphysical, that "subjects are both *carried by* a truth – they compose the 'finite' points of an always 'infinite' truth – and provide its literal material 'support'" (Ibid., x). Yet this process must perform a delicate balance of "normalizing" experience for the victim to facilitate very necessary healing and also resist in some way the paradox of relieving powerful actors from responsibility through such normalization. It functions such that "by allegedly liberating the individual from her traumatic experience, the language simultaneously normalizes that very trauma and, moreover, requires that the victim continue functioning within the same structure (communal, cultural, historical) that originally inflicted the trauma upon her" (Aleksić 2013, 153).[8] As outlined by Subotić earlier, narratives have very real power in the former Yugoslavia, and by fostering multidirectional memory's intricate balance of narrative and justice in a more theoretical space, divisive national narratives can potentially be overcome.

IV. Building multidirectional memory in the former Yugoslavia

To explicitly illuminate the possibility for a multidirectional memory in the traumatic wake of the Yugoslav wars, it is helpful to explore the work of Tatjana Aleksić, a Serbian comparative literature scholar now working in the United States. Her work offers necessary nuance, especially that of particular embodiment, to Rothberg's proposal, as well as a thickness of place specific to the context. Using Aleksić, it is clear that multidirectional memory in the former Yugoslav territory must resist the tendency within state-sanctioned stories of the past to reduce "political space for debate and conflict" and foreclose free rhetorical space (Subotić 2013, 309). It must also recognize and defy more metaphysical narratives that encourage two dominant cultural trends: (1) the thrust toward a neoliberal capitalist economy above all other concerns, and (2) "a falsely spiritual and egalitarian pursuit of common identity" (Aleksić 2013, 15). Finally, multidirectional memory in the former Yugoslavia must function to effectively counter the hegemonic imposition of meaning, instead turning toward fostering ethical relationality.

To accomplish such ambitious goals, Aleksić reads literature, art and film focused on the Western Balkans and uncovers a more insidious tendency toward a "sacrificial economy" in the region. Just as the regional conflicts functioned as "cosmic wars" manipulated by those in power, Aleksić exposes foundational myths that represent a deeply embedded tendency toward sacrifice in the Western Balkans, namely, the suppression of liminal bodies in service to the collective. She uses a Balkan edifice-building myth to clarify her point. *The Building of Skadar* is a Serbian epic that repeats in slightly different iterations throughout the entire region. It tells the story of builders who murder the lead contractor's wife and bury her within the walls of the structure they are creating to satisfy the demands of the powerful, omniscient narrator of the story. The killing occurs to sate the god figure, but also to sublimate the conflict present between the workers themselves. The myth further reveals that "both the perpetrators and the victims of the communal enterprise eventually come to share a sense of inevitability and imperative collaboration with the incomprehensible demands made by the invisible authority" (Aleksić 2013, 4–5).[9] Sacrifice in this story is more than just a myth and continues to function within society as a way to encourage the ongoing repression of the individual to the collective. Aleksić warns of the less explicit but still present power of the sacrificial narrative in postwar zones, that

> laws are not infrequently overridden by much more ancient and rooted communal traditions. . . [and] regardless of their "bloodlessness," such insidious administrative (legal) forms of discrimination and cleansing are barely less inhumane, and their ultimate effects not infrequently lead to the same deadly outcome.
>
> (Ibid., 11)

Importantly, the sacrificial narrative is not limited to the region of the former Yugoslavia but is instead an arguably global phenomenon with mythic, even religious, power.

To further explore the sacrificial impulse in the Yugoslav successor states, as well as point toward hope of resistance to its power, Aleksić purposefully focuses on the victim. It is the victims who reveal socially

> undesired bodies. . . [whose] bodies themselves are a visible reminder of the fragility of communal ideologies based on restrictive and exclusive identities. Such bodies, on the contrary, by necessity offer a glimpse at the possibility of a different community, constructed on heterogeneity and mutual respect of differences.
>
> (Ibid., 17)[10]

This brings into distinct embodiment Rothberg's more theoretical multidirectional memory. In the former Yugoslavia, the mythological victim killed and entombed in the walls of the structure is very real and alive in the bodies of the diversity of people who suffered through the violent conflict. It is these individuals who, in reflecting upon their experience in a cultural context, demand recognition of their unique experience, but remain bound together by common trauma. However, Aleksić points out that the vacuum of true regional community has long allowed groups to "live alongside each other although rarely *with* each other" (Ibid., 10). In this way, while experience has taught most of the former Yugoslav citizenry to be wary of state power, groups continue to foster myths of division among themselves that support the "building of an important, endlessly postponed structure," a myth both political and social, "paid for in blood" to supposedly secure safety and identity (Ibid.). Divisive, sacrifice-based narratives continue to gain power and influence in the former Yugoslav region. For example, throughout the spring of 2014, protests in Bosnia and Herzegovina erupted, focused on economic insecurity and dissatisfaction with the leadership. While some citizens saw the actions as focused on building a better future, others believed that the unrest was fostered as a "state of preparation for genocide" (Vahidin Omanović, interviewed by Zoodsma 2014, 7). This reaction may have been tied to the experience of the demonstrations in Sarajevo that marked the beginning of the war in Bosnia and Herzegovina, but it also reflected the continuation of divisive ethno-nationalist narratives that those in power continue to interweave into politics and economics. Aleksić is less than hopeful that radical structural change will occur to alter such an environment, and believes instead in gradual grassroots movements that can resist both the temptations of capitalism and a perhaps overly utopian drive to communalism. It is only such small-scale efforts that can reveal the subliminal sacrificial economy and support those who seek to resist its power. Aleksić writes that it is

> many individual acts of subversion of the hegemonic narrative that, however minuscule, still succeed in expanding the limits of freedom. Such individual

> acts of subversion are found in the very sacrificed body and at the exact moment when its "immurement" in and for the structure becomes certain, on the invisible boundary between the body's obvious defeat and its humble victory: in the half-buried woman cursing the edifice that is about to eat her alive. . . . The small acts of determination and revolt by small people gradually expand the public space and create potential for its further expansions.
> (2013, 194, 197)

These efforts usually happen completely outside the "official" system. They are neither sanctioned nor supported by those who, as Edkins reminds us, are seeking to support their own power rather than create space for authentic change. Such "small acts" are often fluid demonstrations of communication and memorialization that attempt to speak toward the creation of a new memory. Aleksić concludes that through these acts, the power of moral obligation is uncovered; that is, communities take on mutual interest for one another and a moral sense of social obligation (Jürgen Habermas as cited by Aleksić 2013, 187).[11] Aleksić recognizes that this is perhaps the hardest thing to accomplish, as even the status of "fellow victim" does not ensure understanding. However, even if genuine liberation from the sacrificial cycle may be impossible, awareness of its existence and power is needed to confront our own base fear of change and open the potential for transformation of this fear (Ibid., 189). Change, then, does not come by replacing political leaders or shifting the focus to different historical events but with the dynamic revolution of attitudes, beliefs and practices that all seek to achieve a truly multidirectional memory.

Echoing critics of the ICTY and recognizing the ongoing tension throughout the former Yugoslavia, Aleksić is very pessimistic regarding the possibilities for the Western Balkans to overcome their divisions and even for the sacrificial drive of the world writ large to be overcome. In some sense, "Historical trauma acts as a somatic hereditary disorder to which no individual is immune or can escape" (Ibid., 19). Aleksić wants to argue for a broader sense of historical responsibility but cannot seem to lay the claim for potential responsibility on anyone but the victims themselves, even as they are subject to the ongoing throes of structural control and traumatic experience. However, as Aleksić and some ICTY detractors argue, even quasi-benevolent interventionism must be resisted, as it too often attempts to suppress the ghosts of history and even ensure their violent reemergence (Ibid., 181–182).

Yet in her assessment of transitional justice in the former Yugoslavia for the Berghof Foundation, peace and development scholar Natascha Zupan (2005) argues that endemic efforts to establish a redefined shared value system are critical to any long-lasting peace and require outside support. As such, some potential lessons for other contexts can be gleaned from the critiques of the ICTY presented here and the attempt to understand what a multidirectional memory could mean in the former Yugoslavia. First, grassroots outreach and support efforts must be of primary importance. As recognized by the ICTY itself, these efforts and corresponding programmatic funding were delayed to the extent that the impacted populations had little to no connection with the processes of the ICTY and no perceived involvement in its proceedings. As Hajra Catic, President of the Srebenica Women's association stated:

> We are glad that the genocide charge has remained [for Bosnian Serb Army General Radislav Krstic]. Any sentence shorter than a life sentence for a criminal such as Krstic is unacceptable for us. Of course, no-one listens to us. We are so disappointed with the Hague Tribunal and unhappy with their sentences. If a criminal who is being tried just admits that he committed crimes, he is forgiven for half [of what he did] and gets a minimum sentence. Thus, we really do not expect justice from them.
>
> (Saxon 2005, 564)

The work of grassroots peacebuilding, including work to discredit false and harmful cultural narratives, must be an essential component to any reconciliation process. By locating this work directly in the communities themselves, victims have more direct access to determine what justice and healing might look like for themselves and their communities – including and apart from strictly legal proceedings. This leads to the second potential lesson from the ICTY and multidirectional memory, that funding should be allocated to physical spaces for community-based reconciliation and meaning-making efforts, culturally appropriate psychological assistance and addressing the concrete needs of impacted populations. While international law may mandate its own due process, it should not be the exclusive driver of reconciliation. Instead, it is within such local spaces that individual as well as collective trauma can begin to be addressed to counter the real or perceived threats to safety and loss of control over one's life that can lead to increased post-traumatic stress disorder (PTSD) and depression in post-conflict zones (Başoğlu et al. 2005). In tandem with the material and psychological healing of communities, individual acts of subverting the hegemonic system (that attempts to mandate certain forms of healing and one "acceptable" narrative) can be bound together through practices such as storytelling, art and play. Such shared "small acts" can resist the combination of "economic interest and human pettiness" (Aleksić 2013, 18) that creates what sociologist and philosopher Jürgen Habermas describes as the apathy of the "satisfied and relatively satisfied" (as quoted by Aleksić 2013, 187). As Zoodsma (2014) and Spahić Šiljak (2016) outline, these small, local group efforts to combat this tendency have long occurred in spaces away from public attention and are directly intended to humanize the "other." Such activities seek not false equality or token diversity but instead attempt to foster a shared life of, at times complex and messy, ethical relationality. Creating spaces of cross-cultural access can provide the space to develop a multidirectional memory (one that cuts with individual truth and binds with universal relation) through hosting locally rooted regional truth commissions endorsed by the states or groups involved and provide networks of counter-narratives to the chosen "truth" of power structures (such as the different histories of the war taught in the segregated educational system of modern-day Bosnia and Herzegovina; Subotić 2012).

V. Conclusion

In this chapter, I have demonstrated the potential for the development of a multidirectional memory in the Western Balkan region. In an ongoing climate of unresolved tension, it is essential for traumatic histories to be read through their structural aspects as well as individual experiences. Herein, an exploration of the Yugoslav conflict as a constructed "cosmic war" and the failed efforts of the ICTY to address ongoing harmful cultural narratives were interrogated as the backdrop for the potential efficacy of a multidirectional memory in the former Yugoslavia. A multidirectional memory provides a different "screen" upon which to read traumatic conflict and supports ongoing peacebuilding efforts in the region.[12] Only when groups reach beyond a competitive, divisive construction of communal memory can the former Yugoslav people reshape their narrative toward generation and peace rather than acrimony and violence.

Notes

1 Lists of destruction of towns, religious and historical sites by religion identity can be found in Sells (2003, 309–331). The Yugoslav wars resulted in one of the first recognitions of rape as a modern warfare tactic. It was not only individualized but also occurred in "rape camps" where women and children were held (see United Nations 2016).

2 "It was territorial aggression, backed by the convenient ideology of ethnic separatism, which justified the crime of ethnic cleansing committed on orders from the politicians" (Broz 2004, xxiv). Broz, the granddaughter of former Yugoslav leader Josip Broz Tito, was able to collect oral histories spanning the three major ethnic groups in Bosnia Herzegovina partially due to her perceived neutrality through her familial ties (2004, xxxv).

3 To battle the dominant, manipulative voices of the creators of conflict, the voices of individuals who suffered are crucially important to the creation of generative cultural memories to combat ongoing acrimony. See also Juergensmeyer (2003, 13). Like Juergensmeyer (although he is addressing terrorism), I undertake a "cultural approach" to considerations of both complicity in and experience of trauma. Focus on the victim is an admittedly ethical move as inspired in this context by Volf and his teacher, Jürgen Moltmann.

4 While retributive justice, such as that sought by the ICTY, can be an integral part of the on-the-ground peacemaking process, to date direct correlation with criminal trials and peace is under-researched. Best practices currently state that a more holistic set of processes has the most hope of establishing satisfactory and lasting peace in postwar areas (Clark 2011).

5 The majority of those apprehended also tended to be "small fry" (Ramet 2012, 6). There is a further discussion of representation of victims in such venues as the ICTY as tokenization and chosen only to represent an "acceptable" version of the victim narrative (Hesford 2004).

6 While Rothberg's (2009) event of concern is the Holocaust, he argues (in 2013) for expanded nuance and application of trauma studies. Thus, Rothberg's work is directly applicable to the Western Balkan situation, as it is essential to consider how the Holocaust not only helped to create trauma theory but arguably remains the backdrop and reference point for all subsequent mass suffering.

7 Edkins draws on Slavoj Žižek's construction of an open social order with an "acceptance of lack" at its center. See also Subotić (2013) who discusses in more detail how the past becomes "social fact" using Steve Stern's concept of emblematic memory.

8 Also important here are the discussions of the role of "witness" and testimony in traumatic experience as explored by Caruth (1996, 2013) and Felman and Laub (1991). Caruth particularly discusses an "ethical relation" to the real that endures through trauma.
9 Also explored are the gender and social location aspects of the narrative, which are too detailed to clarify here. A potential further exploration would be into a dialogue with the Girardian mimetic cycle of violence broken by the scapegoat mechanism, as well as the direct overtones of religious motivations.
10 Aleksić frames sacrificial bodies as "pathogens." She also discusses the subversion possible through self-sacrifice of individuals who "inscribe themselves on the prohibited space" as a way of asserting power but then ultimately are brought under the communal demands for cleansing in the name of purity (Ibid., 19). History is played out on bodies, and must be read in such a manner. See Aleksić's (2013) Chapter 5 and specifically her discussion of the work of performance artist Marina Abramović (especially relevant for this discussion is *Rhythm 0,* 1974).
11 For reflections on practices and processes of peace as well as the related roles of complicity and responsibility, I refer to Spahić Šiljak (2016) as well as Zehr (2002), Sullivan and Tifft (2003), Johnstone (2011), Lederach (2005) and Kutz (2000).
12 A nod to Sigmund Freud's concept of screen memory.

References

Aleksić, Tatjana. 2013. *The Sacrificed Body: Balkan Community Building and the Fear of Freedom*. Pittsburgh: University of Pittsburgh Press.

Arzt, Donna E. 2006. "Views on the Ground: The Local Perception of International Criminal Tribunals in the Former Yugoslavia and Sierra Leone." *The Annals of the American Academy of Political and Social Science* 603.1: 226–239.

Başoğlu, Metin, Maria Livanou, Cvetana Crnobarić, Tanja Frančišković, Enra Suljić, Dijana Ðurić, and Melin Vranešić. 2005. "Psychiatric and Cognitive Effects of War in Former Yugoslavia: Association of Lack of Redress for Trauma and Posttraumatic Stress Reactions." *Jama* 294.5: 580–590.

Biro, Mikloš, and Petar Milin. 2005. "Traumatic Experience and the Process of Reconciliation." *Psihologija* 38.2: 133–148.

Broz, Svetlana. 2004. *Good People in an Evil Time: Portraits of Complicity and Resistance in the Bosnian War*. New York: Other Press.

Caruth, Cathy. 1996. *Unclaimed Experience: Trauma, Narrative and History*. Baltimore: Johns Hopkins University Press.

Caruth, Cathy. 2013. *Literature in the Ashes of History*. Baltimore: Johns Hopkins University Press.

Clark, Janine Natalya. 2008. "The Three Rs: Retributive Justice, Restorative Justice, and Reconciliation." *Contemporary Justice Review* 11.4: 331–350.

Clark, Janine Natalya. 2009a. "The Limits of Retributive Justice Findings of an Empirical Study in Bosnia and Herzegovina." *Journal of International Criminal Justice* 331–350.

Clark, Janine Natalya. 2009b. "Plea Bargaining at the ICTY: Guilty Pleas and Reconciliation." *The European Journal of International Law* 20.2: 415–436.

Clark, Janine Natalya. 2011. "Peace, Justice and the International Criminal Court Limitations and Possibilities." *Journal of International Criminal Justice* 521–545.

Edkins, Jenny. 2003. *Trauma and the Memory of Politics*. Cambridge: Cambridge University Press.

Erikson, Kai T. 1976. *Everything in Its Path: Destruction of Community in the Buffalo Creek Flood*. New York: Simon & Schuster.

Erikson, Kai T. 1994. *A New Species of Trouble: The Human Experience of Modern Disasters*. New York: W.W. Norton & Company.

Felman, Shoshana, and Dori Laub. 1991. *Testimony: Crises of Witnessing in Literature, Psychoanalysis and History*. New York: Routledge.

Gill, Duane A. 2007. "Secondary Trauma or Secondary Disaster? Insights from Hurricane Katrina." *Sociological Spectrum* 27: 613–632.

Hallward, Peter. 2001. "Translator's Introduction." In *Ethics: An Essay on the Understanding of Evil*, edited by Alain Badiou, vii–xlvii. London: Verso.

Hesford, Wendy S. 2004. "Documenting Violations: Rhetorical Witnessing and the Spectacle of Distant Suffering." *Biography* 27.1: 104–144.

ICTY. 2017. "ICTY Marks Official Closure with Moving Ceremony in The Hague." United Nations International Criminal Tribunal for the Former Yugoslavia. Accessed 14 August 2018. www.icty.org/en/press/icty-marks-official-closure-with-moving-ceremony-in-the-hague.

Johnstone, Gerry. 2011. *Restorative Justice: Ideas, Values, Debates*. 2nd ed. New York: Routledge.

Juergensmeyer, Mark. 2003. *Terror in the Mind of God: The Global Rise of Religious Violence*. Berkeley: University of California Press.

Kissell, Judith Lee. 1999. "Complicity in Thought and Language: Toleration of Wrong." *Journal of Medical Humanities* 20.1: 49–60.

Krebs, Ronald R., and Jennifer K. Lobasz. 2007. "Fixing the Meaning of 9/11: Hegemony, Coercion, and the Road to War in Iraq." *Security Studies* 16.3: 409–451.

Kutz, Christopher. 2000. *Complicity: Ethics and Law for a Collective Age*. Cambridge: Cambridge University Press.

Lederach, John Paul. 2005. *The Moral Imagination: The Art and Soul of Building Peace*. New York: Oxford University Press.

Miller, Nancy K., and Jason Daniel Tougaw, eds. 2002. *Extremities: Trauma, Testimony, and Community*. Champaign: University of Illinois Press.

Ramet, Sabrina P. 2012. "The ICTY-Controversies, Successes, Failures, Lessons." *Southeastern Europe* 36.1: 1–9.

Rothberg, Michael. 2009. *Multidirectional Memory: Remembering the Holocaust in the Age of Decolonialization*. Stanford: Stanford University Press.

Rothberg, Michael. 2013. "Preface: Beyond Tancred and Clorinda – Trauma Studies for Implicated Subjects". In *The Future of Trauma Theory: Contemporary and Cultural Criticism*, edited by Gert Buelens, Samuel Durrant, and Robert Eaglestone, xi–1. London: Routledge.

Saxon, Dan. 2005. "Exporting Justice: Perceptions of the ICTY Among the Serbian, Croatian, and Muslim Communities in the Former Yugoslavia." *Journal of Human Rights* 4.4: 559–572.

Scarry, Elaine. 1985. *The Body in Pain: The Making and Unmaking of the World*. New York: Oxford University Press.

Sells, Michael. 2003. "Crosses of Blood: Sacred Space, Religion, and Violence in Bosnia-Hercegovina." *Sociology of Religion* 64.3: 309–331.

Spahić Šiljak, Zilka. 2016. "Women, Religion and Peace Leadership in Bosnia and Herzegovina." EWI Fellowship Programme. Accessed 21 December. www.eiz.hr/wp-content/uploads/2014/12/Zilka-Spahic-Siljak-ENG.pdf.

Spoerri, Marlene. 2011. "Justice Imposed: How Policies of Conditionality Effect Transitional Justice in the Former Yugoslavia." *Europe-Asia Studies* 63.10: 1827–1851.

Spoerri, Marlene, and Annette Freyberg-Inan. 2008. "From Prosecution to Persecution: Perceptions of the International Criminal Tribunal for the Former Yugoslavia (ICTY) in Serbian Domestic Politics." *Journal of International Relations and Development* 11.4: 350–384.

Subotić, Jelena. 2012. "The Past Is Not Yet Over: Remembrance, Justice and Security Community in the Western Balkans." *Journal of Regional Security* 7.2: 107–118.

Subotić, Jelena. 2013. "Stories States Tell: Identity, Narrative, and Human Rights in the Balkans." *Slavic Review* 72.2: 306–326.

Sullivan, Dennis, and Larry Tifft. 2003. "What Are the Implications of Restorative Justice for Society and Our Lives?" In *Critical Issues in Restorative Justice*, edited by Howard Zehr and Barb Toews, 387–400. New York: Criminal Justice Press and Willan Publishing.

United Nations. 2016. "Background Information on Sexual Violence Used as a Tool of War." Accessed 22 December. www.un.org/en/preventgenocide/rwanda/about/bgsexualviolence.shtml.

Volf, Miroslav. 2010. *Exclusion & Embrace: A Theological Exploration of Identity, Otherness, and Reconciliation*. Nashville: Abingdon Press.

Zehr, Howard. 2002. *The Little Book of Restorative Justice*. Intercourse, PA: Good Books.

Zoodsma, Marieke Maria Anna. 2014. "Then We Came to Understand That I Was Hurt and You Were Hurt Too: The Role of Islamic Initiatives and the Interreligious Dialogue in the Reconciliation Process in Bosnia and Herzegovina." MA thesis, University of Amsterdam.

Zupan, Natascha. 2005. "Facing the Past and Transitional Justice in Countries of Former Yugoslavia." Working Group Development and Peace, Bonn. http://center.theparentscircle.org/images/aea261e141c5488186fae473cc107576.pdf.

7 Remembering side by side

Transforming relationships through storytelling

Edita Čolo Zahirović

Deep ethnic divisions and negative historical narratives, reinforced by institutional policy frameworks, continue to inhibit reconciliation in Bosnia and Herzegovina (BiH). Personal and collective traumas are commonly transformed into retelling historical narratives and used to intensify feelings of hostility and vengeance toward "others," hindering the processes of healing and social reconstruction. A strong culture of denial and non-acceptance of the other's narrative is an everyday occurrence and is accompanied by ethnic and religious divisions, stirring up insecurity and increasing the threat of future conflicts. It is present on both the individual and collective level, reinforcing mainstream politics against "others." Educational curricula omit perspectives of different ethnic and religious groups, and history of the 1990s has not yet found its way into the textbooks (see Jeftić's contribution in this volume). Poverty and economic underdevelopment accompany these conditions, contributing to a climate that fosters a culture of violence rather than a culture of nonviolence and prosperity. Such an atmosphere permeates social life, but simultaneously suggests multiple arenas for intervention, multiple agents of interventions and a multiplicity of interventions in a dynamic process of social change (e.g., Kriesberg 1991; Senehi 2002). Despite numerous structural and infrastructural projects where state institutions and homes were rebuilt and conditions for returnees improved, the process of social reconstruction in BiH failed, indicating the need for different interventions aiming to provide new opportunities for a positive social transformation in BiH.

Catholic Relief Services (CRS), in partnership with Caritas of Bosnia and Herzegovina, acknowledged the need for intervention and designed the project Choosing Peace Together (CPT), financed by the United States Agency for International Development (USAID) from 2009 to 2013. Recognizing former soldiers and war survivors of different ethnic and religious backgrounds as highly influential individuals in their ethnic groups, CPT tailored a methodology that enabled them to overcome traumas and bring forth constructive personal narratives as alternatives to dominant narratives. Through a storytelling project called Public Speaking Events: My World, My Words (hereafter PSE), they shared their personal and intimate life stories about the war, the postwar period and peace.

Although originating in the CPT project, PSEs became the foundation of a larger CRS peacebuilding project called Trust, Understanding, Responsibility for the Future (hereafter: PRO-Future).[1] For the past six years, under the auspices of the CPT, the PRO-Future project convened 161 public speaking events in over 40 local communities, exposing 4,597 citizens (mainly youth) to alternative narratives. The main goal of the PRO-Future project was to build trust among citizens of all ethnic groups in Bosnia and Herzegovina and to support the environment in which BiH citizens, encouraged by key influencers, advocate for new social changes resulting in the improved quality of life.

Drawing from six years of participant observation of this project, in addition to participant's evaluations results produced after every public speaking event, in this chapter I provide insight into personal paths toward attitudinal and behavioral change of war survivors who decided to contribute to peacebuilding processes in BiH through constructive storytelling.

Trauma healing

Conflict and violence causes damage across multiple spheres, reducing the capacity of individuals and communities to find change options and act. Trauma and other effects of war disempowers individuals and community structures, fragments memories, relationships and settlements, creates destructive cycles and breaks down social networks, cohesion and ethics (Khuzwayo 2013). Healing individual and collective trauma in a post-conflict society is complex. Mental health professionals and peacebuilding activists are constantly engaging with individual trauma experiences, navigating the impact of current events and changing interpersonal and intergroup relationships. Therefore, it is important to link individual trauma to collective trauma by giving greater attention to synergies between mental-health and psychosocial work with processes of social change and family and/or communal recovery. Psychosocial support provided to individuals and groups is crucial for reducing pain and transforming hate and negative beliefs about others into healing (Halpern and Weinstein 2004; Justad 2006). Psychosocial approaches generally share the view that armed conflict not only impacts the mind of an individual but also the family and the community. In cases of collective trauma, individual trauma counseling has its limits, not only because of the number of people affected but – possibly more importantly – because people suffer from "social wounds" (Richters 2010, 185; Bubenzer and Tankink 2015).

In BiH, these deep individual and collective wounds are exacerbated by different interpretations of historical facts. Events ranging from Ottoman occupation to World War II have created specific ethno-political traumas and corresponding narratives between different groups that have continued to influence the psychological reactions of groups and individuals within BiH for years and centuries. In the wake of World War II, Yugoslav political elites gave little attention to trauma reduction or transforming the violent narratives from the war into reconciliatory narratives (Agger 2001). As a result, many of the crimes committed during the war in the 1990s were driven by these violent narratives and unresolved trauma.

Recognizing the importance of understanding ethno-political trauma and narratives and seeking to interrupt new cycles of violence, CRS started programs to work with individuals and groups to come to terms with the pain of the past. Without dealing with this pain, there is no bridge to a nonviolent future, and emotional and social wounds will continue to fuel cycles of violence (Wessells 2007).

Storytelling's potential for social transformation

Storytelling consists of language, narrative and dialogue. As language, it encodes the culture of a particular community, including a shared understanding of identity, power, history, values and utopian visions. As a narrative, it can serve as the rationale for action, because it encodes knowledge that everyone in the group buys into and therefore holds narrative potency. And as dialogue, it is a direct interpersonal interaction and can generate and sustain person-to-person relationships (Senehi 2002). As such, public speaking events (PSE) hold the power to raise awareness, change attitudes and initiate socio-transformative processes.

Senehi (2002) illustrates two ways in which storytelling can be significant in conflict resolution, peacemaking and peacebuilding. First, storytelling invites a paradigm shift – it catalyzes transformation – and second, it is accessible both technically and intellectually to the listener, something unusual when hearing from the "other." Bar-On and Kassem (2004) found that storytelling among Palestinian and Jewish students contributed to their ability to listen to one another and to construct a more complex image of the other than usually conveyed by the media. As a method to communicate personal truth, storytelling encourages social healing and reconciliation by promoting individual responsibility over general group blaming and collective assignment of guilt. When the truths of past crimes are exposed, individuals – not entire ethnic, religious or cultural groups – are exonerated from guilt (Mendelof 2004). Therefore, as Halpern and Weinstein (2004) note, the storytelling process helps to individualize members of opposing groups and challenges dehumanization of their behavior and nature. Storytelling can help individuals and groups to learn, experience and acknowledge that both groups are victims of the conflict and have experienced loss, albeit uniquely (Justad 2006).

Trauma healing workshops as potential for personal transformation

In 2010, CRS and Caritas BiH published an open call for individuals who suffered during the war to participate in the CPT project and attend a series of psychosocial workshops and seminars aimed at helping them overcome war trauma and grievance by providing a safe space and supportive environment to tell their war and postwar accounts. Over 200 individuals who had traumatic war experiences, mainly members of victims' associations from 38 municipalities across BiH, applied to attend and 52 actively participated in the CPT project from its beginning to its end. The war survivors were of different ethnic, religious, gender and geographical backgrounds, similarly representative of the general population.

The tailored program consisted of a series of psychosocial workshops and seminars (e.g., nonviolent communication, trauma and forgiveness), aiming to address personal trauma, build self-confidence and improve interethnic relationships among participants (Hart and Čolo 2014). The program offered psychosocial workshops and seminars for more than a year and half, providing over 200 hours of trauma healing and capacity-building sessions for participants. Follow-up psycho-support sessions were offered to those who decided to speak publicly about their war experiences.

During the first year-and-a-half of the CPT project, I observed individual cognitive change as part of a process with different phases. The *first phase* is linked to beneficiaries' motives to be part of the reconciliation process. While in this phase, individuals are primarily connecting with their deep need to resolve personal trauma, as well as developing a curiosity about the experiences of others. During the *second phase*, individuals engage empathy, initiated through a safe space for storytelling and listening, as well as discussion about the past. During the *third phase*, the relationship between the victim and the perpetrator becomes clearer, regardless of ethnic background, and the idea of exemption from collective guilt is accepted. After humanizing the "other side" with similar war experiences and separating their personal from collective identities, positive personal change and joint activities become possible. This progress emerges from constructive discussion in a safe space and leads individuals into a *fourth phase* of activism in their transformational journey (Hart and Čolo 2014).

Prior to the second phase, 29 percent of beneficiaries decided to drop out of the project. The participants who dropped out were either in need of greater psychosocial support (e.g., persons with little or no previous therapeutic work to address their trauma), or they had been motivated to participate in the workshop by different things, such as material and economic gain. Further, some had an entrenched attitude that reconciliation was impossible or a strong connection with nationalistic politics (Hart and Čolo 2014).[2]

Of those who continued to participate in the trainings and seminars (N=52), 71 percent indicated improved capacity to address personal trauma, while 64 percent indicated readiness to reach out to others affected by trauma (Catholic Relief Services 2014). Workshops helped participants a great deal in learning how to communicate and how to deal with their pain. Regardless of their ethnicity, participants found a common experience in the pain and suffering they had gone through, and the fact that they can help themselves and others with similar issues. This therapeutic experience helped survivors to develop a group identity of those who suffered heavily and overcame personal traumas (Bosankic, Mesic and Sosic 2012). They revised previous positions and internalized new identities and partnered to create space for peer support. Kelman finds that identity "negotiation" is essential to reconciliation: "each party (must) revise its own identity just enough to accommodate the identity of the other" (Kelman 2004, 119; Funk 2013). These new attitudes and more positive perspectives about self and others helped participants to find closure and develop an ability to look ahead and rebuild new positive identities (Bosankic, Mesic and Sosic 2012).

On many occasions, I observed participants in these groups encourage each other to view themselves no longer as victims but as survivors. Regardless of their ethnic and religious backgrounds, they developed friendships, helped each other find jobs, collected money to support those with less, found strength within each other and jointly visited places which they previously considered triggers for their traumatic experience. In 2013, one Croat participant and former war camp prisoner decided to engage with his trauma even more deeply by walking around Mostar's east ("Bosniak") side with his fellow participants (a Bosniak and a Serb) for the first time in 20 years after a public speaking event held near the city.[3] According to him, their support was crucial, as he considered them the only two people who could understand his feelings and actions truly and completely.

Storytelling's potential for personal transformation

Through the workshops, 22.5 percent of training participants decided to take a further step in their transformation through public speaking events to the wider community (Catholic Relief Services 2014). For them, who suffered greatly during the war, sharing their personal stories of transformation became something they could do to help individuals and communities better understand and accept alternative and historical narratives of "other groups," helping them to think critically about dominant narratives and paving the way to reconciliation.

For many of the speakers, the motivation to engage in public speaking events was deeply connected with their will to participate in truth-telling and peacebuilding processes. They found the PSE project very important for reaching out to youth and to encourage young people to start questioning their beliefs about other ethnic groups. Other speakers found it to be a continuation of their trauma healing process (Bosankic, Mesic and Sosic 2012). Therefore, as peacebuilding activists and advocates, they started a joint initiative to present their personal narratives to the broader community through PSEs.

PSEs include stories about human lives before, during and after war. They are structured into approximately 15-minute testimonies for each of the three main speakers (one Bosniak, one Serb and one Croat) who jointly and openly talk about their experiences, maltreatment, loss of loved ones, emotions, thoughts and coping styles developed to maintain dignity and life during the war and in the postwar period. These testimonies are unique in that the reflections are individual and personal rather than from a historical or political perspective. The speakers talk about life after war, endeavors to overcome hostility toward "others," trauma, and their transformations from past war victims to peace activists today. After these stories, they take questions and comments from the audience (another approximately 45 minutes) as a post-story dialogue between storytellers and listeners (youth, peers, academics and others).

Attendees of PSEs are of different ages, genders, ethnic and religious backgrounds. Depending on location, the group may be ethnically homogenous or heterogeneous; it may consist mainly of youth, but at times it will have people of different ages. The group's size could vary from 500 to more than a couple of hundred. Many people who have attended PSEs come from communities affected by conflict and a sense of victimhood. That sense of victimhood is often woven into their socially constructed identities along with the collective group's chosen trauma and chosen identity. They bring to the PSE their own war memories, emotions, reflections, doubts and their experiences of living in a postwar and transitional society. They also are generally most familiar with their own ethnic group's dominant political and historical narratives. It is unlikely that they would have participated in a similar activity previously, leaving their attitudes about others and about reconciliation processes previously unchallenged. In particular, the effect of PSEs is likely highest for youth, since youngsters in BiH live most often in homogenous enclaves where one group's prejudices and stereotypes are maintained while many of these youth have not had the opportunity to meet "others" and hear their stories.

In order to influence change, a number of inner cognitive processes have to occur during the PSE. Listeners have to personally understand and recognize the relevance of the PSE so they are *motivated* to listen; if motivated, they must have the *ability to process* what they hear. Since there is sometimes silence or unawareness around conflict, speakers' personal narratives provide a unique perspective of history and as such hold the power to influence the perceptions and attitudes of those who listen. This process could be more or less helpful. If listeners are open to hearing about the experiences of other religious and ethnics groups, a PSE could open a place for their personal growth and better understanding of the past conflict. However, if listeners hold strong opinions and beliefs about the facts of what happened during the war, and are less willing to hear war testimonies of other groups, an internal conflict may occur and as such could block potential for change.

During the post-story dialogue, listeners are concurrently relating new information to their prior knowledge and experiences and *validating those information* according to own personal identities, experiences, histories and visions. Personal wartime stories may also help listeners to better understand the context, as well as accept new stories; listeners (especially youth) often comment that they have never heard of atrocities committed by their own ethnic group or say they were unaware that "such things" happened at all. Very often, listeners trust all speakers very quickly, mainly because members of their own religious and/or ethnic group do not publicly judge but support narratives of different ethnic groups. That is when listeners start to feel empathy or resistance toward the speakers and develop more or less favorable thoughts about their stories. For those with more favorable thoughts, a powerful relationship between the narrator and listener is likely to occur, which may facilitate a collaborative process of meaning-making (Senehi 2002). Without having to give up one's social identity, listening, experiencing and understanding should give people the possibility to change some of those group beliefs that are destructive to the intergroup relationship. For others with lack of motivation and/or understanding or with less favorable thoughts toward stories and speakers, attitudes will remain the same as before or become even more deeply entrenched against the "others." Some listeners might hold that PSEs relativize the different groups' roles during war, question the truthfulness of the testimonies and consider public acceptance of structures and states as more relevant to reconciliation processes than PSE testimonies. In practice, however, observations and qualitative data gathered through internal evaluations suggest that such comments are rare. If present, they are mainly expressed by individuals who had suffered heavily during the war and are themselves in need of psychosocial support, ones with strong nationalistic political active involvement or those whose close family members were prosecuted or convicted for war crimes during the 1990–1995 conflicts.

As two participants (ex-war camp prisoners) stated in a focus group interview (Ibid.):

> If only, during our public speaking we affect five people from one hundred, I feel that we have accomplished something. We do not have to change someone's attitudes completely. . . . I am aware that I cannot change anyone, but I can influence some people to a certain degree and maybe some other people seeing our work will feel inspired to do something or at least to speak differently (about others).
>
> (Banja Luka, focus group participant)

> The first time I told my story in the workshop it was very difficult, and it is difficult every time I tell it, but every time I tell it, I am breaking down barriers and I feel more free. Until then, I did not have strength. . . [to tell the story] and nobody ever heard it until then . . . and now after all the seminars and workshops it is easier to talk about it; now I feel better after telling my story
>
> (Tuzla, focus group participant)

These responses indicate the potential of storytelling for both personal and collective transformation.

Results: transformation through storytelling in Bosnia and Herzegovina

For Bosnia and Herzegovina, storytelling implemented through the CPT and PRO-Future projects indicates similar positive trends cited by authors previously described. The findings of an internal CRS evaluation of the PSEs[4] show that 48 percent of respondents[5] considered PSEs important and that they contributed to the peace process in BiH, 38 percent considered this type of activity very important and able to bring peace processes to a conclusion. None of them considered PSEs detrimental to the peacebuilding process. Furthermore, 86 percent said that this kind of dialogue significantly increases trust between different ethnic groups in BiH, and 78 percent thought that the activity increased intercommunity collaboration on public policy issues of common interest, regardless of ethnic background. This is supported by data collected through the PRO-Future project's qualitative survey with a data sample of 637, which found that 57 percent of respondents considered PSEs to be highly or very relevant for peacebuilding processes. As stated by one PSE attendee in Brčko:

> These stories are endless and painful. Sharing your personal experiences on this topic, in my opinion, is a great contribution to the establishment of coexistence within the entire territory of Bosnia and Herzegovina and beyond. Showing that even after all the horror, loss and pain, someone may continue in unity, and tolerance is the first step and most important one. For something like this, you should primarily have a lot of courage and energy. Given that I was in Bosnia during the aggression, it was very difficult and distressing to listen to some of the details that were presented. But on the other hand, I believe that this moment of emotional reactions is normal; any other response would be weird.
>
> (Čolo 2013)

Twenty-eight percent of respondents considered it important but less effective than other methods and processes,[6] and five percent considered such initiatives to have almost no influence.

While data analysis shows tendencies that PSEs within the program have a positive effect, it will be essential to consider how re-traumatization of PSE speakers and attendees can occur in order to fully avoid re-traumatization in the future. After a PSE, a speaker can potentially experience negative feelings and thoughts; therefore, it is essential to be careful and aware of such situations and provide constant support (such as supervision and psychotherapy) so as not to set back the trauma healing process. For the wider public (attendees), very careful guidance of the PSE process is crucial, so that professional and quality facilitation leads to more positive final outcomes.

Postwar situations create the need to bridge the work for healing to the wider work on building peace. The reconstruction necessary for peace and many other democratic processes includes: (a) rebuilding social trust; (b) facilitating the return of displaced people and building a sense of community; (c) addressing issues of intolerance; (d) nurturing respect for human rights; (e) encouraging prosocial values and education for peace; (f) supporting norms of nonviolence and law; and (g) rebuilding a civil society (Wessells 2007). Hopes and fears for the future, personal security, historical understanding and identity issues are not easily negotiated, at least not at the community level. These issues are bound to the personal and identity group level. The citizens' perception of the situation and their relationships with each other need to change in order for deep-rooted conflicts to be resolved (Lederach 1997).

Although important in helping people understand their collective wounds and the basis for action in historicized consciousness, PSEs cannot stand alone in reconciliation and peacebuilding processes in BiH – in the absence of other transformative processes, their effect will be diminished. In order for the program to have an impact beyond the people participating and in the society at large, it is essential to develop a critical mass of people that can challenge stereotypes, prejudice and out-group hatred within respective identity groups (Justad 2006). Young people active in politics, leaders of organizations and journalists, among others, have an impact on society and are expected to take leading roles in the future that are especially needed in sustained dialogue.

Such a premise is present in the PRO-Future project, based on its efforts to encourage key influencers to demonstrate support by, for example, leading or engaging in interreligious events, promoting reconciliation in speeches and through the media, and providing sponsorship or co-funding of initiatives that work across ethnic or party lines to address local concerns. Political and religious leaders, for many years after the war, have used divisive rhetoric in public speeches, which discourages citizens from acting upon positive social transformation. PRO-Future is working to provide safe spaces and encourage citizens by initiating and supporting positive messages and actions of their leaders, assuming that in such environment, citizens could find value and participate in civic initiatives across ethnic lines to address/resolve local problems. In such a resulting atmosphere of solidarity and consensus, citizens may then identify that working in solidarity will help them not just solve common problems but also restore and establish new relationships with their neighbors regardless of their religious and ethnic background, hold political leaders accountable and create political, economic and social stability in their communities (Catholic Relief Services 2013).

Conclusion

A complete assessment of the impact of CPT and the PRO-Future projects needs to be evaluated, but practical model is presented here, with its background in several theories on personal and group transformation, supports the use of PSEs in social reconstruction. Data gathered through these two projects shows that PSEs have the potential to positively influence healing processes and social reconstruction, both on individual and community/social levels. Many times, members of war victims' associations who participated in these projects self-evaluated their improved mental health, heightened readiness to interact with "others" and increased willingness to influence social change by sharing experiences and bringing different people together.

A number of NGOs have also used PSEs to enrich their reconciliation programs, and many journalists wrote articles and/or created TV stories about how those who suffered the most were able to forgive, work together and advocate for peace. Such media stories helped bring various reconciliation perspectives into the public discourse and emphasized the need for peacebuilding work in a time when political structures are dedicated to quite the opposite.

War trauma is human-made, created and maintained through social structures. To heal, therefore, individuals and groups need opportunities to change society, but also to draw energy and strength from society itself. Social reconstruction is more effective alongside individual and social healing processes. There is more chance for individuals and societies to heal by changing their perspectives and replacing hatred with actions. Such action could lead to new policies and laws within institutions, and new policies or laws can foster peacebuilding principles and impose the adoption of new, positive social norms in postwar societies. Peace without endogenous, equitable sustainable development cannot be a permanent viable peace. At the same time, development cannot be sustained without broad, positive peace (Mayor 1995). Therefore, projects like CPT and PRO-Future supported and implemented more complex and comprehensive social peace work, suggesting critical steps toward the long-term and superordinate goal of peaceful and sustainable peace and prosperity in BiH.

Notes

1 PRO-Future is a four-year project (2013–2017) financed by USAID and implemented by CRS and partners: Mozaik Foundation, Caritas of Bosnia and Herzegovina, Forum of Tuzla Citizens, Helsinki Citizens Assembly Banja Luka and the Interreligious Council in Bosnia & Herzegovina.

2 War victims' associations in BiH, although registered as nongovernmental organizations, are unofficially extensions of mono-ethnic nationalistic politics and their actions are mainly financed by and serve politics that omit such initiatives as building relationships and reconciliation.

3 Different political and historical narratives about the war in Mostar and the destruction of its historic and symbolic Old Bridge pose a barrier for reconciliation between Bosniaks and Croats still today. Most residents have not crossed to the "other" side and many youth have never visited the UNESCO heritage Old Bridge. Therefore, crossing the Old Bridge is perceived by local and international communities as a peacebuilding act.

4 "Case Study: Public Speaking Events (Not) Influencing Audience's Attitudinal and Behavioral Change" is an internal CRS document developed to measure the impact of PSEs on the public. It contains both quantitative and a qualitative components. It was conducted among a group of young people of different genders and ethnicities involved in the project "Youth building a future in Brčko Distrikt" (N=42). 57 percent of the respondents were female and 43 percent were male, out of which 41 percent were Serbs, 38 percent were Bosniaks, 7 percent were Croats and 14 percent who declared themselves "others."

5 42 young people – listeners to a PSE in Brčko in 2012.

6 There is no evidence-based data of why respondents considered PSEs less effective or not influential, but attendees' comments provide some clues about what they think is missing. The most usual comments were: (a) truth telling and bringing war criminals to justice is crucial for reconciliation; without this coming to terms, any peacebuilding initiative or model has no effect; (b) perpetrators and victims have to be clearly defined and perpetrators should acknowledge crimes and ask victims for forgiveness; (c) talking about the past will keep us in the past; we have to speak more about future; (d) economic prosperity would speed the process of reconciliation and make it more realistic; (e) PSEs support the process of relativization, making everybody equally guilty, which is not the case in BiH; (f) it is too late, or it is too early for this method; (g) to have any effect, PSEs need to be part of a larger structure (for example, to be obligatory in schools) to have any broad effect.

References

Agger, Inger. 2001. "Reducing Trauma During Ethno-Political Conflict: A Personal Account of Psycho-Social Work Under War Conditions in Bosnia." In *Peace, Conflict, and Violence: Peace Psychology for the 21st Century*, edited by Daniel J. Christie, Richard V. Wanger, and Deborah DuNann Winter, 240–251. Englewood Cliffs, NJ: Prentice-Hall.

Bar-On, Dan, and Fatma Kassem. 2004. "Storytelling as a Way to Work Through Intractable Conflicts: The German-Jewish Experience and Its Relevance to Palestinian-Israeli Context." *Journal of Social Issues* 60.2: 289–306.

Bosankic, Nina, Enisa Mesic, and Bojan Sosic. 2012. "Choosing Peace Together (CPT) Project. Final External Evaluation Report." Unpublished Report for USAID, Catholic Relief Services, Sarajevo.

Bubenzer, Friederike, and Marian Tankink. 2015. "Healing Communities, Transforming Societies: Exploring the Interconnectedness Between Psychosocial Needs, Practice and Peacebuilding." Conference Report, Institute for Justice and Reconciliation and the War Trauma Foundation. https://peacebuildingandmentalhealth.files.wordpress.com/2015/04/ijr-healing-communities-conference-web.pdf.

Catholic Relief Services. 2013. "Povjerenje, Razumijevanje, Odgovornost za Buducnost (PRO-Future) Project." Technical Application for USAID.

Catholic Relief Services. 2014. "Choosing Peace Together: Final Report." Submitted to USAID Sarajevo.

Čolo, Edita. 2013. "Case Study: Public Speaking Events (Not) Influencing Audience's Attitudinal and Behavioral Change." Unpublished Report for USAID, Catholic Relief Services, Sarajevo.

Funk, Julianne. 2013. "Towards an Identity Theory of Peacebuilding." Centre for Research on Peace and Development, Working Paper No. 15.

Halpern, J., and H.M. Weinstein. 2004. "Empathy and Dehumanization After Mass Violence." In *My Neighbour, My Enemy: Justice and Community in the Aftermath of Mass Atrocity*, edited by E. Stover and H.M. Cambridge: Cambridge University Press.

Hart, Barry, and Edita Čolo. 2014. "Psychosocial Peacebuilding in Bosnia and Herzegovina: Approaches to Relational and Social Change." *Journal of Mental Health and Psychosocial Support in Conflict Affected Areas* 12.1: 76–88.

Justad, Lars Otto. 2006. "Post-Conflict Peacebuilding and Reconciliation Through Dialogue." Master's thesis, University of Oslo, Norway. www.duo.uio.no/bitstream/handle/10852/13993/33708.pdf?sequence=1.

Kelman, Herbert. 2004. "Reconciliation as Identity Change: A Social-Psychological Perspective." In *From Conflict Resolution to Reconciliation*, edited by Yaacov Bar-Siman-Tov, 111–124. Oxford: Oxford University Press.

Khuzwayo, Khethokuhle. 2013. "The Role of Trauma Support Work in Peace-Building." Coursework dissertation, School of Social Sciences University of KwaZulu-Natal, South Africa.

Kriesberg, Louis. 1991. "Formal and Quasi-Mediators in International Disputes: An Exploratory Analysis." *Journal of Peace Research* 1.28: 19–28.

Lederach, John Paul. 1997. *Building Peace: Sustainable Reconciliation in Divided Societies*. Washington, DC: United States Institute of Peace Press.

Mayor, Federico. 1995. "How Psychology Can Contribute to a Culture of Peace." *Peace and Conflict Journal of Peace Psychology* 1: 3–9.

Mendelof, David. 2004. "Truth-Seeking, Truth-Telling, and Postconflict Peacebuilding: Curb the Enthusiasm?" *International Studies Review* 6.3: 355–380.

Richters, Annemiek. 2010. "Suffering and Healing in the Aftermath of War and Genocide in Rwanda: Mediations Through Community-Based Sociotherapy." In *Mediations of Violence in Africa: Fashioning New Futures From Contested Pasts*, edited by L. Kapteijns and A. Richters, 173–210. Leiden: Brill.

Senehi, Jesica. 2002. "Constructive Storytelling: A Peace Process." *Peace and Conflict Studies* 9.2: 41–63. http://nsuworks.nova.edu/pcs/vol9/iss2/3.

Wessells, Michael G. 2007. "Post-Conflict Healing and Reconstruction for Peace: The Power of Social Mobilization." In *Fear of Persecution: Global Human Rights, International Law and Human Well-Being*, edited by Timothy J. White and Anthony J. Marsella, 257–278. New York: Lexington.

Part III

Women's resilience

8 Victim or survivor? Choosing identity after wartime sexual violence

Zilka Spahić Šiljak

Introduction

After terrible crimes in Bosnia and Herzegovina and the region, including mass killings and the rape of women and men, many survivors and victims still live in the shadow of a stigma and silence imposed by ethno-nationalist agendas as well as cultural and religious norms, in order to protect their families' and nation's pride and honor. The production and reproduction of cultural and political narratives deepen trauma and suffering through the politicization and ethnicization of victimhood. The predominant discourse of neoliberal and ethno-national matrices (mis)use survivors for their own policies and goals, while playing at the same time the role of guardian of the survivor's interests. Through reading Bosnia and Herzegovina (BiH) women's narratives, I explore how the ethno-national victimhood discourse silenced many women and alienated them from survivors of other ethnic groups. Coupled with a neoliberal understanding and the expectations of victim/survivor identities, ethno-national victimhood discourse further alienates women from the same ethnic group, because many of them refuse the politicization of their experience and the inscription of ethnic narratives on their bodies. One of the solutions for the imposed positioning and labeling might be to claim the right to self-identification, as Rebecca Stringer (2014) and Alyson Cole (2006) suggest in their work, or to enable a "liberatory epistemology" with a woman's body as the locus of meaning and experience, as Tamy Spry (1995, 27) proposes in her oral history work.

Through oral history processing work with women peacebuilders (Spahić Šiljak 2014) and participation in inclusion projects for women returnees in Bosnia from 2008–2012 in Eastern and Western BiH, I collected narratives from wartime rape survivors. These narratives were analyzed against the larger portrait of the social inclusion of women who returned to their prewar villages after the conflict. In this chapter I look into: (1) body politics and the ethnicization of women's bodies; (2) how the feminist debate and the language about victimhood, survivorship and agency empower or disempower women in dealing with their identities; (3) how to go beyond the victim/survivor binary imposed by international donor politics, scholarship and women's organizations and how to enable new vocabulary for self-identification.

Contextualization: ethnicized bodies?

Sexual violence and other forms of violence in BiH and in the entire Balkans are gendered and ethnicized (Spahić Šiljak 2014, 188), because gender and nation, as Julie Mostov concludes, "intimately participate in the formation of one another" (2002, 89). During the wars (1991–1995) in the former Yugoslavia, women were the main targets of sexual violence and mass rape, and they were targeted because their bodies represented one of the three main ethno-national groups – the body of the nation. Sexual violence was a tool of ethnic cleansing according to UN reports, and depending on the region, it was systemic or sporadic. Helsinki Watch reports say that all sides committed sexual violence in the former republics of Yugoslavia, but the Yugoslav Army and Serbian paramilitary groups "appeared to be using rape on the largest scale and with impunity. . . . The fact the rapes occur[red] before witnesses indicates that the rapists ha[d] nothing to fear" (Laber 1993, 4).[1]

Feminists in the Yugoslav region had opposing views about the war and wartime rape crimes and some of them condemn all men on all sides, while others single out Serbs as the main perpetrators of these crimes. Women on all sides were raped in the wars dividing the former Yugoslavia, so while we should not get into the trap of ethnicization of suffering, the fact of systematic rape of Bosnian Muslim women cannot be neglected. Elisa Helms in her anthropological study in BiH wrote that rape was used "as systemic tool primarily by Serb forces" (2003, 6), or as "highly organized and calculated systemic rape of the Bosnian Muslim women by the Bosnian Serb army," as Olivera Simić (2012, 132–133) found in her work in the region. Stasa Zajović, the anti-war activist from Belgrade states that "ethnic cleansing was not a consequence, but rather one of the main aims of the war" (Ibid., 132), and elaborating further on that, she contended that "cleaning in our language (Bosnian/Serbian/Croatian) is a local word for abortion" (Zajović 1995, 176–177), or to clean (out) oneself; the main objective of ethnic cleansing was to completely clean the territories of the other ethnic group.

The prevailing media and political discourses portray women who survived sexual and other forms of violence as either victims or survivors, with certain expectations imposed on them (Helms 2013). Torn between these two identities, some brave women became agents of change for themselves and for other women, while some remained silent under the pressure of the imposed narratives. Some rose up against binary victim/survivor labels and claimed the right to articulate their own experiences. While working in the field on various human rights projects, I had an opportunity to talk to many women who survived wartime rape and who were active in local organizations or who individually tried to encourage other women to testify, or seek help in women's centers. Some of them embrace the existing labels of victims or survivors, while others do not find them compelling and resonant with their own feelings and perceptions of the violence that was done to them.

While much has been written about the ethnic dimensions of rape, feminists insist on referring to these atrocities as "gender-based violence" (Petrović 2000).

They view this gender-based violence as deeply rooted in the patriarchal value system, in which women are treated as the property or territory of men, nations or people. This type of violence is closely related to power and feminists confirm, "Rape serves to prove power and establish hierarchy" (Anić 2006, 91). This hierarchy, however, as Cynthia Cockburn (1998) found in her research, is part of militarized, masculinized patriarchal cultures that continue to oppress women with hierarchical gender policies and structural violence of the inefficient governmental institutions even after wars end.

Femininity, masculinity and heterosexuality, as Dubravka Zarkov (2006) explored in the Balkans, were crucial in the production of ethnicity and ethnicized bodies. In feminist literature, the female body was discussed as a domain of power and dominance, and in ethno-national ideologies the female body was used as paradigm for territory, homeland and nation that should be protected, nurtured and respected or defeated if it is the enemy's body or territory. Women's bodies were and are still a battlefield and object for many scholars, practitioners and ethnic and religious communities. That body represents primarily the ethnic and national paradigm of purity, chastity and sacredness. Women are not generally invited to speak out about their own bodies, simply because those bodies do not belong only to themselves. Actually, their bodies belong more to a male, to a family, to a community and a country and they are either celebrated or glorified as holy mothers and a paradigm of ethical virtues of a perfect woman, or rejected as fallen Madonnas who should bear the stigma of shame and guilt (Spahić Šiljak 2010). Since a woman is considered the guardian of her family's moral life, it is expected that she be silent about sexual violence for the sake of those who claim the right to her body. By complying with the social gender norms, she maintains her family's dignity (Ibid.).

Given the moral double standards of patriarchal societies in which women survivors of sexual violence live, only some dare to report these crimes. Public acknowledgment of such crimes could have devastating results on survivors' family life. When I asked one survivor why she chooses silence she responded with the question: "Who would want to associate with the family of a woman who was raped and consider marriage with her children and socialize with them"?[2] The cultural "blame and shame" complex perpetrated by the patriarchy strongly discourages survivors from sharing their personal stories (Spahić Šiljak 2010). Women were pushed into the role of "safeguards" for family values and by extension, protectors of the entire moral fabric of their societies and they had to internalize their pain and suffering in order to maintain a "dignified" silence.

Conceptualization of victim/survivor identity

Victimhood, survivorship and agency are widely debated in the scholarship of many disciplines (Karp 1986; Bell 1999; Mahmood 2009; McNay 2000; Ahall and Shepherd 2012; Stringer 2014), but understanding the interplay between them in the lives of women who survived wartime rape and other forms of violence in the recent Bosnian war (1992–1995) requires the exploration of various social, political and cultural factors in the postwar Bosnian context. In this chapter, however, I will focus on language as one of the very important factors in learning, knowing and reflecting. Through discourses we determine knowledge and truth, and discourses construct power and knowledge, as Michel Foucault (1984) explains. In discursive frameworks people learn about themselves, but they also learn how to position themselves. Since language not only reflects but also constitutes a social reality, the subject as well as her/his experience are revealed through language. When scholars, practitioners or women who survived sexual violence use certain words like victim, survivor, raped woman (en) agents or woman (en) who survived rape, these are political acts. They convey the message and image that they as survivors want to present or what those who are exploring the subject matter have interpreted from their study.

The notion of victim (*žrtva*) in everyday communication refers to persons who survived various types of violence, including wartime rape inflicted outside the control of the person and under coercion. In BiH, "victim" is an official label used by some women's organizations and activists as well as the media and state institutions that regulate the status of women and men who survived violence. Some women use it, finding it important to draw attention to the status of those who need help. Women War Victims from Sarajevo and Our Voice from Tuzla use this term, while underlining that they work against the "conspiracy of silence" in order to regain dignity for women who should not bear shame or stigma for something for which they were not responsible. They claim the proactive agency of victims who struggle to position themselves in Bosnian society, and they do not want the government to pity them but to secure their social and economic rights.

Another label is survivor (*preživjeli*), which requires another word or words following it to explain what they survived; making it necessary that one needs to say women or persons who survived violence. Some women and feminist organizations like Medica Zenica, Vive Žene in Tuzla, La Strada in Mostar and many others in BiH use the term survivor as an empowering notion with positive traits for active agents who experienced violence but decided to live and move on with their lives despite the challenges. It seems that in this way survivors attempt to preserve their dignity through the message that they are above the violence they suffered and that they do not want to be perceived as helpless victims. The individualism discourse encourages women to show that they are responsible, strong and decisive in their intent to overcome the pain and suffering.

Many women use both terms interchangeably, without assigning particular weight of meaning to either notion. However, some women's NGOs and media, as Elissa Helms (2013) noticed in her research, selectively use these notions depending on the context and the audience. The pervasive media image of the woman who survived rape is a poor refugee village woman in traditional clothing. While the majority of refugees and raped women come from rural areas, many urban and educated women's activists opposed this portrayal as a misrepresentation of BiH women. They assert that there were so many urban, highly educated women who survived sexual violence and so reject being represented monolithically and being referred to as poor helpless women. Not surprisingly therefore, they attempt to avoid their identity's "balkanization": the Bosnian woman is "other" first to the men of her own ethnic group and the larger ethno-nation. Second, she is "other" to neighboring ethnic groups in BiH and the region, and finally, she is "other" to the Western world, which uses a neo-colonial lens to define its periphery, which requires civilizing and rescuing. Compounded marginalization and multiple processes of othering make some women's activists oppose the victim label. If they use it, they understand it as a transitional process from victim to survivor. Some scholars explain this (Young and Maguire 2003), and some women refer to it as in: "It's not that you *are* a victim or that you *are* a survivor. Instead, you move from one end where something was done to you (victim) to where you do something about it (survivor)" (Ibid., 49).

Some women, however, do not want to be labeled as victims or survivors but as women who experienced certain types of violence or simply human beings who suffered or who experienced injustice. For them any narrative, any story about violence, is contextualized and personalized; thus, they do not want to dwell in either of these two categories but instead want to have the freedom to self-conceptualize their experience. They want their own story to articulate what they experienced as women and human beings. Dubravka Zarkov (2006, 223) also warns about the limitations of agency and victimization narratives as well as lack of other possible narratives and experiences, which should include the space for women to label their experiences outside the victim/agent binary.

Theoretically and practically, the victim/survivor binary has limitations, but the question is about what kind of language women have at their disposal to accurately represent what has happened to them without essentialization, alienation and expectation. I am particularly interested in the feminist debate about victimhood, survivorship and agency because of the predominant neoliberal feminist discourse that insists on the term survivor as something active, positive and agentive vs. the notion of a victim which is understood as passive, negative and lacking agency (Wolf 1993, 154). Chris Gilligan, for instance, confirms this essentialist understanding:

> Victims are, by definition, passive objects who have been acted upon by other forces, not active agents. They are defined by the mark that has been made on them rather than the mark that they have made on the wider world. In as far as they are victims, they are devoid of volition or intent.
>
> (2003, 30)

Some anti-victim feminist scholars like Katie Roiphe (1993), Christina Hoff Sommers (1994) and Naomi Wolf, who coined the term "victim feminism" and "power feminism" (1993, 154), criticize the perpetual victimization of women as passive and highlight that the concept of survivorship connotes the choice, agency, resilience and responsibility of an individual. But as Gudrun Dahl (2009) notices, these anti-victim feminist scholars dwell on personal agency and responsibility, which is important, but neglect the roots and causes of structural violence and social and political circumstances that enable it. They see portrayals of women as victims of the capitalist system and neoliberal economy as false or bad "gender feminism" that insists on structural changes of the system and dismantling traditional femininity. Although Wolf criticizes capitalism as exploitive, she finds it inevitable.

One of the biggest feminist scholars, Judith Butler, also concluded that feminists should provide counter positions beyond the paradigm of victimization, in terms of the negative connotation of the notion (Osborne and Segal 1996), but she did not exclude structural violence and oppression. In the feminist debate, as Stringer explains in her recent work on the anti-victim debate, which "legitimizes and normalizes the values of neoliberalism" (2014, 6), there is need to question the anti-victim feminist discourse because it reinforces a neoliberal discourse of power and neglects the origins of structural oppression and discrimination.

One of the ideas is to reclaim victimhood, but as Stringer proposes, "reclaiming" lies between the poles of celebration and jettison" (Ibid., 160). It is important to go beyond the victim/survivor binary and reclaim victimhood, which should not be essentialized and reduced to a passive non-agentive subject. Victims also have agency and that agency should also be reclaimed, but not at the cost of making the survivor fully responsible for the violence he/she survived. Carine Mardorossian clarifies that "being a victim did not mean being incapacitated and powerless. It meant being a determined and angry (although not pathologically resentful) agent of change" (2002, 767).

Identity paradoxes

How should one identify as a raped woman today in the postwar BiH context, and how can one survive the social stigma of shame and personal feelings of guilt and responsibility for her well-being and for her family? How does one cope with the imposed identities of victim or survivor? How may one position oneself and narrate the experience of rape? Does rape define who one is, or should the woman define what she survived and who she is? Women responded in different ways to these questions, and struggled to understand what happened, why it happened to them and how to live with the experience. The majority of women have chosen silence as a method of survival and sacrificed their own subjectivity, pain and suffering for a "bigger" cause – for the sake of their own families. They internalized the narratives of victimhood and oppressive scripts (Young 1990, 55), and they did what Uma Narayan calls "bargaining with patriarchy" (quoted in Oshana 2015, 147) in order to survive the social norms imposed on them. Helms brings examples in her study about women in BiH and says: "Even when accepted by their families, no woman wanted to be branded a raped woman in the community" (2013, 201). It is primarily, as one woman from Srebrenica explained, that they "still had to live with people" (Ibid.). They made preference-maximizing choices from within their constraints, being aware of injustice and the patriarchal social norms that suppress their subjectivity (Narayan in Oshana 2015). Women victims, survivors or raped women have the agency to decide how they will deal with their experiences, because agency is not limited to one of these identities, as anti-victim feminist scholars claim. Agency is also not only related to liberation, advocacy and subversion of the patriarchy, as Saba Mahmood (2005) elaborate; it can also be a voluntary act of submission. In the case of some Bosnian women who do not want to be labeled raped women, their agency was expressed in their voluntary act of submission to the social norms.

It is important is to recognize not only the oppression of patriarchal societies, but also the disguised oppression of the well-intended neoliberal discourse (Young 1990, 41) that perceives gendered structural oppression "as individual problems of personal responsibility, or as a depoliticized social problem" (Stringer 2014, 14). The rhetoric of personal responsibility, agency and gender-neutral language make victims, survivors and women who suffered from violence responsible for recovery and healing; if they are unsuccessful, as some women never fully recover from these experiences, they are responsible for this as well.

Women cope with sexual violence and trauma in different ways, and so many factors influence how they identify themselves and how that identification evolves over time. Many women have accepted and internalized the victim label and feel entitled to claim certain rights as victims, but sometimes they internalize their traumas so intensely and dwell on it so much that they cannot escape the victim circle. They seem fully absorbed by the victim narrative. The identity of a victim is the only one that matters for some women or the only one that resonates as an acceptable form of expression:

> We are victims and we will keep saying that as long as we live, because we lost everything; this is what we have. We do not give up and we will not allow perpetrators to live in peace and we will not allow the state to forget our suffering and pain. Every time we show up we will remind everybody of the crimes committed over our bodies. They cannot silence us.
>
> (Women War Victims, Sarajevo[3])

According to the recent studies about women in BiH who survived wartime rape, 57 percent suffer from posttraumatic stress disorder (PTSD), 70 percent say that the rape still fully governs their lives, 65 percent report that they use drugs, while 76 percent confirm that their trauma influences their relationships with men (Husić et al. 2014, 91). Many women who reported rape and identify themselves as victims do not find it necessary to seek psychological support because they know what they need. One example is the group Women War Victims who state on their website that what they need is to provide for the economic and social well-being of their members, as well as documentation of the crimes and prosecutions. Helms (2013) had similar findings in her research in BiH with the Sarajevo NGO, Women War Victims.

According to Medica Zenica's study (Husić et al. 2014), some women who were empowered through therapy programs managed to move from being a "helpless victim" to "agentive survivor" and became strong enough to continue life and help other women to cope with their trauma, as they variously narrated:

> I am strong and became a fighter; I am much stronger now; I can bear everything for my children to help them live without suffering what I have been through; through therapeutic work in Medica Zenica I understood that what happened to me was not my fault, and that I should not bear shame and guilt; I learned that we should help those who suffer and now I am helping those who are ill.
>
> (Ibid., 122)

Although most of these women have never fully recovered, they have rediscovered meaning in their lives and have goals, including raising their families and helping those in need. Despite the pain they still feel, they report that they successfully cope with their trauma. The survivor label thus better explains and articulates their inner struggle to overcome shame and guilt.

Some women, however, faced difficulties in meeting the expectations of the survivor identity – to be strong, empowered and ready to change. A woman who was 14 when she was raped got married after the war, but did not find meaning in her marriage and her environment. She narrates:

> When I reported my rape for the first time everybody was talking about me as a victim, and in the beginning I did not mind. When I noticed that people felt pity for me, referring to me as "that poor woman" (*jadnica*), I could not accept it anymore, so I decided to embrace the label survivor, which was something powerful and something that tells people "she is not some "poor woman," she is a fighter, she can handle this." But, over time I realized I could not handle it, I did not feel better, and despite all the therapy I have been through, I am really scared and have the same fears . . . and yet everybody expects me to feel better and be courageous as a survivor.
>
> (woman wartime rape survivor from Zenica)[4]

This is the typical victim/survivor paradox, which discloses a deep psychological dilemma over her identity and the way she copes with her trauma and expectations. Thompson explains it this way:

> Being a victim maximizes the possibility that the awfulness of rape can be appreciated. But adopting a victim identity also runs a risk of being pitied . . . and regarded as weak. . . . If one adopts a survivor identity then the trauma of rape must be minimized and salience given to (one's recovery) from the rape. While this may afford the survivor respect from others . . . it renders her unable to talk about her experience or elicit support and sympathy from others should the need arise
>
> (Thompson 2000, 330)

The paradox we find in this statement from a woman wartime rape survivor shows the limitations of these two labels and how women struggle with the transition from one to the other. This might be one of the reasons why some of the women reinstated silence as a viable model of survival that does not place expectations upon them that they cannot fulfill.

Some women, although vocal about their experience, do not want to embrace any of these identities, because they find them hegemonic, intrusive, exclusivist and divisive. They choose to be women who have been raped, or simply women who experienced violence, and the very narration of that experience constructs their identity, which is not fixed and stable. For them rape is not the first word that should identify who they are, because they are first and foremost women: "I am not a raped woman, I am not the one [who was raped], I am not "the poor woman" . . . I do not feel well in these boxes, I do not want to let anybody define me" (a woman from Prijedor who survived sexual violence).[5] If a woman refuses one of the available identities (victim or survivor) and if it does not resonate with how she feels, what else is there for her? What kind of language does she have at her disposal? Knowing that language reflects and constructs the reality in which we live, can the language include and describe individual feelings and situations?

Tami Spry (1995) answers that our lived reality does not recognize the complexity and diversity of women's experiences with sexual violence. She wants women to make new language and meanings, because the existing categories of victim and survivor are phallocentric, describing a woman as the object of a man's action. Some women do not want to be defined by someone else's actions, but by their primary identities as women and human beings whose integrity was violated by someone else's actions. Women's bodies are colonized and culturally detached from a woman and her experience, and when she narrates painful experience, she should have agency to define it but not separately from her own body. Spry therefore suggests a "liberatory epistemology," which is a "liberation of ways of knowing, of exploring how we know what we know, the discovery of a "room [body] of one's own," a site where a woman might tell a story of sexual violence . . . where she – her body – is the locus of meaning for her experience" (Ibid., 27). Woman's body cannot be dislocated from her experience and thought. Spry further concludes that a woman's body should be a "meaning making agent, and that the telling of her experience is a performative act of liberation (Ibid., 28).

The problem remains: how can we develop women-centered language that is emancipatory and liberating within the hegemonic power of socially constructed views about sexual violence? What are the tools available, how can we make them accessible to women and make the new vocabulary acceptable in the society, knowing that most of us use cognitive shortcuts to define something without due respect for another's experience? How shall we develop new vocabulary in Bosnian society and culture, where a woman and her body are objects owned by men, the family or the nation? How can we produce new knowledge and pursue emancipatory practices when the linguistic discourse is masculinized and subordinated to oppressive gender roles?

One of the ways is to provide a forum to narrate women's experiences and open dialogue with the new vocabulary that they will bring through their narrations or that they will accept from other women or scholars who are attuned to these kinds of experiences. Through stories and dialogue, women can gain recognition and build self-respect. With the new language tools, women can self-identify how they choose and authentically express how they feel. They need to be subjects who will narrate and teach us how to present their experiences and not mere objects of ethno-national ideologies that generate divisions over women's bodies and claim to protect Bosniak, Serb or Croat women rather than women who survived sexual violence, whatever their ethnic identity.

Postmodern feminist scholars propose that the gesture of reclaiming the right for self-identification "lies between the poles of celebration and jettison, making 'reclaiming' a satisfactory way to frame the response that is needed" (Stringer 2014, 160). If women feel safe and comfortable with the victim or survivor identity, they should not be pressured to meet the expectations of victim and anti-victim feminist claims. If they want something else that they feel best reflects how they want to be perceived, then they need to be allowed to construct a new language shaped by their experience. The language comes through narration of their stories, which makes their experience known and provides self-recognition and recognition by others. However, the challenge is not only to provide the space for these narratives but also to prepare other women and men to listen to these experiences without ethnicizing the pain, suffering and survivor/victim agency that is limited by the dominant ethno-national discourses.

Conclusion

We can say that women who survived different types of violence during wars and conflicts should not be theorized as mere objects of power but as agents who can claim and reclaim their identities. This is important to acknowledge in each context, because as Kathy Davis (1997, 15) argued, women's bodies and what they symbolize and represent in a particular culture are produced through a variety of social and political relationships. Production and reproduction of women's bodies is closely related to language; therefore, women should have safe channels to tell their stories and through their own narrations create proper naming of what they have experienced.

Notes

1 See also UN Security Council, *Security Council resolution 808 (1993) [International Criminal Tribunal for the Former Yugoslavia (ICTY)]*, 22 February 1993, S/RES/808 (1993), accessed 8 December 2016, www.refworld.org/docid/3b00f15d30.html; and "Report on the Situation of Human Rights in the Former Yugoslavia", U.N. Doc. E/CN.4/1993/50. *International Journal of Refugee Law* 5.2 (1993): 319–333.
2 Personal interview with S.B. from Prijedor, June 2008.
3 Personal Interview with A.M. from Sarajevo, October 2010.
4 Personal Interview with E.O. in Tuzla, September 2009.
5 Personal Interview with A.S. in Prijedor, June 2010.

References

Ahall, Linda, and Linda J. Shepherd. 2012. *Gender Agency and Political Violence*. New York: Palgrave McMillan.

Anić, Rebeka. 2006. *Nasilje nad ženama u obitelji: teološko-pastoralni vid*. Split: Franciscan Institute for Culture of Peace.

Bell, Vikki. 1999. *Performativity and Belonging*. London: Sage.

Cockburn, Cynthia. 1998. *The Space Between Us: Negotiating Gender and National Identities in Conflict*. London: Zed Books.

Cole, Alyson. 2006. *The Cult of True Victimhood: From the War on Welfare to the War on Terror*. Stanford: Stanford University Press.

Dahl, Gudrun. 2009. "Sociology and Beyond: Agency, Victimization and the Ethics of Writing". *The Asian Journal of Social Science* 37: 391–407.

Davis, Kathy. 1997. "Embodying Theory: Beyond Modernist and Postmodernist Reading of the Body." In *Embodied Practices: Feminist Perspectives on the Body*, edited by K. Davis. London: Sage.

Foucault, Michel. 1984. *Space, Knowledge and Power*. New York: Pantheon.

Gilligan, Chris. 2003. "Constant Crisis/Permanent Process: Diminished Agency and Weak Structures in the Northern Ireland Peace Process." *The Global Review of Ethnopolitics* 3.1: 22–37.

Helms, Elissa. 2003. "Gendered Visions of the Bosnian Future: Women's Activism and Representation in Post-War Bosnia-Herzegovina." PhD dissertation, University of Pittsburgh.

Helms, Elissa. 2013. *Innocence and Victimhood: Gender, Nation and Women's Activism in Post-war Bosnia-Herzegovina*. Madison: University of Wisconsin Press.

Hoff Sommers, Christina. 1994. *Who Stole Feminism? How Women Have Betrayed Women*. New York: Simon & Schuster.

Husić, Sabiha, Elvira Duraković-Belko, Irma Šiljak, Monika Hauser, Simone Lindorfer, Kirsten Wienberg, and Karin Griese. 2014. *We Are Still Alive: Research on the Long-Term Consequences of War Rape and Coping Strategies of Survivors in Bosnia and Herzegovina*. Zenica: Medica Zenica, medica mondiale.

Karp, Ivan. 1986. "Agency and Social Theory: A Review of Anthony Giddens". *American Ethnologist* 13.1: 131–137.

Laber, Jery. 1993. "Bosnia: Questions of Rape". *New York Review of Books*, 25 March: 4.

Mahmood, Saba. 2005. *Politics of Piety: The Islamic Revival and the Feminist Subject*. Princeton, NJ: Princeton University Press.

Mahmood, Saba. 2009. "Agency, Performativity and the Feminist Subject." In *Pieties and Gender*, edited by Lene Sjorup and Hilda Rømer Christensen, 11–46. Leiden: Brill.

Mardorossian, Carine. 2002. "Towards a New Feminist Theory of Rape." *Signs: Journal of Women in Culture and Society* 27.3: 743–775.

McNay, Lois. 2000. *Gender and Agency: Reconfiguring the Subject in Feminist and Social Theory*. Cambridge: Polity Press.

Mostov, Julie. 2002. "Sexing the Nation/Desexing the Body: Politics of National Identity in Former Yugoslavia." In *Gender Ironies of Nationalism – Sexing the Nation*, edited by Tamar Mayer, 89–112. London: Routledge.

Osborne, Peter, and Lynne Segal. 1996. "Gender as Performance: Judith Butler." In *A Critical Sense: Interviews with Intellectuals*, edited by Peter Osborne, 109–125. London: Routledge.

Oshana, Marina A.L. 2015. *Personal Autonomy and Social Oppression: Philosophical Perspectives*. Oxon: Routledge.

Petrović, Mirko. 2000. "O povijesnom revizionizmu Vesne Kesić." *Zarez* 45–46: 22–35.
Roiphe, Katie. 1993. *The Morning After: Sex, Fear and Feminism*. London: Hamish Hamilton.
Simić, Olivera. 2012. "Challenging Bosnian Women's Identity as Rape Victims, as Unending Victims: The Other Sex in Times of War." *Journal of International Women's Studies* 13.4: 129–142.
Spahić Šiljak, Zilka. 2010. "Images of Women in Bosnia, Herzegovina, and Neighboring Countries, 1992–1995." In *Muslim Women in War and Crisis: From Reality to Representation*, edited by Faegheh Shirazi, 213–226. Austin: University of Texas Press.
Spahić Šiljak, Zilka. 2014. "Nation, Religion and Gender." In *Politicization of Religion, the Power of Symbolism the Case of Former Yugoslavia and Its Successor States*, edited by Gorana Ognjenović and Jasna Jozelić, 185–210. New York: Palgrave MacMillan.
Spry, Tami. 1995. "In the Absence of Word and Body: Hegemonic Implications of 'Victim' and 'Survivor' in Women's Narratives of Sexual Violence." *Women and Language* 18.2, 22 September: 27–32.
Stringer, Rebecca. 2014. *Knowing Victims: Feminism, Agency and Victim Politics in Neoliberal Times*. London: Routledge.
Thompson, Monica. 2000. "Life After Rape: A Chance to Speak?" *Sexual and Relationship Therapy* 15.4: 326–343.
Wolf, Naomi. 1993. *Fire with Fire: The New Female Power and How It Will Change the Twenty-First Century*. London: Chatto & Windus.
Young, Iris M. 1990. *Justice and the Politics of Difference*. Princeton, NJ: Princeton University Press.
Young, Stacy L., and Kathryn C. Maguire. 2003. "Talking About Sexual Violence." *Women and Language* 26.2: 19–38.
Zajović, Staša. 1995. "Abuse of Women on National and Militarist Basis." In *Women for Peace*, 67–76. Belgrade: Women in Black.
Zarkov, Dubravka. 2006. "Towards a New Theorizing of Women, Gender and War." In *Handbook of Gender and Women's Studies*, edited by Mary Evans, Kathy Davis, and Judith Lorber, 214–233. London: Sage.

9 "The war changed me"

Bosnian women, resilience and the search for peace

Marie E. Berry

The war in Bosnia and Herzegovina between 1992 and 1995 left more than 100,000 people dead, nearly half the country displaced, and families scattered across the globe. In the aftermath, tens of thousands of women were reeling from sexual violence, the loss of loved ones, financial destitution, and many other traumatic experiences. Like armed conflicts before and since, the end of the violence did not bring durable peace to affected communities or ensure that justice was served. Instead, the 1995 Dayton Accords bifurcated the country into two semi-autonomous entities and installed a precarious consociational government that granted significant power to those political leaders who had championed the war in the first place. Women were left out of this formal peace process, though they were the targets of millions of dollars of international humanitarian aid.

Social scientists have long understood war to be a period of widespread social and institutional destruction. Acknowledged, but less well understood, is how war is simultaneously a period of rapid social and institutional transformation (see Cramer 2006; Marwick 1988). During armed combat, institutions can be destroyed and rebuilt, political systems can be reimagined, and critically, the gender status quo can fluctuate. This is often because the traditional gender roles women hold in many places around the world – such as caring for children, securing food and maintaining the home – are disrupted because of the disproportionate conscription, displacement, imprisonment and death of men. Further, international humanitarian actors that arrive during war and target aid delivery toward women can give women access to financial capital, training and even international networks that were previously unavailable, shifting women's economic power within their homes and broader community. War can also shift norms about women's social importance, making their ability to bear children part of a broader national political project and elevating them as the "more peaceful" gender that can operate in public spaces more safely and easily than their "more violent/political" male counterparts (see Berry 2015, 2018).

Women suffered tremendously during the Bosnian war. While men comprised over 90 percent of the dead, thousands of women were also killed (Ball, Tabeau and Verwimp 2007). Many more were subjected to horrific sexualized abuse and lived under conditions of scarcity and constant fear of aerial shelling and sniper attacks in cities like Sarajevo. Women also suffered greatly from the loss of their family members – especially their sons, husbands, brothers and fathers. A vast amount of research has been dedicated to this topic (see Mertus 2000; Skjelsbaek 2006; Stiglmayer 1994).

In this chapter I focus on something less often explored: the way in which the conditions of war catalyzed women's resilience and mobilization in explicitly political ways.[1] As one woman put it, "The war changed me. I understand what is important and what is not important" (Interview #67, 6/2013). Drawing from literature on the micro-politics of resistance, including work by James Scott (1985, 1990) and more recent work by Asef Bayat (2010), in addition to feminist literature on the ways in which women's political actions often occur outside the formal political sphere (see Gal and Kligman 2000; Yuval-Davis 1997), in this chapter I illustrate some of the ways that war's devastation simultaneously opened space for social transformation.

To do so, I draw on interviews and focus groups I have conducted with more than 110 women in Bosnia since 2010. I conducted the majority of these interviews in three places: Sarajevo, Tuzla and the region around Prijedor (see Berry 2018, for an explanation of this case selection). I conducted most of the interviews one-on-one, but spoke with approximately 20 women in small groups (often with individual follow-up interviews later), as part of a collaborative project.[2] I spoke with women involved in formal politics, women who had founded or worked for community organizations focused on women's needs and with many women who were the beneficiaries of these organizations. Overall, my goal in each interview was to understand the varied ways that the war had shaped each woman's life during the decades since the armed violence ended.

In what follows, I illustrate some of the ways women's lives were affected by war in Bosnia and Herzegovina, focusing particularly on the way in which war catalyzed a new sense of agency or urgency. I also explore the way some activities, which appear to be confined to an essentially feminine logic at first glance, are in fact remarkable examples of some of the innovations women in Bosnia and Herzegovina have made in order to rebuild their lives and communities after war. As I argue elsewhere (see Berry 2018), these activities may appear to be apolitical and yet they reflect an understudied reality: war can often precipitate women's political mobilization in innovative ways. Better understanding how women mobilize to effect change in their homes and communities during and after war should be of critical importance to international humanitarian agencies and peacebuilding efforts, which have yet to fully harness the potential of women's organizing amid violence.

Survival and resilience during war

The war in Bosnia and Herzegovina was characterized by different logics, levels and speeds of violence in different regions of the country. In Sarajevo, which was subjected to the longest siege of a capital city in modern history, residents worked to stay alive and also to carve out spaces of normalcy while under constant attack.

One powerful way that residents did this was through art and satire, which Ivana Maček has described as a product of their "determination to resist the omnipresence of war" (2009, 54). During the 1,425 days of siege, Sarajevans staged art exhibitions, performed radical anti-war musicals like "Hair," founded the Sarajevo War Theater and Film Festival and more. Yugoslav celebrities, such the members of *Top lista nadrealista*, captivated the city with humorous skits broadcast via radio or television (when it functioned). Maintaining this vibrant art scene during the war required Sarajevans to take great risks, as they quite literally dodged shelling to attend performances or record satirical videos (Maček 2009, 56; Interview with Zenit Đozić, 5/2016).

Women participated in many of these subversive artistic activities. They set up counter-barricades around the city to oppose the barricades maintained by armed actors, serving favorite local foods like čevapčići and burek as a way of rejecting the war and maintaining some semblance of normalcy, culture and community (Udovicki and Štitkovac 1997, 182). They staged the "Miss Besieged Sarajevo '93" beauty contest, which was then broadcast across the world. During the event, participants held up a banner reading "Don't Let Them Kill Us," explicitly converting their barely-clad bodies into a powerful political statement condemning the war. Women also painted and created art, some of which was put on public display in the bombed-out central post office after the war (Maček 2009, 58). All of these examples of creativity during the siege were part of a collective rejection of the war and of the violence that was orchestrated by a few but affected all.

Ismeta, a politician, emphasized how women utilized gendered understandings of femininity and beauty to make a powerful political statement during the siege. For instance, in order to make their lives as normal as possible, she described how she and her colleagues made sure to wear lipstick and nail polish everyday when outside their apartments; they also made sure their clothes were clean and pressed before leaving the house. As she put it,

> The women showed unbelievable strength in Bosnia-Herzegovina – courage. . . . I think that so many women in Bosnia-Herzegovina during this period did great things, because we really tried to make our lives as normal as possible. It means that we really did not mind everything, that we did not have water or electricity.
>
> (Interview #2, 4/2013)

This insistence on normalcy – even through beauty standards – was an actively political way of rejecting the war's aims and feeling less defeated by the nationalists who orchestrated it.

Svjetlana, a Bosnian Serb who stayed in Sarajevo during the siege, described how the challenges women were exposed to during the war created a sense of "survival solidarity" that continued in the war's aftermath. Because the war "was a time with no lies," she noted how Sarajevans from all ethnic backgrounds worked together to survive. Svjetlana described how many of the city's residents often risked their lives to help others. Women risked their lives to gather water, firewood and food for their families and others in need – men often risked their lives in other ways, such as in defense of the city. These everyday tasks became highly political during the siege, as such tasks were necessary for the survival of the population of Sarajevo and thereby a rejection of the war aims of nationalist politicians.

Outside Sarajevo, women also played critical roles ensuring the survival of their families and others during the war. During this process, they often engaged in bold or risky behavior in order to reject the war and its aims. Aida, a woman from a village in the Drina valley, described how paramilitaries came to her house at the outset of the war. They beat her husband severely and forced him to dig trenches in order to bury a body. They then turned to her and demanded she tell them details about the death of a soldier in the area. She refused, even as one of the men "grabbed me from my neck and raised me off the ground and starting cursing at me." Still, she refused to give him any information, even as he threatened to kill her. Rather than caving under that very real threat, Aida recalled smiling and taunting the soldier by saying, "I have two sons who are alive and you can't get them" (Interview #25, 4/2013).

Aida's risky behavior provoked the soldier, who then sexually assaulted her. And yet upon describing this profoundly traumatizing experience, Aida displayed a strong and fierce sense of pride in her statement that taunted the soldier and demonstrated the futility of his actions. For Aida, having two sons out of reach of her assailants meant that her family was doing its part to preserve their ethno-national identity that the aggressors aimed to destroy. While we might see Aida as a victim in this instance, she articulated her experience as one of surviving – an act that she saw as a small contribution to the broader anti-war effort. As she put it, "I am sad but life goes on."

Another woman, Merima, was a housewife before the war. As the violence intensified in the area around Sanski Most, she fled with her family to Travnik. Militias had killed scores of people in the region and raped numerous women, so many of the refugees Merima met in Travnik were in desperate need of basic goods and psychological aid. Because many of the men who arrived in Travnik left immediately to join the Army of the Republic of Bosnia and Herzegovina, Merima described how the "women had to take on all the responsibilities from kids to food . . . they had to live with fear because they were throwing grenades at them still. They had to take care of both the whole family and other things" (Interview #56, 5/2013). Merima and other women in Travnik formed a small organization dedicated to helping the most vulnerable displaced women. As the war ended, Merima and others returned to their village where they found animals in the streets, no electricity, no water and their homes destroyed. So they continued to work. Soon, with some funding and training from a Swiss NGO, Merima's organization began to organize women for human rights advocacy, income-generating projects and psychosocial support. While she noted that she has always been an ambitious person, she had no idea that the war would push her to become involved with work on social issues and women's rights. Today, she described how the war led women to "have power, more than people would expect."

These examples of women's activities during wartime reveal how war can simultaneously devastate and transform women's lives and political subjectivities. By taking grave personal risks to make artistic statements condemning the war or to appear well dressed and polished, women's actions implicitly rejected the bloodshed as "the new normal." Women like Aida also bore the brunt of physical violence because they spoke defiantly to their attackers and refused to acquiesce to their demands. Years later, Aida's continued pride reflects her sense that she stood on the "right" side of history – despite its heavy personal cost. Many women like Merima found themselves leading grassroots efforts to protect and heal women during the war, marking a proud shift from their prewar occupations as housewives confined largely to the domestic sphere.

Community organizing in the wake of war

With the end of armed conflict in 1995, many women began to do the essential work of rebuilding their communities. There was tremendous work to be done: families sought reunion, the displaced needed to return to their homes or a new place of residence and the dead and missing had to be identified. Many international actors assisted with this process, but they relied heavily on local knowledge to do so, often because local actors were the best positioned to identify those most in need and facilitate rapid aid delivery.

During this period, donors provided significant funding for women and other "vulnerable groups," such as orphans and survivors of sexual violence, concentration camps or torture. This led to a rapid formation of many community organizations to meet the needs of these groups. These organizations began to form during the war, while the postwar period featured an even more rapid proliferation of local humanitarian organizations. In many cases, women with some resources, skills or background in activism founded these community-based organizations (CBOs) in order to meet the critical needs of their communities. As one of the founders of Udružene Banja Luka put it, these organizations were founded "because we recognized some problems that . . . the state would not help people with" (Interview #57, 5/2013). This meant that CBOs, often led by women, became a critical parallel structure that provided many of the services a state would normally provide (see Berry 2018; Cockburn 1998, 2013; Helms 2013).

For instance, Beba had been the principal of a school before she was displaced during the war. While living in an internally displaced persons camp, she organized some other displaced women to knit socks and warm sweaters, which provided them some income and helped occupy their time. They learned how to apply for formal status as a "humanitarian" organization, which granted them the ability to then solicit funding from international agencies. She described how she applied to Oxfam to fund the purchase of the wool they needed for their knitting projects. Their first grant was for 300 kilos, which they used to create socks and sweaters for schoolchildren. During the next funding cycle, Oxfam gave them 4,000 kilos of wool, taking the organization to the next level. As she put it,

> There were a lot of bad moments during the war of course. But there were of course some great moments as well. Having this great group of people that works together creates a special kind of connection, and that is one of the greatest moments of this time. This is what helps the person to go through it; you learn new things and you don't think about the war.
>
> (Interview #22, 4/2013)

As these comments suggest, women often experienced pain and suffering during war alongside a sense of pride in their accomplishments, creativity and community.

Widows and mothers of those killed during the war were also quick to organize. Munira Subašić, President of the Mothers of Srebrenica, described how women "did the work that the government wouldn't do." Furious, but committed to documenting the truth, she described how early members of her organization "marked the places of the massacre, [we gave] questionnaires to 12,500 people, we found the mass graves, we helped identify the victims, we pressed charges against the UN" and so forth. According to Munira, the women were motivated not by revenge but rather by a firm commitment that "we did not want to turn to hate, we wanted to turn to dialogue" (Interview #60, 6/2013). Women of Srebrenica, another group based in Tuzla comprised of women who lost sons, husbands and fathers during the massacre and their supporters, began organizing protests on the 11th of every month in central Tuzla. These protests continue to this day, highlighting the continued need for truth and justice about what happened during Srebrenica's fall in 1995. As one participant in this organization described, "We are healing ourselves in this process" (Interview #67, 6/2013).

These groups played a critical role in supporting women's emotional and material needs in the aftermath of the war. Women's organizations have provided resources and emotional support to women who testified at the International Criminal Tribunal for the Former Yugoslavia (ICTY) about their experience, provided group therapy and other forms of psychosocial healing and facilitated income-generating projects. For many of the women I interviewed, the real value of these women's organizations was the act of being together in a group, regardless of the organization's mission. Being in a group allowed many women to realize that while they themselves had suffered, other women suffered even more, which helped motivate them to move forward while helping those less fortunate. These groups supported individual women as they sought reparations and pensions from government and navigated the judicial process. Groups also allowed women to participate in political claims-making on issues related to women's rights, justice and accountability, such as the movement to destigmatize rape or, more recently, advance UN Security Council Resolution 1325 (Rošul-Gajić 2016). While many of these organizations were officially registered as "humanitarian organizations," many also engaged in highly contentious political processes related to refugee return, community rebuilding and security (Berry 2018; see also Helms 2013; Sivic-Bryant 2016).

In part as a result of the important work that many community organizations took on in the aftermath of the war, some women I interviewed expressed a sense of being motivated – rather than disheartened – by the war. Vesna, a politician, noted how she had planned to move away from Bosnia and Herzegovina before the war broke out, but changed her mind when she realized that, as a woman in an interethnic marriage, she had an important symbolic role to play in staying and actively rejecting the virulent rhetoric coming from her own group's politicians. She described her own feeling of motivation and commitment to her country, Bosnia and Herzegovina, increasing dramatically during the war, exclaiming that "you cannot put a price on it" (Interview #29, 5/2013). Lejla, an attorney, said that the war introduced her to a sense of injustice and the idea that good does not always prevail (Interview #33, 5/2013). Decades later, she remains fiercely committed to protecting women and human rights and noted that this commitment stems directly from her war experience. Seida, a community leader from the Prijedor region, recounted that simply seeing how many people needed help after the war motivated her to join together with others in her community to form organizations that could pick up the pieces left by the dysfunctional state. If government was not going to help them, and if men were often unable (or unwilling) to help, she described how women took on critical roles helping their communities recover (Interview #6, 4/2013). For those reasons, Seida – and many women like her – became motivated to do the challenging work of rebuilding their communities and searching for some semblance of peace.

Re-territorialization and gendered aesthetics of peace in Bosnia today

In the 25 years since the end of the war, many residents of Bosnia and Herzegovina still note how Dayton may have ended the violence, but it did not end the war. There is a pervasive sense that the war continues to live on, through ethnicized politics, the ever-growing divide between the Republika Srpska and the Federation, endemic structural violence and even in the legacy of intimate partner violence that affects countless women's lives. As a result, many women are still actively engaged in daily efforts to counter the war's effects on their lives, families and communities.

In this section, I outline one of the innovative ways that women continue to combat the war's legacy, which encompasses an effort to re-territorialize physical spaces through an explicitly feminine aesthetic of beauty and self-care (see also Berry and Rana 2019). Drawing on Dusselier (2005, 173), these efforts are centered around the idea of creating normalcy by converting hostile spaces into arenas of identity articulation where women from Bosnia and Herzegovina can enact subjectivity. This concept of "re-territorialization" draws on the work of Akhil Gupta and James Ferguson (1992) to emphasize the active process of creating spaces of normalcy and subjectivity amid displacement or hostility. War, as Gupta and Ferguson note, can amplify the meaning of place because it often severs the tie between people with certain identities and a physical location (1992, 11).

Such a framework is particularly useful to employ in Bosnia and Herzegovina, as women reclaimed physical spaces – including their homes and villages – both emotionally from the memories of war and physically from those who had occupied their homes and villages in the aftermath. For many who were displaced as part of the process of "ethnic cleansing," returning home after the war was not as simple as just moving back. Instead, it required reentering spaces associated with the opposing side after lengthy petitions and negotiations with government officials and resettlement agencies. Moreover, upon return, many women discovered that their homes were in terrible condition, damaged by the war and scattered with the abandoned possessions of the people who had lived there in their absence. Thus, moving back into the homes and communities they had lived in before the war required more than simply cleaning and rearranging possessions: it required spiritually reclaiming the space for themselves and their families.

What does this look like in practice? Women across the world go about "making place" in different but patterned and gendered ways. In Bosnia and Herzegovina, this often involves creating items and spaces that are beautiful through feminine(ized) representations like flowers, light colors, good scents and embroidery. It can also involve incorporating highly gendered activities, such as cooking, hosting guests, serving coffee and sweets or raising children. In the decade I have been working in Bosnia, many women have described to me how they planted flowers or did needlework because it soothed them and allowed them to feel at peace in their homes. While not articulating such activities as intentional political acts, I see these forms of self-care as part of an informal but powerful effort to reclaim physical spaces that were attacked by armed actors simply because they constituted the Bosnian way of life.

Some women's organizations have also assisted in this process. For example, Snaga Žene, an organization based in Tuzla, provided seeds, starter plants and greenhouses to their members for growing lavender, echinacea and roses. The ostensible motivation for this project was to provide an income-generating activity for the organization's members, and particularly for those who had returned to Srebrenica and the surrounding area after being displaced in Tuzla after the war. It soon became clear that the market demand for these plants was minimal; nevertheless, growing beautiful plants that had medicinal qualities (e.g., lavender for relaxation) served a profoundly therapeutic purpose for the women involved. When I asked members of the organization how they thought it had helped them, several responded that the rose project "helped bring beauty back" into their lives. One woman who had survived rape during the war described how she had been so excited when her echinacea had bloomed that she had called her friend just to celebrate (Interview #71, 6/2013). Participating in the act of creating beauty – through growing flowers or herbs, knitting cross-stitch or embroidery, or creating art or music – gains salience in the aftermath of violence as something that is deliberately in contrast to the ugliness of violence. Moreover, plants, in particular, represent something permanent and hopeful, as one can watch a rose bush bloom year after year.

In interviews with other women in Bosnia and Herzegovina, I often asked what they were most proud of in their lives. Almost all mentioned something they created, built, crafted or grew. Many explained that this was because they found pride in returning beauty to a place where they also remembered pain and darkness. Roses, lavender and needlework reflected the transformation of a barren, war-scared environment into a place of comfort. One woman who survived physical torture and several concentration camps during the war noted that she was able to feel a small sense of peace when she sat by a fountain she had installed in her garden:

> It is so peaceful sitting by the fountain. After everything I've been through, I thank God that I have that. The water runs out a small stream and [I like] the sound of it. . . . I have a place that's covered like a patio where I sit and have my coffee. I sit and make scarves out there. Coffee, breakfast, lunch and everything – I do it outside. I cannot imagine myself being locked inside, I don't like being inside where it's dark with the blinds [closed], I don't like the dark.
> (Interview #111, 7/2016)

For some women, this process of re-territorializing physical spaces also included the art of performing traditional roles in the family, but for the explicit purpose of undermining the purported goals of the war itself. Many women understand that they were attacked during the war because, as one woman put it, "when you attack women, you break down family" (Interview #94, 7/2016). Thus for some women, performing traditional gender roles has become part of resisting the war's aims, even more than two decades after the end of the bloodshed. For instance, one woman proudly mentioned how before meeting me and my research team, she had made a sandwich for her husband (Interview #93, 7/2016). He did not expect this, she noted, but doing so allowed her a daily reminder that she had managed to preserve the family unit and some semblance of the traditional Bosnian family life that had been attacked during the war. She put it clearly: making sandwiches everyday for her husband is her own private way of declaring that nationalists failed to succeed.

Creativity centered around a gendered aesthetic of beauty – during the war and in the decades since – suggests a way that women in Bosnia and Herzegovina continue to actively resist the war and its legacy. While growing flowers or stitching needlepoint can most easily be seen as an apolitical, distinctly feminine activity, here I urge us to consider it part of something more politically substantive. For women who have survived war, creating beauty to simultaneously resist the war's aims and engage in self-care might be considered political in the same way that Audre Lorde considered Black women's self-care in the United States to be "an act of political warfare" (1988). When contrasted with destruction and suffering during wartime, the combined effort of thousands of women working peacefully to "bring beauty back" into physical spaces reflects a way that women are actively engaged with healing themselves, rebuilding their communities and promoting peace in the long run.

Conclusion

In this chapter I have described several of the ways that the Bosnian war transformed women's lives by catalyzing innovative forms of resilience and grassroots mobilization. During the war, women across Bosnia and Herzegovina used their creativity and boldness of spirit to reject the logic of war and those perpetrating it – often at great risk to themselves. In the aftermath of the armed conflict, women led many of the postwar recovery efforts by founding small community organizations dedicated to addressing urgent material and emotional needs. In the decades since, these organizations have served as critical service providers that have taken on many of the roles normally belonging to the state, situating the women involved in these organizations at the center of critical, highly political efforts, such as refugee resettlement, justice and accountability for war crimes. Many women, especially those who returned to places that had experienced massive violence, have also engaged in a process of re-territorialization where they have planted flowers, stitched embroidery, or even made meals for their loved ones in a deliberate effort to bring beauty back into physical places where the horrors of war unfolded. Such acts reflect a "politics of the ordinary," to use Asef Bayat's (2010) term, where the accumulation of many small, seemingly apolitical activities can manifest in a widespread movement for positive social change.

While these examples do not capture the full range of ways that war transformed women's mobilization and resilience, they suggest that while the war in Bosnia and Herzegovina was destructive and devastating, it simultaneously catalyzed new, gendered forms of engagement in public spaces and in contentious political projects. To be sure, there were women from all ethno-national backgrounds who actively championed the war and embraced the logic of violence as it unfolded. Yet among the women I have been privileged to meet over the course of my research, there was a resounding sense that the war transformed many women's roles within society. As one woman put it, "[N]ow women are, and me as well, we are louder" (Interview #69, 6/2013). Recognizing the ways that war is simultaneously destructive and transformative for gender power relations should be a critical part of future postwar recovery and peacebuilding efforts.

Notes

1 See also work by Bop 2001; Meintjes 2001; Sharoni 1995; Tripp 2015.
2 The collaborative project was conducted jointly with Jessica M. Smith, Ph.D. Candidate at George Mason University's School of Conflict Analysis and Resolution. As such, some qualitative data from the project appears in both of our data sets.

References

Ball, Patrick, Ewa Tabeau, and Philip Verwimp. 2007. *The Bosnian Book of Dead: Assessment of the Database*. Brighton: Institute of Development Studies, Households in Conflict Network, University of Sussex.

Bayat, Asef. 2010. *Life as Politics: How Ordinary People Change the Middle East*. Redwood City, CA: Stanford University Press.

Berry, Marie E. 2015. "From Violence to Mobilization: War, Women, and Threat in Rwanda." *Mobilization: An International Quarterly* 20.2: 135–156.

Berry, Marie E. 2018. *War, Women, and Power in Rwanda and Bosnia-Herzegovina*. New York: Cambridge University Press.

Berry, Marie E. and Trishna Rana. 2019. "What Prevents Peace? Women and Peacebuilding in Bosnia and Nepal." *Peace & Change* 44.3: 321–349.

Bop, Codou. 2001. "Women in Conflict: Their Gains and Their Losses." In *The Aftermath: Women in Post-Conflict Transformation*, edited by Sheila Meintjes, Meredeth Turshen, and Anu Pillay, 19–34. London: Zed Books.

Cockburn, Cynthia. 1998. *The Space Between Us: Negotiating Gender and National Identities in Conflict*. London: Zed Books.

Cockburn, Cynthia. 2013. "Against the Odds: Sustaining Feminist Momentum in Post-War Bosnia-Herzegovina." *Women's Studies International Forum* 37.1: 26–35.

Cramer, Christopher. 2006. *Civil War Is Not a Stupid Thing: Accounting for Violence in Developing Countries*. London: Hurst & Co.

Dusselier, Jane. 2005. "Gendering Resistance and Remaking Place: Art in Japanese American Concentration Camps." *Peace & Change* 30.2: 171–204.

Gal, Susan, and Gail Kligman. 2000. *The Politics of Gender After Socialism: A Comparative-Historical Essay*. Princeton, NJ: Princeton University Press.

Gupta, Akhil, and James Ferguson. 1992. "Beyond 'Culture': Space, Identity, and the Politics of Difference." *Cultural Anthropology* 7.1: 6–23.

Helms, Elissa. 2013. *Innocence and Victimhood: Gender, Nation, and Women's Activism in Postwar Bosnia-Herzegovina*. Madison: University of Wisconsin Press.

Lorde, Audre. 1988. *A Burst of Light: Essays*. Ithaca: Firebrand Books.

Maček, Ivana. 2009. *Sarajevo Under Siege: Anthropology in Wartime*. Philadelphia: University of Pennsylvania Press.

Marwick, Arthur, ed. 1988. *Total War and Social Change*. London: Palgrave Macmillan.

Meintjes, Sheila. 2001. "War and Post-War Shifts in Gender Relations." In *The Aftermath: Women in Post-Conflict Transformation*, edited by Sheila Meintjes, Meredeth Turshen, and Anu Pillay, 63–77. New York: Zed Books.

Mertus, Julie. 2000. *War's Offensive on Women: The Humanitarian Challenge in Bosnia, Kosovo, and Afghanistan*. Bloomfield, CT: Kumarian Press.

Rošul-Gajić, Jagoda. 2016. "Women's Advocacy in Postwar Bosnia and Herzegovina: Implementation of UNSCR 1325 on Women, Peace and Security." *Journal of International Women's Studies* 17.4: 143–159.

Scott, James C. 1985. *Weapons of the Weak: Everyday Forms of Peasant Resistance*. New Haven: Yale University Press.

Scott, James C. 1990. *Domination and the Arts of Resistance: Hidden Transcripts*. New Haven: Yale University Press.

Sharoni, Simona. 1995. *Gender and the Israeli-Palestinian Conflict: The Politics of Women's Resistance*. Syracuse, NY: Syracuse University Press.

Sivic-Bryant, Sebina. 2016. *Re-Making Kozarac: Agency, Reconciliation, and Contested Return in Post-War Bosnia*. London: Palgrave Macmillan.

Skjelsbaek, Inger. 2006. "Victim and Survivor: Narrated Social Identities of Women Who Experienced Rape During the War in Bosnia-Herzegovina." *Feminism & Psychology* 16.4: 373–403.

Stiglmayer, Alexandra, ed. 1994. *Mass Rape: The War Against Women in Bosnia-Herzegovina*. Lincoln: University of Nebraska Press.

Tripp, Aili Mari. 2015. *Women and Power in Postconflict Africa*. New York: Cambridge University Press.

Udovicki, Jasminka, and Ejub Stitkovac. 1997. "Bosnia and Herzegovina: The Second War." In *Burn This House: The Making and Unmaking of Yugoslavia*, edited by Jasminka Udovicki and James Ridgeway, 174–214. Durham: Duke University Press.

Yuval-Davis, Nira. 1997. *Gender & Nation*. Thousand Oaks, CA: Sage.

10 From subjects of stories to agents of change

Countering dominant discourses of gender and peacebuilding

Jessica M. Smith

Introduction

The complexity of challenges in the aftermath of conflict necessitates participation from a broad range of actors. To ensure postwar policy is informed by different perspectives and expertise, individuals whose voices have been marginalized must be meaningfully engaged in the development of sustainable solutions. Research has shown women to be central to the success of peacebuilding[1] efforts, yet they continue to be underrepresented in these processes. International attention to the different experiences and levels of vulnerability women face during and after war, alongside global recognition of the important role women play in peacebuilding (Pratt and Richter-Devroe 2011, 489–503; Strickland and Duvvury 2003; Greenburg and Zuckerman 2006), has resulted in international policy frameworks intended to better support and engage women affected by conflict. For example, the systematic use of sexualized violence during the conflict in Bosnia and Herzegovina brought global awareness to the gendered nature of violence during war.[2] Experiences of women in Bosnia and Herzegovina (BiH)[3] were a catalyst for the adoption of United Nations Security Resolution (UNSCR) 1325,[4] and the subsequent creation of the United Nations Women, Peace and Security (WPS) Agenda which shapes contemporary postwar policy and programming for women in the aftermath of conflict.

Looking to women's experiences in postwar Bosnia and Herzegovina offers much, for scholars and policymakers alike, to learn about the challenges of translating peacebuilding policy into practice and the ways in which international intervention has both supported and forestalled women's engagement in these processes in the years since violent conflict ended in the region. Although global attention has largely moved on from conflict in the Western Balkans, Bosnian and Herzegovinian women still have much to teach us about the ways in which women in postwar settings, formally and informally, facilitate peacebuilding and positive social change in their daily lives. These lessons can be useful for other women facing similar challenges in the aftermath of war, such as women in Syria or the Democratic Republic of Congo and for organizations with vested interests in promoting gender and peacebuilding agendas.

Layout of the chapter

The chapter begins with a brief overview of UNSCR 1325 and the resulting WPS agenda, highlighting the influence these policy instruments have had on shaping postwar gender interventions. Next, the chapter introduces a narrative lens to reveal how dominant discourses have influenced contemporary approaches to gender and peacebuilding, in BiH and globally, and the implications this has for women's expression of agency in these contexts. The chapter then explores the transformative potential of an arts-based method called photovoice, arguing that photovoice allows for a multiplicity of women's narratives to emerge and opens up pathways for individuals to have more ownership over the storytelling process. Finally, the chapter concludes by highlighting the potential for photovoice to support the evolution of more empowered narratives among participants, a finding that emerged in a photovoice project with 29 women across BiH. Excerpts from a photovoice interview with Ferida are shared to illustrate how the process of narrative evolution works in practice.

A women, peace and security approach to women's empowerment

Contemporary gender and peacebuilding practice is overwhelmingly characterized by a women, peace, and security approach, which is broadly focused on (a) inclusion of women in peacebuilding, and (b) preventing and addressing conflict-related gender-based violence.[5] UN Security Council resolutions like UNSCR 1325 and the others that make up the UN WPS Agenda[6] have not only structured the type of gender programming on the ground but have also embodied the dominant narratives of women and war. Some have argued that heightened global awareness around gender-based violence in conflict has led to an overemphasis on prevention and protection (Scully 2009), which has in turn shaped donor priorities and thus the nature of peacebuilding interventions for women (Helms 2013). The concern is that this overemphasis has the potential to overshadow dimensions of the WPS framework that push for greater engagement of women in the decision-making processes of peacebuilding, which could sideline efforts to increase women's participation in peacebuilding. Fifteen years after passing the landmark United Nations Security Resolution 1325, which solidified the issue of women, peace and security within the international peacebuilding agenda, women remain underrepresented in decision-making processes (Porter 2007, 38; Oudraat 2013), revealing that the policy rhetoric in which gender is prioritized does not always translate into practice.[7] The significant role of women in conflict transformation[8] underscores the critical importance of understanding not only the role they play in restoring the social fabric of their communities but also what it means to them to "participate" in peacebuilding (De la Ray and McKay 2006) and how international postwar policy and programming can better support women in shaping these processes.

The reality of women's increased risk of violence in situations of conflict and crisis is well documented (IRC 2013; UNFPA 2014), but so is their capacity to be agents of change (UN Women 2015; Porter 2007; Schnabel and Tabyshalieva 2012, 21). For example, women in BiH were subject to particularly horrific forms of gendered-violence during the war, but they also played a crucial role in sustaining families and communities during and after violent conflict and have continued to actively facilitate positive social change in the country (see Berry's contribution in this volume). As is the case in many patriarchal societies, women in BiH are central to families and communities, and thus have a key role to play in how communities recover from violence and how they move forward toward peace. Sustained attention to the multiplicity of women's experiences (see Spahić Šiljak in this volume) – not focusing exclusively on women's vulnerability to victimization but also highlighting their resilience – will increase the likelihood that policy instruments such as UNSCR 1325 work to support women's capacity to participate in their own protection and emancipation. For this reason, empowerment of women in these contexts must be prioritized alongside efforts to prevent and address gender-based violence.

However, this prompts the question of what it means to women to be "empowered" in these contexts. Literature on women's empowerment reflects overall inconsistency in how the concept is understood and measured (Duffy 2011; Aston et al. 2006; Bradbury-Jones, Sambrook and Irvine 2008; Tew 2006). Malhotra and Schuler conducted a review of 45 studies, the majority of which used quantitative methods to try to capture "women's empowerment" (2005, 81). Although specific definitions of empowerment varied across studies, Malhotra and Schuler found underlying consensus that the concept of empowerment entails "enhancement of women's ability to make strategic life choices" with elements of process (change occurs over time) and agency (women participate in this change) as defining features of the concept (Ibid., 84).

The rise in popularity of the term "empowerment" within development discourse has led to what Cornwall and Anyidoho refer to as "empowerment-lite," a "depoliticized and instrumental version of empowerment" (2010, 145). They claim the term has taken on a liberal notion of agency located within the individual, arguing, "The anaemic forms of 'empowerment' that are promoted by international development agencies and their national government partners do not acknowledge global inequalities" (Ibid., 147). The danger in the proliferation of empowerment-lite, to which Cornwall and Anyidoho call attention, is that it does not adequately question "how women can be empowered within disempowering structures and systems" (Ibid., 145).

This concern seems especially salient not only in contexts where patriarchal norms are particularly disempowering to women but also in situations in which state institutions are dysfunctional or corrupt. For example, in the case of Bosnia and Herzegovina, interethnic conflict has become embodied in political parties' struggles for power, forestalling the realization of a thriving democratic state and leading to broad political disenfranchisement for both men and women across the country (Griffiths 1999). These challenges, alongside a strong history of traditional gender norms, necessitate approaches to women's empowerment and engagement in peacebuilding that extend beyond quota arguments for women's inclusion in existing systems and structures ("empowerment-lite") toward a reimagining of how to support BiH women in effectively maneuvering for change. As scholars such as Pupavac argue, quota systems designed to increase women's participation in decision-making processes may benefit a select number of "female members of the urban elite" but fail to generate "real changes in the political, social and economic opportunities of Bosnian women" (2005, 403). Without ongoing attention to intersecting forms of oppression[9] that constrain women's expression of agency in these spaces, including disempowering discursive factors embedded within policy discourse, efforts toward women's empowerment will continue to fall short of any kind of sustainable transformation that is truly emancipatory for women.

A narrative lens on gender and peacebuilding

Narrative, as both an analytic tool and a form of praxis, is a useful resource for rethinking postwar interventions for women. A narrative lens on gender and peacebuilding is helpful because it reveals the power dynamics operating in the narrative landscape (Cobb 2013), which materialize in the nature of stories being circulated at all levels, from the interpersonal to the institutional. Foundational to narrative theory is a belief that individuals understand themselves and others through the stories they tell, and a narrative lens is keenly focused on both the relational and social dimensions of experience. This is important because discursive power dynamics shape individuals' beliefs and actions (Jabri 1996) and influence the relationship between structure and agency (Shepherd 2008, 385). From a narrative point of view, the formation of policy initiatives such as UN Security Council resolutions, is seen as a discursive practice (Shepherd 2008), with institutions like the United Nations functioning as sites of discursive power.

A narrative lens draws attention to gendered assumptions embedded in the discourse of policy instruments like UNSCR 1325, offering critically needed insight given the hegemonic force this particular resolution has in structuring gender policy and programming, including its central role in guiding country-specific National Action Plans (NAPs) on gender (Miller, Pournik and Swaine 2014).[10] For example, some have argued that UNSCR 1325 has embedded within it a biological conception of gender, in which women are viewed to be inherently more peaceful than men (Pratt and Richter-Devroe 2011). Linking biology to a predisposition to peace reflects a lack of attention to the diversity of women's lived experiences in conflict situations and can have a de-politicizing effect on women's agency (El-Bushra 2012, 12). This type of logic presents an essentialized narrative of women and neglects factors that contribute to the social construction of gender and gender roles, such as issues of power embedded in social relations and structures (Swaine 2009, 421; El-Bushra 2012, 9).

Women, in fact, often take on a wide variety of roles before, during and after conflict (Afshar and Eade 2003; Moser and Clark 2001; El-Bushra 2012; Myrttinen, Naujoks and El-Bushra 2014; Bouta and Frerks 2002). To the extent that "women as peacemakers" embodies a singular narrative of agency reflected in the discourse of UNSCR 1325, the framework will fall short in accounting for and encouraging a range of opportunities for women's participation (Cohn 2003, 13). Another problematic concept folded into the discourse of the WPS framework is the frequent reference to women as victims, often combined with other vulnerable populations through phrases like "women and children" (Puechguirbal 2010; Carpenter 2005). Collapsing "womenandchildren" (Enloe 1990) into one category is a disservice to the complexity of women's experiences and undercuts a framing of women as active agents capable of pushing for change on their own behalf (Puechguirbal 2004; Carpenter 2005).

Essentializing discourse, in any of its forms – women as victims or women as peacemakers – has implications for the positioning[11] of women as legitimate moral actors, those with the capacity to make moral decisions. For example, in the case of Bosnia and Herzegovina, Elissa Helms (2013) argues that frameworks used by scholars, activists and policymakers inadvertently contributed to the dominance of an essentialized narrative that portrays women as victims instead of agents. According to Helms, women in postwar Bosnia and Herzegovina were positioned by the international community through a dominant discourse of victimhood, such that some women felt "victimhood" became the only thing of value they could leverage to access international aid (Ibid., 235; Berry 2017). By discursively constructing female war survivors as innocent victims, women were invited into the political arena (public space) primarily as apolitical peacemakers or agents of reconciliation (Helms 2013, 139). Helms illustrates the discursive politics between moral agency and legitimacy by showing the implications a dominant narrative of victimhood had on the range of agency available to women in BiH and the impact of this on the ways in which women's activists maneuvered in the postwar space (Helms 2013).

For example, following the end of armed conflict in the Balkans, a conflict famous for its use of rape as a weapon of war, international organizations and donors prioritized postwar women's programming focused on addressing the aftermath of sexual violence (Helms 2013; Walsh 2000). International attention to "protection" of women meant that in order to get international funding and support, grassroots women's groups working in BiH had to frame their work in terms of international donor priorities (Walsh 2000), which resulted in a (re)structuring of activities around "protection" and "victimization" (Helms 2013) with less emphasis on women's political empowerment or increasing women's engagement in peacebuilding.

Attention to the political nature of narratives originating from these spaces and their resulting influence on peacebuilding policy and practice reveals the power of discursive politics to determine what kind of stories of gender and peacebuilding can be told by whom and how those stories then unfold within people's lives. It is hard to imagine how women, invited into the public sphere in largely apolitical ways, could be viewed as moral agents without a shift in the discursive landscape. For transformation to occur, meaningful participation of women in peacebuilding processes would entail the ability of women not only to "speak and be heard"[12] in these spaces but to have the moral authority to alter, if not define, the politics of the speaking space and the narratives produced therein.

Furthermore, from a relational understanding of agency,[13] the extent of women's moral authority would be dependent upon dominant voices already present within the space to that acknowledge and reinforce women's contributions, a requirement that may entail a full-scale reorganization of the nature of these conversations. The quality of voice in these settings would thus be dependent upon the ability of women to exercise agency over the terms of the conversations, which would require much more than the simple inclusion of women in existing structures and institutions. Viewing institutional bodies, such as the United Nations, as sites of discursive power suggests narrative as a useful resource for transforming the discursive sphere so that more emancipatory storylines can emerge. To this end, a narrative lens enriches the field's understanding of what is needed to meaningfully engage women in peacebuilding.

A narrative approach to photovoice

Narrative offers an analytic lens but also an approach to praxis. A central goal of narrative praxis is the evolution of stories circulating in the narrative landscape, which is achieved using techniques like circular questioning, externalization and reflective practice to support the elaboration of narratives such that more complex, better-formed stories emerge (Cobb 2013, 226–227).[14] The better formed the story is, the more likely it is to travel across time and have traction within social networks, which is critical to the success of counter-stories.[15] Narrative praxis can be used to facilitate a process that supports narrative evolution by designing the conversation such that shifts toward better-formed stories occur.[16] Stories become "better-formed" as participants uncover new, more empowered, insights and understandings from the stories that structure their experiences, which allows new perspectives to emerge and with them, new avenues for action (Cobb 2013, 223–227; Smith 2016, 180). This reflexive process of generating conversation becomes the platform for facilitating the possibility for change and redressing marginalization by elaborating underdeveloped narratives in which individuals are positioned without legitimacy.

Arts-based methods like photovoice, which also facilitate self-reflection and a process of new meaning-making, may be particularly complementary to this kind of narrative work. Photovoice is a participatory action research methodology developed by Carolyn Wang and Mary Ann Burris (1997) and has been used to study a variety of community-based issues such as race relations, environmental issues, cultural diversity and homelessness (Hergenrather et al. 2009, 690). The method involves supplying cameras to research participants who, through a series of workshops, take photographs around themes that relate to the research questions of the project. Photovoice works to promote marginalized voices (Wang and Burris 1997; Wang 1999; Molloy 2007; Teti et al. 2013) by using the photographs produced by participants as a platform for critical dialogue. Furthermore, a central goal of photovoice workshops is that knowledge generated by participants is then elevated into the public sphere, such as through public photography exhibitions, as means to foster community-level dialogue and ultimately influence policy change (Wang and Burris 1997).

For individuals who have often been objects of the researcher's gaze, photography offers a means by which participants can direct the gaze outward (Parrella and Del Loewenthal 2013, 110). This has been shown to be an empowering process for photovoice participants (see, for example, Teti et al. 2013), allowing them agency over the aspects of their experience they wish to discuss or share, as they ultimately have control over what makes it into the frame and what does not. Additionally, photovoice serves as a resource for self-representation in which participants have an opportunity to counter essentialized narratives of their experiences.

There is also evidence to suggest that photovoice, as an arts-based method, may be particularly useful with individuals who have experienced trauma (Rolbiecki et al. 2016; True, Rigg and Butler 2015). Research on neurophysiology and the role of art in trauma healing (Appleton 2001; van der Kolk and Fisler 1995) has demonstrated the effect of trauma on the brain (Bremner 2002) and how traumatic experiences become encoded in parts of the brain that are inaccessible to the region of the brain responsible for speech, rendering these experiences literally unspeakable. Studies have shown how artistic processes have been used to successfully access these encoded experiences, providing a means by which individuals can begin to articulate these stories (Riedal 2013; Klorer 2005; Nanda et al. 2010). The process of making art allows access to the experiences, while the object created through the art provides an external, tangible representation of the experience from which individuals can begin to construct a narrative. Photovoice works in much the same way, offering an artistic process that results in an image, an object from which participants can story their experiences.

A discussion of the therapeutic benefits of speaking about traumatic experiences is outside the scope of this chapter;[17] however, I wish instead to highlight here the connection between trauma and narrative and suggest the utility of a narrative approach to photovoice to support survivors' ability to overcome challenges associated with reconstructing coherent narratives of their experiences, and through that process, assert a greater sense of agency. Susan J. Brison writes, "Trauma undoes the self by breaking the ongoing narrative, severing the connections among remembered past, lived present and anticipated future" (1999, 41). Experiences of trauma thus become un-narratable (van der Kolk and Fisler 1995) such that individuals are unable to capture them within narrative structure. If we adopt the perspective that identity is narratively constructed (Nelson 2001, 106), the implications of this rupture in an individual's meaning-making system can be quite profound.

Brison draws a distinction between traumatic memory and narrative memory, explaining traumatic memory as a somatic type of memory often accompanied by physiological symptoms over which survivors often have little control (1999, 42). She argues the shift from traumatic to narrative memory transforms "traumatic memory into a coherent narrative that can then be integrated into the survivor's sense of self and view of the world" (Brison 1999, 39). Illustrating how narrative can be useful in facilitating this shift she writes,

> Narrative memory is not passively endured; rather it is an act on the part of the narrator, a speech act that diffuses traumatic memory, giving shape and a temporal order to the events recalled, establishing more control over their recalling, and helping survivors remake the self.
>
> (Ibid., 40)

To the same end, Cobb argues, "[T]alking about violence is critical to containing violence within and through narrative, as it provides a structure to experience that orders it both causally and morally" (Cobb 2013, 171).

This process takes place at an individual level, but as both authors point out, has a relational dimension. "In order to construct self-narratives we need not only the words with which to tell our stories, but also an audience willing to hear us and to understand our words as we intend them" (Brison 1999, 46) – in other words, we need to "speak and be heard." Thus, arts-based methods such as photovoice, which allow for an articulation of voice that expands beyond the boundaries of speech, and may indeed support the shift from traumatic memory to narrative memory, can be a resource for survivors to access "the words with which to tell." Furthermore, there is agency in constructing one's narrative, as Brison writes, "narratives are the result of certain obvious choices (for example, how much to tell, in what order, and so forth)" (1999, 47). By positioning individuals as their own visual storytellers, photovoice gives participants greater control over how their story is told and how their experience is represented, and can help avoid essentializing representations.

Photovoice with female war survivors in Bosnia and Herzegovina

During the summer of 2016 I ran a photovoice project with 29 women from four regions across BiH.[18] The project, entitled *Her Wisdom, Her Wings*,[19] was broadly focused on using photovoice to explore with BiH women how they make sense of their role in positive social change and to learn directly from women affected by war what has been helpful over the past 20 years, what challenges they continue to face and any wisdom they have to share with other women who may find themselves facing the aftermath of war. I provided women with digital cameras and encouraged them to take pictures around project themes; these images were then used as the platform for dialogue in individual interviews and in some cases, focus groups. After the women had several days to take photographs, I met with each of them to review their images and learn the story and meaning behind each photograph, their motivation for creating particular images and the story they hoped to convey. This process gave women the opportunity to share what they determined to be the most salient aspects of their experience and gave them agency within the interview process.[20]

For the purposes of this chapter, I will focus on one interview in particular, which captures a broader trend of narrative evolution that emerged in interviews with women throughout the project. My conversation with Ferida below illustrates how photovoice can support participants in articulating and reframing their experiences, and facilitate the emergence of better-formed stories:

> *The afternoon had grown warm by the time we arrived at Ferida's house. She heard our car pull up and poked her head through the beaded curtain that covered the front door. Her long dark hair glistened in the sunlight, and with a warm smile and bright eyes, she beckoned to us to come in. Leaving our shoes near the steps outside, we followed her down the hallway and into the living room. The blinds were drawn and it was cool and dark inside. Ferida chatted casually with us as she brought a tray of coffee and sweets from the kitchen. After placing the tray on the table, she proudly produced her camera, taking a seat next to me on the couch as I opened my laptop and plugged in the memory card.*
>
> *As the images began to load, she said, "I have one story to share!" I smiled and asked her which image she wanted to start with and she replied, "Well, they are all the same theme, about being a victim of war. They show the story of how I got my scar." The images popped up on the screen, one after another, each of the frames filled with a long, silvery pink scar etching its way across her torso. As I clicked on the first image, she said, "There was a grenade explosion, and there's shrapnel inside my body, it's still in my lung. One piece they got out, but one is still in [there]. I didn't know what life, or the pain of life, was until I felt the physical pain of the grenade and the emotional pain of having my brother in the concentration camp."*
>
> *Looking together at the screen, I asked her, "How does seeing the scar make you feel?"*
>
> *"Well, I don't know, I haven't looked at it in a long time. I avoid looking at it in the mirror on purpose. It reminds me of the time I died and woke up. . . . This picture reminds me of the whole experience of the war. I pull my shirt up all the time to cover the scar. It reminds me of the times when we didn't have anything to eat, to wear, when we lived a very difficult life. . . . The war was like dying. Not having food, worrying all the time, it was so painful."*
>
> *Curious about her experience of choosing to focus her images on the scar, I asked, "What made you decide to take a photo of the scar? What was it like to photograph it?"*
>
> *"I would have never remembered to take a picture of the scar if the theme wasn't brought up at the first group meeting. . .*[21] *I had 100 other ideas, but this one came from my heart."*
>
> *"How did it feel?" I asked.*
>
> *"I haven't seen the images at all until now. I myself don't enjoy seeing them, but I enjoy sharing the story with someone else. . . . Actually, I am really glad that this is what I took a picture of. That was a really good idea. I feel fulfilled right now. I feel really good about taking the pictures."*

> *"Can you tell me more?" I asked.*
>
> *"It's because I was a child back then and I survived it. And after the surgery I didn't have anything to eat, and I survived again. I am happy to share what is not only a testament to surviving the grenade blast, but also everything that came after it. The operation, the hospital, not having the necessary bandages, waiting for the military to bring supplies . . . this is a reminder of survival – my memory of survival. Last year, I had back surgery and I never think about it, it doesn't mean anything. But this was so important."*
>
> *At the end of the interview I asked her, "What story do you hope this photo will tell?"*
>
> *"My message to other women would be that whatever happens, whatever hits you in life – whether it's a bullet or a fist – get back up, put your head up high, and keep going."*[22]

Ferida offers a powerful and complex account of herself as both victim and survivor. The photographs she took facilitated a telling of her story that moved beyond a recitation of a sequence of events, toward a reflexive process of meaning-making which becomes visible as she articulates and (re)frames the symbolism of the scar and her traumatic memory. Through the course of Ferida's story, it is possible to see her narrative of the scar evolve and increase in complexity. Initially she identifies the scar as something she avoids looking at, a reminder of war and all the suffering she and those she loved endured. Given the emotional weight of that symbolism, I wish to acknowledge her courage in choosing the scar as the subject of her photographs. When we began to look at the images, she told me that it was the first time she was seeing them. Although it was possible to review images in the digital camera, she said she had not wanted to look at them. I mention this not simply to underscore her bravery, but because it holds significance relative to the shift in her narrative of the scar over the course of our interview and the strength of photovoice to facilitate the emergence of better-formed stories.

The images were an opportunity for her to share a story about her experience during the war, which she said was meaningful for her, and through the process her description of the symbolism behind the scar grew more complex, from a traumatic memory initially to "a reminder of survival – my memory of survival." This is not to imply that the scar no longer holds a memory of trauma for her; what I wish to highlight is that through the process of taking the photographs and sharing the meaning behind them, a new perspective of the scar emerged and the narrative grew in complexity. This mirrors the shift in how she positions herself within the narrative, which she begins describing herself as a victim of war, and ends identifying as a survivor. Through a process of reflection, details are added in along the way, and the narrative grows more complex as she stories herself as both victim and survivor, moving between the two and sometimes occupying both at once.

Rolbiecki et al. conducted a study using photovoice with trauma survivors and found, "Survivors who participate in photovoice have the opportunity to explore how they view themselves and how they wish to be seen by others in the future" (2016, 243). It is possible to see this process unfold in Ferida's case as well. Ultimately, Ferida wanted people who viewed her photograph to know her story of resilience, and to encourage other women that they too can survive, "My message to other women would be that whatever happens, whatever hits you in life – whether it's a bullet or a fist – get back up, put your head up high, and keep going." The narrative reflects her suffering, but also her resilience, and the process of participating in the photovoice project allowed her to project into the public sphere a self-authored representation of her experience that reflected how she prefers "to be seen by others in the future" (Ibid.). Her story includes both an account of victimization and an account of survival, which counters an essentialized narrative of the female war victim. Although she was initially nervous about the idea of taking the pictures, she reported that she was glad she had taken them, and that she felt fulfilled. The telling of the story was also important to her. To this end, Ferida's story reinforces findings from additional studies that have shown photovoice to be an empowering experience for participants (Teti et al. 2013).

Ferida's experience in the photovoice project illustrates three core strengths of the method: (1) It encourages individuals to engage in self-reflection through the use of artistic process, which creates a space for them to "frame" their experiences in a new way; (2) This reflexive process of meaning-making supports an evolution of their perception of self as agent and facilitates narrative evolution as participants story these perceptions; and (3) It provides an avenue of engagement with marginalized populations that allows them agency over the aspects of their experience they wish to discuss or share and positions participants as their own visual storytellers and experts. In the context of gender and peacebuilding, this type of intervention provides an avenue for engagement, which allows women to articulate storylines not beholden to essentialized narratives. In the case of BiH, a dominant discourse of women's victimhood has in many ways structured not only the speaking space but also which types of stories can be told by whom. For women who have often been the *subjects* of stories, instead of the *storytellers*, photovoice as an avenue for self-representation and narrative authorship offers a valuable resource for promoting postwar agency and empowerment. This approach disentangles itself from liberal assumptions about women's empowerment, looking instead to women affected by conflict, positioning them as experts and legitimate voices in the public sphere.

Conclusion

Around the world, women's voices continue to be underrepresented in virtually all aspects of peacebuilding, warranting additional research that seeks to understand how to elevate their status as agents of change. However, *inclusion* of women in existing processes is not enough. It is critically important to understand how to support women in shaping the terms of their participation in peacebuilding interventions such that they are able to dictate how, in which way and when they engage. A narrative lens draws attention to discursive features embedded within the current WPS framework that are inherently disempowering and function to forestall women's agency. Furthermore, narrative, as both an analytic lens and a form of praxis, offers a valuable resource for advancing policy and practice focused on gender and peacebuilding globally. For this reason, NGOs engaging in women's empowerment efforts after war might consider incorporating a narrative component into their local grant giving and programming.

Additionally, interventions like narrative praxis and photovoice, which provide women with opportunities to counter essentialized representations, could be especially useful for supporting women in challenging disempowering gendered discourses. Photovoice has been used for this purpose in diverse contexts, such as with female sex workers in Indonesia (Smith forthcoming),[23] conflict-affected women in Guatemala (Lykes, Blanche and Hamber 2003), lesbian and bisexual women in South Africa (Zway and Boonzaire 2015), women in Northern Ireland (McIntyre 2003; Side 2005) and Latina women in the United States (Mejia et al. 2013). Echoing findings of this study, additional research has also shown photovoice to be an excellent vehicle for supporting experiences of empowerment (Foster-Fishman et al. 2005), including studies with women in Guatemala (Chomat et al. 2016), Canada (Duffy 2011) and the United States (Teti et al. 2013). Larger funding entities, such as the UN and other multinational organizations, should prioritize funding for initiatives that incorporate feminist forms of praxis and evaluation that actively counter or disrupt essentialized gendered representations. By bringing forth local wisdom and highlighting individual and collective expressions of agency, narrative and photovoice methods elevate the voices of women, empowering individuals to craft narratives that counter oppressive dominant discourses and creating opportunities to reposition themselves as agents of change.

Notes

1 The term peacebuilding can take on a wide range of meaning. Within the literature, "peacebuilding" is often used to describe structural process associated with post-conflict reconstruction efforts (De la Ray and McKay 2006; Boutros-Ghali 1992). It is also used to refer to formal processes, which scholars like Galtung (1969) refer to as "peacemaking" including mediation, international negotiations, cease-fires, etc. Peacebuilding is used less often to refer to work that is culture-specific (De la Ray and McKay 2006) or gender-specific (Anderlini 2000), although scholars such as Lederach (1995a, 1995b) and Fisher (1993) were influential in expanding the concept of peacebuilding beyond its initial structural understanding (De la Ray and McKay 2006).

2 The conflict in the Western Balkans marked the first instance in which an international war crimes trial included charges of sexual violence. For additional information, please see the United Nations International Criminal Tribunal for the former Yugoslavia (ICTY) judgments on sexual violence available at: www.icty.org/en/features/crimes-sexual-violence/landmark-cases.

3 BiH has been a leader in the region with regard to the adoption of international gender policy into state law and was the first postwar country to develop a comprehensive National Action Plan (NAP) on UNSCR 1325 (Miller, Pournik and Swaine 2014, 12).

4 Full text of the United Nations Security Resolution 1325 is available at https://documents-dds-ny.un.org/doc/UNDOC/GEN/N00/720/18/PDF/N0072018.pdf?OpenElement.

5 For a comprehensive description of this approach, please see United Nations (2002). *Women, Peace and Security*. Study submitted by the Secretary-General pursuant to Security Council Resolution 1325 (2000). New York: United Nations. Available at www.un.org/womenwatch/daw/public/eWPS.pdf.

6 At the time of publication, the UN WPS Agenda is comprised of the foundational policy document UNSCR1325, strengthened by nine additional Security Council Resolutions, beginning with SCR 1820 in 2008, following with SCR 1888 and SCR 1889 in 2009, SCR 1960 in 2010, SCR 2106 and SCR 2122 in 2013, SCR 2242 in 2015, and most recently SCR 2467 and SCR 2493 in 2019. The full text of each Security Council Resolution is available at https://www.securitycouncilreport.org/un-documents/women-peace-and-security/.

7 For an overview of the impact of UNSCR 1325, see Maureen Shaw (2010).

8 For examples of research showing women as central agents of change in the aftermath of war, see the following sources: UN Women 2015, 41–42; Porter 2007; Schnabel and Tabyshalieva 2012, 21. For an overview of scholarly work related to the centrality of women to peace, see Ellerby (2013) and Zuckerman and Greenburg (2004). For examples of international organizations that affirm women's central role in peace, see the analysis of WOMANKIND World Wide's work by Lockett (2008) and the work of the Institute for Inclusive Security, available at www.inclusivesecurity.org. In additional to policy within the UN, see, for example, Women's International League for Peace and Freedom (n.d.) overview of WPS policy within the United States, including links to the US NAP and US Strategy on Women, Peace and Security available at http://peacewomen.org/nap-usa.

9 A discussion of intersectional theory is beyond the scope of this chapter, but the work of Kimberlé Crenshaw (credited with creating the term intersectionality), Audre Lorde, Chandra Talpade Mohanty and Patricia Hill Collins has been central to the development of the concept and theoretical frame.

10 Miller, Pournik and Swaine (2014) offer an extensive overview of UNSCR 1325 and National Action Plans.

11 Positioning theory (van Langenhove and Harré 1999) is helpful for tracking how individuals or groups are positioned within a particular discourse and who is seen to be a legitimate interlocutor.

12 Klugman et al. describe voice as "having the capacity to speak up and be heard and being present to shape and share in discussions, discourse, and decisions" (2014, 155).

13 According to Cobb, "[A]gency is not produced because the Self pronounces itself; it can be produced only relationally because the Self advances descriptions of itself that are adopted, contested, and elaborated by Others" (2013, 153). Agency, from a narrative perspective, is thus viewed not as an intrinsic human quality, but as a relational practice in which agency is produced through discursive positioning (Shepherd 2008).

14 For additional resources on practices to support narrative evolution, please see White (2007) and Winslade (2009).

15 According to Hilde Lindemann Nelson, a counter-story is "a story that resists an oppressive identity and attempts to replace it with one that commands respect" (2001, 6). Nelson suggests counter-stories as a means by which marginalized voices can begin to reposition themselves as legitimate interlocutors.

16 The term "better-formed story" was originally coined by Carlos E. Sluzki (1990) to describe narrative transformation within the context of family therapy, and adapted as a model for narrative approaches to conflict resolution by Sara Cobb (2013).

17 It has been well established, especially within psychology and social work fields, that speaking about trauma can contribute to a process of healing (for example, see: Brison 1999; Mansfield, McLean and Lilgendahl 2010; Agger and Jensen 1990). Other scholars have critiqued the link between speaking and healing, cautioning that the assumption that speaking leads to healing reflects dominant Western approaches to

healing that may not be culturally relevant in other contexts, and may in fact hide the political motivations (and agency) that can underlie an individual's choice not to speak (for example, see Dwyer 2009; Henry 2009; Becker 2015).

18 Traditional focus groups and interviews were conducted alongside the photovoice workshops, a selection of which were co-facilitated with my colleague Dr. Marie Berry, assistant professor at the Josef Korbel School at the University of Denver. As such, some qualitative data from the project appears in both of our data sets.

19 Participants in *Her Wisdom, Her Wings* each selected one photograph to be included in public photography exhibitions and to be displayed in an online gallery. The online gallery featuring photographs from the full project can be accessed at https://herownwings.org/projects in both English and B/C/S (*Njena Mudrost, Njena Krila*).

20 This data was collected as part of my dissertation research. A fuller description and analysis of the project will be featured in my forthcoming dissertation, "Visualizing Voice: Framing Peace & Agency in Bosnia-Herzegovina."

21 During the initial photovoice workshop in which the project was introduced to the group and the cameras were distributed, the women brainstormed ideas for photos they might like to take. The women in this group have been friends for many years, and one of them suggested that Ferida photograph her scar. She was apprehensive about the idea, despite encouragement from her friends, and nervous about showing images of the scar. I told her that she did not have to share any pictures she wasn't comfortable with, and that if she wanted to try taking them, she could always delete them right away, but suggested that the process might be helpful for her. When she left the workshop, she was still undecided.

22 Though presented as a narrative, the quotes from Ferida are taken directly from the interview transcript (R6_July 2016). This is an abbreviated version of the interview, with passages that are most relevant to the current discussion.

23 An online gallery of the photovoice exhibition for this project entitled "I AM ME" is available at https://herownwings.org/i-am-me.

References

Afshar, Haleh, and Deborah Eade, eds. 2003. *Development, Women, and War: Feminist Perspectives*. Bloomfield: Kumarian Press.

Agger, Inger, and Søren Buus Jensen. 1990. "Testimony as Ritual and Evidence in Psychotherapy for Political Refugees." *Journal of Traumatic Stress* 3.1: 115–130.

Anderlini, Sanam Naraghi. 2000. *Women at the Peace Table: Making a Difference*. New York: United Nations Development Fund for Women.

Appleton, Valerie. 2001. "Avenues of Hope: Art Therapy and the Resolution of Trauma." *Art Therapy, Journal of the American Art Therapy Association* 8.1: 6–13.

Aston, Megan, Donna Meagher-Stewart, Debbie Sheppard-Lemoine, Adele Vukic, and Andrea Chircop. 2006. "Family Health Nursing and Empowering Relationships." *Pediatric Nursing* 32: 61–67.

Becker, Heike. 2015. "Against Trauma: Silence, Victimhood, and (Photo-) Voice in Northern Namibia." *Acta Academica* 471: 116–137.

Berry, Marie E. 2017. "Barriers to Women's Progress After Atrocity: Evidence from Rwanda and Bosnia-Herzegovina." *Gender & Society* 31.6: 830–853.

Bouta, Tsjeard, and Georg Frerks. 2002. "Women's Roles in Conflict Prevention, Conflict Resolution, and Post-Conflict Reconstruction: Literature Review and Institutional Analysis." Netherlands Institute of International Relations. http://gender.care2share.wikispaces.net/file/view/Bouta+%26+Frerks+Survey+of+Gender+and+IOs.pdf.

Boutros-Ghali, Boutros. 1992. *An Agenda for Peace*. New York: United Nations Publications.

Bradbury-Jones, Caroline, Sally Sambrook, and Fiona Irvine. 2008. "Power and Empowerment in Nursing: A Fourth Theoretical Approach." *Journal of Advanced Nursing* 62: 258–266.

Bremner, J. Douglas. 2002. "Neuroimaging Studies in Post-Traumatic Stress Disorder." *Current Psychiatry Reports* 4: 254–263.

Brison, Susan J. 1999. "Trauma Narratives and the Remaking of the Self." In *Acts of Memory: Cultural Recall in the Present*, edited by Mieke Bal, Jonathan Crewe, and Leo Spitzer, 39–54. Hanover: University Press of New England.

Carpenter, R. Charlie. 2005. " 'Women, Children and Other Vulnerable Groups': Gender, Strategic Frames and the Protection of Civilians as a Transnational Issue." *International Studies Quarterly* 49.2: 295–334.

Chomat, Anne Marie, Paola Letona, Eleanor Platt, Maria Garcia Maldonado, Kristine G. Koski, and Marilyn E. Scott. 2016. "Photovoice Reveals Narratives of Hardship and Resilience Among Rural *Mam*-Mayan Women in the Western Highlands of Guatemala." In *Maternal Stressors Impact Maternal Wellbeing and Cortisol and Infant Growth in Rural Guatemala: Insights from Qualitative and Quantitative Approaches*, 194–224. Doctoral dissertation, Institute of Parasitology & School of Environment, McGill University, Montreal, Canada.

Cobb, Sara. 2013. *Speaking of Violence: The Politics and Poetics of Narrative in Conflict Resolution*. New York: Oxford University Press.

Cohn, Carol. 2003. "Mainstreaming Gender in UN Security Policy: A Path to Political Transformation?" Consortium on Gender, Security, and Human Rights. http://cgshr.resonetrics.com/sites/default/files/mainstreaming_gender_in_un_security_policy-_a_path_to_political_transformation_0.pdf.

Cornwall, Andrea, and Nana Akua Anyidoho. 2010. "Introduction: Women's Empowerment: Contentions and Contestations." *Development* 53.2: 144–149.

De La Rey, Cheryl, and Susan McKay. 2006. "Peacebuilding as a Gendered Process." *Journal of Social Issues* 62.1: 141–153.

Duffy, Lynne. 2011. " 'Step-by-Step We Are Stronger': Women's Empowerment Through Photovoice." *Journal of Community Health Nursing* 28.2: 105–116.

Dwyer, Leslie. 2009. "A Politics of Silences." In *Genocide: Truth, Memory, and Representation*, edited by Alexander Laban Hinton and Lewis O'Neil, 113–146. Durham: Duke University Press.

El-Bushra, Judy. 2012. "Gender in Peacebuilding: Taking Stock." International Alert. www.international-alert.org/sites/default/files/Gender_TakingStock_EN_2012.pdf.

Ellerby, Kara. 2013. "(En)gendered Security? The Complexities of Women's Inclusion in Peace Processes." *International Interactions* 39.4: 435–460.

Enloe, Cynthia. 1990. "Women and Children: Making Feminist Sense of the Persian Gulf Crisis." *Village Voice* 25.9: 29–32.

Fisher, Ronald J. 1993. "The Potential for Peacebuilding: Forging a Bridge from Peacekeeping to Peacemaking." *Peace and Change* 18: 247–266.

Foster-Fishman, Pennie, Branda Nowell, Zermarie Deacon, M. Angela Nievar, and Peggy McCann. 2005. "Using Methods That Matter: The Impact of Reflection, Dialogue, and Voice." *American Journal of Community Psychology* 36.3–4: 275–291.

Galtung, Johan. 1969. "Violence, Peace and Peace Research." *Journal of Peace Research* 6.3: 167–191.

Greenburg, Marcia, and Elaine Zuckerman. 2006. "The Gender Dimensions of Post-Conflict Reconstruction: The Challenges to Development Aid." United Nations University World Institute for Development Economics Research (UNU-WIDER). www.responsibilitytoprotect.org/files/rp2006-62.pdf.
Griffiths, Hugh. 1999. "A Political Economy of Ethnic Conflict Ethno-Nationalism and Organised Crime." *Civil Wars* 2.2: 56–73.
Helms, Elissa. 2013. *Innocence and Victimhood: Gender, Nation, and Women's Activism in Postwar Bosnia-Herzegovina*. Madison: University of Wisconsin Press.
Henry, Nicola. 2009. "Witness to Rape: The Limits and Potential of International War Crimes Trials for Victims of Wartime Sexual Violence." *International Journal of Transitional Justice* 3.1: 114–134.
Hergenrather, Kenneth C., Scott D. Rhodes, Chris A. Cowan, Gerta Bardhoshi, and Sara Pula. 2009. "Photovoice as Community-Based Participatory Research: A Qualitative Review." *American Journal of Health Behavior* 33.6: 686–698.
International Rescue Committee (IRC). 2013. "Syria: A Regional Crisis." www.rescue.org/sites/default/files/resource-file/IRCReportMidEast20130114.pdf.
Jabri, Vivienne. 1996. *Discourses on Violence: Conflict Analysis Reconsidered*. Manchester: Manchester University Press.
Klorer, P. Gussie. 2005. "Expressive Therapy with Severely Maltreated Children: Neuroscience Contributions." *Art Therapy: Journal of the American Art Therapy Association* 22.4: 213–220.
Klugman, Jeni, Lucia Hanmer, Sarah Twigg, Tazeen Hasan, Jennifer McCleary-Sills, and Julieth Santamaria. 2014. *Voice and Agency: Empowering Women and Girls for Shared Prosperity*. Washington, DC: World Bank Group.
Lederach, John Paul. 1995a. *Building Peace: Sustainable Reconciliation in Divided Societies*. Tokyo: United Nations University.
Lederach, John Paul. 1995b. *Preparing for Peace*. Syracuse, NY: Syracuse University Press.
Lindemann Nelson, Hilde. 2001. *Damaged Identities, Narrative Repair*. Ithaca: Cornell University Press.
Lockett, Kathryn. 2008. "The Mechanisms of Exclusion: Women in Conflict." *Feminist Legal Studies* 16.3: 369–376.
Lykes, M. Brinton, Martin Terre Blanche, and Brandon Hamber. 2003. "Narrating Survival and Change in Guatemala and South Africa: The Politics of Representation and a Liberatory Community Psychology." *American Journal of Community Psychology* 31.1–2: 79–90.
Malhotra, Anju, and Sidney Ruth Schuler. 2005. "Women's Empowerment as a Variable in International Development." In *Measuring Empowerment: Cross-Disciplinary Perspectives*, edited by Deepa Narayan-Parker. Washington, DC: World Bank.
Mansfield, Cade D., Kate C. McLean, and Jennifer P. Lilgendahl. 2010. "Narrating Traumas and Transgressions: Links Between Narrative Processing, Wisdom, and Well-Being." *Narrative Inquiry* 20.2: 246–273.
McIntyre, Alice. 2003. "Through the Eyes of Women: Photovoice and Participatory Research as Tools for Reimagining Place." *Gender, Place & Culture* 10.1: 47–66.
Mejia, Angie Pamela, Olivia Quiroz, Yolanda Morales, Ruth Ponce, Graciela Limon Chavez, and Elizabeth Olivera y Torre. 2013. "From Madres to Mujeristas: Latinas Making Change with Photovoice." *Action Research* 11.4: 301–321.
Miller, Barbara, Milad Pournik, and Aisling Swaine. 2014. "Women in Peace and Security Through United Nations Security Resolution 1325: Literature Review, Content

Analysis of National Action Plans, and Implementation." Institute for Global and International Studies, The George Washington University. www.peacewomen.org/assets/file/NationalActionPlans/miladpournikanalysisdocs/igis_womeninpeaceandsecuritythroughunsr1325_millerpournikswaine_2014.pdf.

Molloy, Jennifer K. 2007. "Photovoice as a Tool for Social Justice Workers." *Journal of Progressive Human Services* 18.2: 39–55.

Moser, Caroline, and Fiona Clark, eds. 2001. *Victims, Perpetrators, or Actors? Gender, Armed Conflict, and Political Violence*. London: Zed Books.

Myrttinen, Henri, Jana Naujoks, and Judy El-Bushra. 2014. "Re-Thinking Gender in Peacebuilding." International Alert. http://international-alert.org/sites/default/files/Gender_RethinkingGenderPeacebuilding_EN_2014.pdf.

Nanda, Upali, H. Lea Barbato Gaydos, Kathy Hathorn, and Nicholas Wakins. 2010. "Art and Posttraumatic Stress: A Review of Empirical Literature on the Therapeutic Implications of Art Work for War Veterans with Posttraumatic Stress Disorder." *Environment and Behavior* 42.3: 376–390.

Oudraat, Chantal de Jonge. 2013. "UNSCR 1325: Conundrums and Opportunities." *International Interactions* 39.4: 612–619.

Parrella, Carmine, and Del Loewenthal. 2013. "Community Phototherapy." In *Phototherapy and Therapeutic Photography in a Digital Age*, edited by Del Loewenthal, 107–120. East Sussex: Routledge.

Porter, Elisabeth. 2007. *Peacebuilding: Women in International Perspective*. New York: Routledge.

Pratt, Nicola, and Sophie Richter-Devroe. 2011. "Critically Examining UNSCR 1325 on Women, Peace and Security." *International Feminist Journal of Politics* 13.4: 489–503.

Puechguirbal, Nadine. 2004. "Women and Children: Deconstructing a Paradigm." *Seton Hall Journal of Diplomacy and International Relations* 5: 5–16.

Puechguirbal, Nadine. 2010. "Discourses on Gender, Patriarchy and Resolution 1325: A Textual Analysis of UN Documents." *International Peacekeeping* 17: 172–187.

Pupavac, Vanessa. 2005. "Empowering Women? An Assessment of International Gender Policies in Bosnia." *International Peacekeeping* 12.3: 391–405.

Riedal, Eberhard. 2013. "My African Journey: Psychology, Photography, and Social Advocacy." *Psychological Perspectives: A Quarterly Journal of Jungian Thought* 56.1: 5–33.

Rolbiecki, Abigail, Kim Anderson, Michelle Teti, and David L. Albright. 2016. "'Waiting for the Cold to End': Using Photovoice as a Narrative Intervention for Survivors of Sexual Assault." *Traumatology* 22.4: 242–248.

Schnabel, Albrecht, and Anara Tabyshalieva. 2012. "Forgone Opportunities: The Marginalization of Women's Contributions to Post-Conflict Peacebuilding". In *Defying Victimhood: Women and Post-Conflict Peacebuilding*, edited by Albrecht Schnabel and Anara Tabyshalieva, 3–47. Tokyo: United Nations.

Scully, Pamela. 2009. "Vulnerable Women: A Critical Reflection on Human Rights Discourse and Sexual Violence." *Emory International Law Review* 23.1: 113–123.

Shaw, Maureen. 2010. "Moving Beyond Rhetoric: Assessing the Impact of 1325." *Rethinking Human Rights*. www.peacewomen.org/content/moving-beyond-rhetoric-assessing-impact-resolution-1325.

Shepherd, Laura J. 2008. "Power and Authority in the Production of United Nations Security Council Resolution 1325." *International Studies Quarterly* 52.2: 383–404.

Side, Katherine. 2005. "Snapshot on Identity: Women's Contributions Addressing Community Relations in a Rural Northern Irish District." *Women's Studies International Forum* 28.4: 315–327.

Sluzki, Carlos E. 1990. "Negative Explanation, Drawing Distinctions, Raising Dilemmas, Collapsing Time, Externalisation of Problems: A Note on Some Powerful Conceptual Tools." *Residential Treatment for Children & Youth* 7.3: 33–37.
Smith, Jessica M. 2016. "Snaga Žene: Disrupting Discourses of Victimhood in Bosnia-Herzegovina." *The International Journal of Conflict Engagement and Resolution* 4.2.
Smith, Jessica M. Forthcoming. "Arts-Based Inquiry and the Emergence of Lines of Flight: Exploring a Narrative Approach to Photovoice." *Special Issue of the Journal of Qualitative Inquiry*.
Stickland, Richard, and Nata Duvvury. 2003. "Gender Equity and Peacebuilding: From Rhetoric to Reality-Finding the Way." International Center for Research on Women (ICRW). www.icrw.org/files/publications/Gender-Equity-and-Peacebuilding-From-Rhetoric-to-Reality.pdf.
Swaine, Aisling. 2009. "Assessing the Potential of National Action Plans to Advance Implementation of United Nations Security Council Resolution 1325." *Yearbook of International Humanitarian Law* 12: 403–433.
Teti, Michelle, Latrice Pichon, Allison Kabel, Rose Farnan, and Diane Binson. 2013. "Taking Pictures to Take Control: Photovoice as a Tool to Facilitate Empowerment Among Poor and Racial/Ethnic Minority Women With HIV." *Journal of the Association of Nurses in AIDS Care* 24.6: 539–553.
Tew, Jerry. 2006. "Understanding Power and Powerlessness: Towards a Framework for Emancipatory Practice in Social Work." *Journal of Social Work* 6: 33–51.
True, Gala, Khary K. Rigg, and Anneliese Butler. 2015. "Understanding Barriers to Mental Health Care for Recent War Veterans Through Photovoice." *Qualitative Health Research* 25.10: 1443–1455.
United Nations. 2002. *Women, Peace and Security*. Study submitted by the Secretary-General pursuant to Security Council Resolution 1325. New York: United Nations. www.un.org/womenwatch/daw/public/eWPS.pdf.
United Nations Population Fund (UNFPA). 2014. "Global Summit Urges to End Sexual Violence in Conflict." New York. www.unfpa.org/news/global-summit-urges-end-sexual-violence-conflict.
UN Women. 2015. "Preventing Conflict, Transforming, Justice, and Security the Peace: A Global Study on the Implementation of United Nations Security Council Resolution 1325." United Nations, New York. http://wps.unwomen.org/~/media/files/un%20women/wps/highlights/unw-global-study-1325-2015.pdf.
van Der Kolk, Bessel A., and Rita Fisler. 1995. "Dissociation and the Fragmentary Nature of Traumatic Memories: Overview and Exploratory Study." *Journal of Traumatic Stress* 8: 505–525.
van Langenhove, L., and Rom Harré. 1999. "Introducing Positioning Theory." In *Positioning Theory*, edited by Rom Harré and Luk van Langenhove, 14–31. Oxford: Blackwell Publishers.
Walsh, Martha. 2000. "Aftermath: The Role of Women's Organizations in Postconflict Bosnia and Herzegovina." Center for Development Information and Evaluation, USAID, Working Paper No. 308, July.
Wang, Caroline. 1999. "Photovoice: A Participatory Action Research Strategy Applied to Women's Health." *Journal of Women's Health* 8.2: 185–192.
Wang, Caroline, and Mary Ann Burris. 1997. "Photovoice: Concept, Methodology, and Use for Participatory Needs Assessment." *Health Education & Behavior* 24.3: 369–387.
Women's International League for Peace and Freedom. n.d. "National Action Plan: United States of America." http://peacewomen.org/nap-usa.

White, Michael. 2007. *Maps of Narrative Practice*. 1st ed. New York: W.W. Norton & Company.

Winslade, John. 2009. "Tracing Lines of Flight: Implications of the Work of Gilles Deleuze for Narrative Practice." *Family Process* 48.3: 332–346.

Zuckerman, Elaine, and Marcia Greenburg. 2004. "The Gender Dimensions of Post-Conflict Reconstruction: An Analytical Framework for Policymakers." *Gender and Development* 12: 70–82.

Zway, Maia, and Floretta Boonzaier. 2015. " 'I Believe That Being a Lesbian Is Not a Curse': Young Black Lesbian Women Representing Their Identities Through Photo-voice." *Agenda* 1–12.

Part IV

From justice to artistic expression

Practices of working with trauma

11 Towards social restoration in Bosnia and Herzegovina

Exploring the place of symbolic forms of transitional justice

Mina Rauschenbach, Stephan Parmentier and Maarten Van Craen

Through the analysis of population-based survey data collected in 2006 in Bosnia and Herzegovina (BiH), this chapter discusses the perceived value of symbolic forms of justice in this "post-conflict"[1] setting. As a significant building block in the expansion of the field of transitional justice (TJ), such forms of justice are gaining prominence. Since the 1980s, TJ has gone through several paradigmatic shifts, which testify to the evolution of the meanings and expectations attached to justice in postwar settings (Teitel 2000). A broader perspective to achieving justice is currently advocated within TJ scholarship in order to achieve thick forms of reconciliation and restore social ties in the aftermath of a violent past. It follows the understanding that TJ processes are meant to achieve various objectives, reaching beyond the aims of accountability and democratization (Bell 2009). Such scholarship has highlighted the limitations of formal and institutionalized top-down forms of TJ, such as trials and truth commissions, highlighting their limited value for thick social reconstruction (Corkalo et al. 2004) or their lack of inclusion of all justice stakeholders (van der Merwe 2008; Shaw, Waldorf and Hazan 2010; Stover 2005). Against the backdrop of such concerns, scholarship is increasingly recognizing the significant potential of nonjudicial, localized and community-based forms of justice practices to help societies restore social ties in transitional contexts (Arriaza and Roht-Arriaza 2010; Isaacs 2009; Quinn 2009). The literature also reflects an emerging consensus for the necessity to account for the various and nuanced meanings that can be attributed to concepts of redress, justice, reparation and social reconstruction (Roht-Arriaza 2006; Shaw, Waldorf and Hazan 2010).

Within this increased consideration for the "local" in TJ scholarship, we focus particularly on the increasing use of more *symbolic forms of justice* (as opposed to concrete or material forms) in postwar settings. These are understood here as those localized and nonjudicial measures that aim at reparation, acknowledgment and community healing through the recognition of victimization and wrongdoing as well as remembrance (Brown 2013; Hamber 2009). Often included within the category of symbolic reparations,[2] such measures of justice can take on various forms and are often context- and experience-specific. Symbolic and material forms of reparation are often distinguished, whether in the legal, academic or policymaking realm (De Greiff 2006: Office of the United Nations High

Commissioner for Human Rights [OHCHR] 2008), yet many scholars debate this distinction, arguing that material reparations are invariably also symbolic in nature in that they will never be commensurate with the harm suffered (Moon 2012). The two forms of reparations may have the same psychological purpose: they "symbolically mark the point of moving into a new phase and symbolize an individual's mastery over the past" (Hamber 2000). We focus this study solely on forms of justice that are symbolic in nature in that they do not consist of monetary compensation or restitution of goods and property. These may include (but are not restricted to) the following: naming a street after someone killed; constructing a museum; exhumations and reburials; rituals; oral histories; building memorials; apologies; public forums of discussions; erecting headstones; or creating a day of remembrance.

Symbolic forms of justice bear particular importance in divided postwar societies as markers of acknowledgment, meaning and narratives of the past. Scholarship has increasingly highlighted their significance in symbolically acknowledging individuals' suffering as well as providing them a voice and status, but also in representing societal recognition of past harm (Hamber 2009). They can also enact or represent specific memories of the past, acting as channels of expression of often conflicting narratives, mediating the dissemination of collective memories as well as personal ones (Brown 2013). We discuss now how symbolic forms of justice can serve a multitude of restorative processes, from acknowledgment of past atrocities to narrative healing.

Symbolic forms of justice: the value of acknowledging suffering and truth-telling

Symbolic forms of justice are generally thought to be significant for victims[3] in the potential to recognize their suffering and their status as victims of undeserved and unjust wrongdoing. On the one hand, the value of such means of symbolic recognition lies in their power to relieve survivors from the "moral ambiguity" they may feel and "redirect blame towards perpetrators" (Hamber and Wilson 2002). They recognize survivors as citizens and as victims, thereby restoring their sense of humanity and dignity and reaffirming their inclusion in the moral community. On the other hand, they symbolically represent empowerment and the possibility to make sense of their undeserved suffering after the uncertainty and stigmatization caused by their experience of violence (Fattah 1991; Herman 1992). Exposure to violence is indeed likely to have shattered their assumptions about who they are and the world in which they live (Janoff-Bulman 1985). They may want to overcome these feelings by creating a "meaningful and coherent" narrative of the experience of victimization (Hamber and Wilson 2002).

Personal truth-telling can represent a key form of symbolic recognition for those who have been exposed to mass violence. It allows them to have a voice (D'Estrée 2006, as cited in Guthrey 2015; van Camp and Wemmers 2013): to tell their story and give meaning to it. This may be even more likely for some victims if it takes place in a private and informal setting (Doak 2011). In addition to truth-telling, scholars such as Hamber (2009) or Quinn (2010) have argued that memory initiatives may constitute another valuable symbolic recognition space, as they can *acknowledge* survivors' experiences as well as allow them to express and make sense of their suffering. Yet measures of symbolic justice are more likely to acknowledge past sufferings if they do so in a meaningful way for their beneficiaries (Hamber 2009).

Some scholars also suggest that symbolic justice measures of *truth-telling* or *acknowledgment* of suffering may have interlinked benefits for victims, while others have pointed to contradictory outcomes attached to both forms of symbolic justice. Memory initiatives, such as memorial museums, can be potential channels for *truth-telling*, in addition to *acknowledgment*, when they provide opportunities for the expression of personal narratives, which are often presented alongside the showcasing of collective narratives of the past. *Truth-telling* can lead to an *acknowledgment* of suffering if it is heard and received by an audience (Guthrey 2015). Yet, this *acknowledgment* is likely to depend on whether the context and process of *truth-telling* constitutes a supportive and sensitive forum for those telling their stories of suffering (Hamber 2009). Moreover, in some cases, victims may prefer private channels of *truth-telling*, such as oral histories or writing a book and may not aim for a public *acknowledgment* of their suffering (Guthrey 2015; Hamber and Kelly 2016). In other cases, victims may find an *acknowledgment* of their suffering in silence, if it is not the result of an imposed silencing (Riaño-Alcalá and Baines 2011; Vinitzky-Seroussi and Teeger 2010).

Yet *truth-telling* and the *acknowledgment of suffering* do not only constitute symbolic recognition. They also reflect a form of social action, which allows survivors to move beyond the victim identity and regain control over their lives and environments (Hamber 2009). This, it is argued, is more likely if one engages in a process of cognitive recovery, which "involves the ability to develop a realistic perspective of what happened, what was done by whom and to whom, and accepting the reality that it happened the way it did" (Danieli 2014). Thus, for survivors, freeing themselves from victimhood may be as important as having their victim status recognized.

Overall, it is thus generally assumed that symbolic forms of justice can be linked to two main valuable functions for victims: *acknowledgment of suffering* and *truth-telling* (Naidu and Torpey 2012). There is a growing consensus concerning their potential to promote peacebuilding and social restoration. Yet scholars such as Lambourne (2009) have suggested that such justice outcomes may be more likely to be achieved if they account for the heterogeneity of needs of those affected by the conflict, especially those representing traditionally marginalized voices. While acknowledgment of suffering or truth-telling may be important for many victims, it may not always be possible or may be counterproductive, depending on the circumstances. As we argue further, there are many reasons why the diversity and structural complexities of justice needs should be considered when devising such initiatives.

Symbolic forms of justice: contested channels to recognize multiple postwar needs

Research focusing on victims' needs and expectations in the aftermath of a violent conflict generally highlight their context-sensitivity and heterogeneity (Naidu and Torpey 2012). Populations who have been affected by a violent conflict constitute a multifaceted cluster of justice stakeholders with heterogeneous needs and claims. Some may be direct victims of violence or persecution, while others may be indirect victims or witnesses of harm during a conflict.

However, such heterogeneity is not only related to the nature of exposure to violence in the conflict but is also due to identity concerns and processes. Violent conflicts cause individual suffering, but they also destroy the social fabric (Fletcher and Weinstein 2002). Social ties and cohesion within a community recovering from a war are likely to have been especially challenged or damaged when the conflict was grounded in identity divides (Haider 2009). Within such a complex identity matrix, diverging justice concerns are likely to be expressed due to conflicting understandings of the past, thereby maintaining and even exacerbating divisions related to various group affiliations.

The fact that symbolic forms of justice, as channels expressing narratives of the past, can act as sites of contestation and power struggles between various justice stakeholders is well documented (Braun 2014; Graham and Whelan 2007; Ramanathapillai 2006). Some of these initiatives may also be attached to hegemonic power agendas and embody narratives of the past which do not reflect the personal memories held by those in the name of which they are created or the needs of local constituents (Naidu 2004). Through the accounts of the past they channel, they can also impose authoritative readings about the involvement of different subgroups within a community, thereby creating or maintaining hierarchies of victimhood and of justice claimants (Ferguson, Burgess and Hollywood 2010). Collective memory can thus be contested and negotiated by different groups claiming the acknowledgment of specific understandings and experiences of the past within various symbolic TJ measures.

The extent to which specific narratives of the past can be propagated is likely to depend on the prevailing power and identity interests in a given social setting (Hammack and Pilecki 2012). As a result, some experiences may be included and allowed to be publicly acknowledged, while others are silenced and marginalized because they are not consonant with dominant narratives (Mannergren Selimovic 2018). This may also lead to the inclusion of some categories of citizens in the class of beneficiaries of symbolic forms of justice, while others may be excluded from these. Exclusion of certain individuals or collectives may be grounded in the fact that their narratives are at odds with mainstream victim narratives or definitions of what victimhood constitutes (De Greiff 2006). In this struggle for the acknowledgment of victimhood, beholders of suppressed experiences may often have no or limited access to sociopolitical spaces of recognition, as well as those institutions which promote it (Ashplant, Dawson and Roper 2000). Resorting to private forms of expressions of memory may be their only possibility to obtain such acknowledgment (Winter and Sivan 1999).

Tensions related to struggles for recognition between individual and collective forms of symbolic justice have also been frequently highlighted (Hamber 2000). Individual forms of justice are generally targeted at a specific individual identified as entitled to these. Collective forms of justice are focused on reparation for a community of individuals who have suffered from a violent past because of their identity (e.g., women, certain ethnic groups) or their status in the armed conflict (e.g., camp detainees). Conflicts between forms of symbolic justice can occur if collective forms are favored over individualized ones. For example, collective reparations such as formal apologies often take on a broad and acontextual focus, with the risk of not bringing forward the whole truth about individual suffering and the responsibilities attached to it. Another example is erecting monuments or memorials in honor of certain categories of the society without consideration for subaltern individuals who were also affected by the conflict. Those forms of collective reparations often constitute political acts which aim at nation-building and restoring the relationship between victims and the state, but which do not target the particular experiences of individuals.

Thus, scholarship increasingly acknowledges the existence of various and often conflicting or marginalized *needs* and interests in specific postwar contexts. This suggests a careful consideration for the individual, political and social symbolic capital of reparations when devising justice initiatives. This could be achieved, as many suggest (Margarell 2007; Naidu 2014), by engaging all those affected by a conflict in consultation processes around such practices. When policymakers and practitioners choose, design and implement justice measures that account for the diversity of experiences and claims of local justice stakeholders, especially those representing traditionally marginalized or subaltern voices, it may increase the chances that they will be contextually appropriate and fit local needs and priorities.

Symbolic forms of justice and their relevance for BiH

Symbolic forms of transitional justice may constitute a key element of social restoration in BiH. Their potential to acknowledge individuals' suffering as well as to provide them a voice and status, but also to symbolize societal recognition of past wrongdoing is particularly significant, due to the complex social reality characterizing this postwar setting.

Current research on symbolic forms of justice in BiH suggests that justice stakeholders do not constitute a homogeneous group (see Čolo Zahirović's chapter in this volume). Justice and acknowledgment needs are not only a subject of conflict between ethno-national groups (Barkan and Becirbasic 2015) but are also contested within these groups, due to individuals' affiliations to other meaningful, often war-related social identities (e.g., urban vs. rural, gender, victim, veteran, refugee, internally displaced, families of the missing, etc.) that are attached to various competing memories of the past. In BiH, wartime experiences and postwar uncertainties crystallize specific moral claims and meaningful war-related identities, which correspond to particular sociocultural categories in competition for resources and recognition (Hronešová 2016). Each group's demands are legitimized by their perceived position within a hierarchical matrix of claims and rights, often upheld by politicians with self-interested agendas (e.g., providing housing opportunities or social benefits to victims from a particular national group) (Grandits 2007). Thus, while the claims of particular groups are recognized, many justice stakeholders are likely to be excluded from the postwar moral community in Bosnia and Herzegovina. (See also Čolo Zahirović's chapter in this volume).

Thus, BiH constitutes a complex social reality within which various social groups struggle to gain recognition and public visibility for their experiences of the past and for their contingent justice needs. This implies also the existence of contrasting and competing understandings of the past held by different groups, understandings that are often contested and negotiated through symbolic TJ measures. BiH has, for that matter, recently seen a growth in the establishment of symbolic measures aimed at countering denial and acknowledging the harms done to all. Such symbolic measures range from state-implemented official national commemorative practices and cultural or artistic initiatives to small-scale and locally rooted initiatives brought about by local communities. Research on these initiatives (Božić 2017; Centre for Nonviolent Action 2016; Moll 2013; Subotic 2016) frequently reveals that such symbolic measures constitute sites of diverging (re)interpretations of the past which are often criticized for being one-sided and attached to self-interested political agendas.

In this chapter, we focus particularly on Bosnian and Herzegovinian citizens' perceptions of initiatives which aim for the symbolic recognition and empowerment of individuals and communities affected by a violent past through *acknowledgment of suffering* and *truth-telling*. Symbolic justice concerns in BiH have been afforded little empirical attention, compared to judicial measures. While the need for grassroots consultation regarding the different meanings afforded to justice is increasingly recognized, those studies that have carried out comprehensive quantitative surveys of needs and expectations have rarely accounted for perceptions of symbolic forms of justice. Research on symbolic justice measures in BiH has mostly taken the form of ethnographic case studies related to specific initiatives, demonstrating generally their contested and divided nature (e.g., Bougarel, Helms and Duijzings 2007). Yet such research has rarely focused on distinguishing between various forms of symbolic justice and how their relevance may depend on specific concerns, which are in turn likely to be contingent upon particular understandings and experiences of the past. Given these gaps and the current calls for a more in-depth understanding of the nuanced meanings that can be attributed to justice, we have studied support for symbolic forms of justice and assume that perceptions are likely to be heterogeneous and shaped by past experiences and present concerns.

Research aims and questions

This study draws on the analysis of data stemming from a population-based survey developed and conducted by members of the Leuven research team as part of a larger research project in BiH and in Serbia, focusing on mass victimization and restorative justice, supported by the Research Council of the University of Leuven (for more details, see Parmentier, Valiñas and Weitekamp 2009; Valiñas, Parmentier and Weitekamp 2009). We aim to explore support for symbolic justice initiatives related to *acknowledgment of suffering* and *truth-telling*, focusing particularly on how respondents' assessments may be attached to particular profiles of reported war experiences, beliefs about the conflict and justice and demographic factors. More specifically, we assess: (1) the extent of support for these two forms of symbolic recognition; (2) whether support for one form is always contingent upon support for the other; and (3) how different symbolic justice concerns can be related to particular profiles of respondents. With this objective, we will categorize respondents according to their relative support for both, acknowledgment of suffering (hereafter referred to as *acknowledgment*) and *truth-telling* forms of symbolic justice. This allows us to investigate (1) whether and to what extent respondents support these symbolic justice dimensions, as well as (2) whether some respondents may support one dimension and not the other. We then evaluate the role of war experiences, relevant conflict or justice beliefs and demographic factors, with a view to identify the factors that may distinguish different respondent profiles. The assumption guiding these objectives is that acknowledgment of suffering and truth-telling refer to overlapping but not equivalent symbolic justice needs in terms of their meaning for justice claimants. *Acknowledgment* is more oriented to one-sided justice interactions in which claimants expect a recognition from the outside world and society, while *truth-telling* is more likely to concern a dialogical form of justice where claimants interact with others to gain a better understanding of their victimization. We argue that whether claimants may perceive these two dimensions as meaningful to them may significantly depend on their experiences and beliefs about the past (i.e., beliefs about the recent conflict in relation to blame and victimhood).

Given these aims, we expect to identify four groups of respondents depending on their attitudes in relation to symbolic justice concerns: (1) those who support *acknowledgment* and *truth-telling*; (2) those who support neither dimension; (3) those who support *acknowledgment* but not *truth-telling*; and (4) those who support *truth-telling* but not *acknowledgment*. Each of these groups is assumed to be attached to distinctive patterns of experiences and understandings of the past and identities.

Methodology

This study is based on the analysis of data collected in 2006 using a population-based survey with 855 respondents recruited from across BiH in the three entities of the state (the Republic of Srpska, the Federation of Bosnia and Herzegovina and the Brčko District). We employed a quota sampling method (for more details, see Valiñas, Parmentier and Weitekamp 2009) to ensure that each religious[4] affiliation was represented in an equal manner in the survey, which meant using a disproportionate sample with regard to their actual representation in BiH. Gender and religious affiliation representation within the sample consisted of: 51 percent of respondents were male and 49 percent were female, 33 percent Catholics, 32.4 percent Muslims, 32.2 percent Orthodox, 0.2 percent declared themselves Jewish, 1.4 percent said they had another religion and 0.7 percent said they had no religion. Snowballing methods were also used to recruit additional respondents. The questionnaire handed out to respondents included questions related to victimization (direct and indirect), perceived subjective suffering (physical, material and psychological during and after the war), accountability, truth, reparation and factors of reconciliation.

Measures

In order to assess respondents' support for the two dimensions of symbolic justice, we derived measures from four items included in a scale measuring various forms of reparations. Respondents had to assess these four items on a four-point Likert scale of agreement going from 1 (Strongly disagree) to 4 (Strongly agree). "I do not know" answers corresponded to the value 5 and were recorded as missing values. These four items were part of the possible options included in the survey that respondents were asked to rate in response to the question "*What would make you feel better about what happened during the war?*

(a) If a memorial would be built in honor of those who have suffered
(b) If my suffering during the war would be acknowledged
(c) If I could tell others about my experience during the war
(d) If I could know the reasons why those who caused me to suffer did this to me

Items (a) and (b) constitute measures which correspond to the *acknowledgment* dimension and items (c) and (d) reflect measures pertaining to the *truth-telling* dimension.

We then computed two variables corresponding to the symbolic justice dimensions of *acknowledgment* and *truth-telling* we wanted to assess by reducing the four items described above to two mean scores.[5] We thus obtained an *acknowledgment* mean score by computing the mean of both *acknowledgment* items and a *truth-telling* score corresponding to the mean of both truth-telling items (see Table 11.1 for the mean scores and their standard deviations). The internal reliability for these two mean scores is acceptable, as shown by the Cronbach Alpha values: *acknowledgment* $\alpha=$ is .599; *truth-telling* $\alpha=$ is .631.

Table 11.1 Mean scores and standard deviations for acknowledgment and truth-telling

	Mean score	*Standard deviations*
Acknowledgment	3.02	1.01
Truth-telling	2.64	1.10

In line with our research questions, we also considered the following experiential and attitudinal factors associated to the profiles of respondents we wanted to identify:

- *Reported war experiences*: measures related to different forms of victimization reported, the identity of victimizers as well as the subjective evaluation of physical, material and emotional suffering during and after the conflict.
- *Conflict and justice related beliefs* about: (1) who to blame for the conflict; (2) the suffering attributed to the out-group; (3) the value of people telling their experience of the war to others and who should be allowed to tell these[6]; (4) where stories about experiences of war should be told; (5) moral and legal forms of accountability; and (6) the reasons for prosecuting perpetrators.
- *Demographic factors* considered concern ethno-religious affiliation, age, gender and employment status.

Findings

(a) Different profiles of symbolic justice needs

In order to check whether our assumed classification of relative support for both dimensions of symbolic justice needs corresponded to the reality of our sample, we carried out a four-solution hierarchical cluster analysis on cases using Ward's Method (Everitt et al., 2011). In line with our assumptions, the cluster analysis yielded four homogeneous groups of respondents, which are clearly demarcated from one another in terms of differences between their acknowledgment and truth-telling mean scores. As one can observe in Table 11.2:

The ***pro-symbolic*** group supports both forms of symbolic justice, as shown by their high mean scores on both dimensions

The ***anti-symbolic*** group does not support any of these forms of symbolic justice, as reflected by their low mean scores on both dimensions

The ***acknowledgment*** group only supports forms of symbolic justice which aim for suffering and victimization to be acknowledged, as shown by a high mean score on acknowledgment and a low mean score on truth-telling

Table 11.2 Acknowledgment and truth-telling mean scores by group (standard deviations in parentheses)

	Acknowledgment mean scores	*Truth-telling mean scores*
Pro-symbolic (n=208)	3.82 (.32)	3.74 (.37)
Anti-symbolic (n=113)	1.38 (.44)	1.47 (.58)
Acknowledgment (n=200)	3.37 (.59)	1.83 (.62)
Truth-telling (n=104)	2.45 (.48)	3.09 (.47)

The ***truth-telling*** group only supports forms of symbolic justice which aim for the truth to be told about what happened to them, as indicated by their high truth-telling mean score and their low acknowledgment mean score.

(b) Patterns of responses attached to these four groups of respondents

Having identified four distinctive profiles of respondents in terms of support for symbolic forms of justice, we explore the response patterns attached to these in relation to reported war experiences, beliefs about the conflict and justice and demographic factors. These findings were yielded through statistical techniques aimed at highlighting significant associations between variables, namely, Chi-Square and multivariate statistics.

War experiences

We analyzed the reported war experiences of the four groups of respondents with the aim of highlighting whether and how they differentiated one cluster from another. We focused in particular on forms of victimization suffered, subjective perceptions of physical, emotional and material suffering and the identity of the victimizers (see Table 11.3).

The *pro-symbolic* justice respondents stand out as a group that was particularly subjected to violence and persecution during the conflict as compared to the other groups of respondents. They are more likely to report having been forced to leave their place of residence during the conflict. Moreover, they are more likely to have suffered an injury and detention during the conflict, as well as to have lost property. They tend also to report high levels of physical and emotional suffering. Their perception of physical suffering is likely to be enduring, as they are

Table 11.3 War experiences by group

	Victimization	*Suffering*	*Victimizer*
Pro-symbolic justice (n=208)	Forced displacement Injury, detention, loss of property and income	High physical (enduring) and emotional suffering during the conflict	Known to the victim Armed group
Anti-symbolic justice (n=113)	Less likely to have been forcibly displaced Less likely to have participated in the conflict	Low physical and emotional suffering	Not known to the victim Not an armed group
Acknowledgment (n=200)	Less likely to have been detained or have lost property	Low physical suffering after the war	
Truth-telling (n=104)	Less likely to have been forcibly displaced	Low material suffering during the war	

significantly more likely to report physical suffering after the conflict compared to the other groups of respondents. Finally, when examining their responses concerning the identity of their victimizers, they are more likely to have known these actors and to have been victimized by a member of an armed group as compared to the other groups of respondents.

The *anti-symbolic* category of respondents shows quite the opposite pattern of experiences. Generally, they are less likely to have suffered physically and emotionally during the conflict, as well as being less likely to have actively participated in the conflict as a civilian or a combatant, compared to other respondents. They are less likely to have known their victimizer, to have been displaced or to have lost property.

The *acknowledgment* group is less likely to have suffered physically whether during or after the conflict, especially as compared to the *pro-symbolic* group. The *truth-telling* group is less likely than the *pro-symbolic* or *acknowledgment* group to have suffered materially during the conflict or to have been forcibly displaced.

Beliefs about the conflict and attitudes about justice

These four groups of respondents can also be distinguished in terms of their beliefs about the conflict and justice (see Table 11.4).[7]

Pro-symbolic justice respondents are more likely to blame the out-group for the conflict, as well as to minimize the suffering the out-group incurred. In terms of their preferred forms of accountability, they are more likely to support prosecutions at the ICTY as well as to want prosecutions for justice to be done and truth to be established via the courts. Moreover, they are more likely to support forms of accountability which have a symbolic and active nature, namely, confessions and apologies. As for their attitudes about personal truth-telling, they are more likely to think that both victims and perpetrators should tell their experiences of the conflict to others and that such personal truth-telling should take place in the court, in public and in groups that exclude the out-group.

The *anti-symbolic* justice group shows again very contrasting attitudes compared to respondents from the other groups. They are less likely to think that it is important for people to tell about their experiences of the conflict to others, to support prosecutions at the ICTY, as well as to agree that prosecutions should be carried out for justice to be done and for the truth to be established in the courts. Moreover, they are the least likely group to support confessions and apologies of perpetrators as forms of active accountability. They are more likely to blame the whole society and the international community for the conflict, while they are least likely to blame the out-group.

The two last groups are similar in terms of their favorable attitudes toward personal truths being told in court. However, they show contrasting attitudes about the targets of blame and whom to include as participants when telling personal truths in small groups. The *acknowledgment* group is less likely than the *pro-symbolic* group to blame the out-group or to blame the whole society for the conflict; they want only victims to tell their personal truths and do not want this

Table 11.4 Beliefs about conflict and justice by group

	Blame and out-group suffering beliefs	*Accountability*	*Personal truth-telling*
Pro-symbolic justice (n=208)	Blame the out-group Minimize suffering of the out-group	Support the ICTY, confessions and apologies Prosecute perpetrators for justice to be done, for the truth to be established in the court and so that it will never happen again	Think stories about the war should be told in court, at public events and in small groups where other ethnic groups' members are **not** present **Victims and perpetrators** should tell their experiences of the war to others
Anti-symbolic justice (n=113)	Blame society and the international community, not the out-group Out-group suffered more than in-group	Less likely to support ICTY	People **should not** tell their experiences of the war to others
Acknowledgment (n=200)	Do not blame the out-group or society	Support the ICTY, confessions and apologies Prosecute perpetrators for justice to be done, for the truth to be established in the court and so that it will never happen again	Stories about the war should be told in court **but not at public events** **Only victims** should tell their experiences of the war
Truth-telling (n=104)	Blame society Do not blame the international community		Stories about the war should be told in the court, at public events and in small groups where other ethnic groups' members **are** present **Victims and perpetrators** should tell their experiences of the war

telling to take place at public events. The *truth-telling group* is more likely to blame the whole society for the conflict, while they are less likely to blame the international community. They also tend to want the truth to be told in small community groups, including to members of the out-group, and to think that victims and perpetrators both should tell their experiences of the war. In terms of the audience for truth-telling, they contrast also with the *pro-symbolic* group, which is more likely to favor telling personal truths in groups which exclude the out-group.

Demographic differences between the four groups

The demographic characteristics attached to each of these four groups of respondents concern only differences in terms of ethno-religious affiliation. The *pro-symbolic* group is more likely to be made up of Muslim respondents, particularly in contrast with the *anti-symbolic* group, which is less likely to include Muslims and thus to be constituted of Catholics and Orthodox. Catholics are more likely to fall into the *truth-telling* group, in comparison with all other groups.

Discussion of findings

Focusing on the symbolic justice needs for acknowledgment and truth-telling, our findings highlight distinctive profiles of responses toward these forms of redress which are contingent upon specific experiences and attitudes.

A first of group of respondents, the *pro-symbolic* justice group, supports both dimensions of symbolic justice and shows a contrasted pattern of reported experiences and beliefs, in comparison to the other three clusters. These respondents are characterized by high levels of victimization, especially physical suffering, which has affected them in an enduring manner. Another characteristic is the personalized character of their victimization, as well as the persecutory nature of the violence they suffered. They are also the group most likely to show conflict-maintaining beliefs, namely holding the out-group responsible for the conflict and minimizing its suffering in the conflict. These findings are in line with research showing a positive relationship between high levels of reported victimization and higher tendencies to blame the out-group (Hewstone et al. 2004) and to have an exclusive focus on one's own group's victimhood (Noor et al. 2012). These two conflict-maintaining beliefs have been found to be positively associated with lower tendencies for intergroup forgiveness and reconciliation (Noor et al. 2008). The fact that they report that their victimizers are more likely to be from a collective acting on behalf of specific community (an armed group) may also explain why they are more inclined to such beliefs about the out-group. Finally, the high representation of Muslims within this group may also be an element associated with their specific pattern of reported experiences and beliefs. Such exclusive and blaming beliefs reflect the dominant narratives about intergroup roles in the conflict that are suggested to be particularly prevalent among Muslim communities (Barkan and Becirbasic 2015), but also by international actors' documentation of ethnic cleansing in BiH (Human Rights Watch 1992). Moreover, because of the persecutory and group-based nature of their victimization and the sense of collective trauma that results from it (Robben and Suarez-Orozco 2000), this group may also be particularly in need of symbolic recognition as a validation of their value as human beings and citizens. Group-oriented forms of recognition may be particularly appropriate for such respondents, because of their potential to restore a sense of belonging in the community and contribute to social repair. However, such recognition should be carried out with consideration for their particular inclination to support intergroup conflict-maintaining narratives of the past conflict and to exclude the out-group from personal truth forums.

The *anti-symbolic* justice group of respondents shows the most contrasting responses, especially in comparison with the *pro-symbolic* one. Their reported experiences of the war suggest that they were not exposed to as much violence and persecution as the other groups of respondents. Their tendency to blame society as a whole as well as the international community, but not the out-group, for the conflict and to agree that the out-group has suffered more than their own group suggests also a more inclusive perspective about the conflict's causes and consequences. They also are least likely to support forms of individualization of responsibility, whether active – through apologies and confessions – or judicial, through prosecutions, especially at the ICTY. They also do not support any form of personal truth-telling. Low levels of victimization as well as not having actively participated in the conflict may provide these respondents with less reason to favor symbolic forms of justice or to stand for public forms of truth-telling. They may also be the least likely group to consider themselves victims in relation to the conflict. Their targets of blame, namely, society and the international community, also constitute a category of actors whose lack of accountability with regard to their role in the conflict has often been criticized. Such perceptions could be reflective of the general lack of trust in civil society and toward international actors observed within BiH (Fischer and Petrović-Ziemer 2013), suggesting that this group's justice claims may be less related to the intergroup conflict and more about the political deadlock plaguing BiH.

The two last groups that favor exclusively either *acknowledgment* or *truth-telling* share some characteristics but can also be distinguished. Both groups report lower levels of victimization severity and suffering than the *pro-symbolic* group as well as less support for conflict-maintaining intergroup beliefs. Nevertheless, some experiential and attitudinal characteristics distinguish these two groups. The first distinguishing element is that the *truth-telling* group is likely to have suffered less persecution during the conflict than the *acknowledgment* group. Another difference concerns the scope of actors who should be allowed to express truths and have their personal truth acknowledged, as well as the favored place for truth to be told. The *acknowledgment* group is more likely to take an exclusive perspective limiting truth-telling to victims and favoring legal truth, while the *truth-telling* group tends to take a broader view toward who should tell the truth and where it should be told. The *truth-telling* group's broad perspective toward truth-telling is probably also related to their greater inclination to blame society and their lesser support for perpetrator-focused active forms of responsibility (apologies and confessions) and prosecutions at the ICTY (compared to the *pro-symbolic* and *acknowledgment* groups). They may be particularly likely to be in favor of a comprehensive search for the truth that would take into account various levels of responsibility and different narratives of the past: going beyond a unique focus on individual responsibility, legal truth and victim accounts to include the normative factors that condoned the conflict and the moral responsibilities attached to these.

In contrast, the *pro-symbolic* and the *acknowledgment* groups show particular support for trial-based forms of accountability and truth. Yet the *acknowledgment* respondents differ from the *pro-symbolic* ones in that they restrict the possibility of expressing personal truth to victims and only in court – and further do not blame the out-group for the conflict. In contrast, those in the *pro-symbolic* group are open to all forums of expression of personal truth, except those which include the out-group. The *pro-acknowledgment* respondents may thus be particularly inclined to want their individual victimhood recognized, excluding those whom they do not consider to be victims from judicial spaces of recognition. This exclusive stance does not, however, involve an inclination for intergroup competition for victim status like the *pro-symbolic* group.

Overall, the four profiles yielded in this study suggest that while one form or another of symbolic justice is supported by a majority of respondents, distinctive patterns of needs can be highlighted. Those who support only truth-telling favor more collective, inclusive and public initiatives bringing together all those affected by the conflict, including the out-group. Those who support only acknowledgment of suffering may be more likely to restrict the possibility of such recognition to victims and to be particularly supportive of the legal realm and its focus on individual accountability. A third category of respondents supporting both forms of symbolic recognition is the most likely to take on a collective vision of justice, which may be more about excluding and delegitimizing the out-group than about redress for individual victims.

Conclusions

These findings provide strong evidence that citizens of Bosnia and Herzegovina perceived symbolic forms of justice to be significant. They also reflect the contention that justice has multifarious meanings for people affected by a conflict and cannot be reduced to a standardized concept. They show how perceptions of justice are contextual; they are shaped by personal experiences but also by collective understandings of the past and what these mean for justice stakeholders in the present. The findings also reveal the influence of specific experiences of the conflict and their contingent war-identities (e.g., whether they were victimized during the conflict, which type of victimization they suffered, whether they were civilians or combatants), which go beyond the influences of religious affiliations. For example, those who fit the pro-symbolic group, in addition to being more likely to fall into the category "Muslim," are also more likely to have suffered high levels of violence, forced displacement and persecution, as well to have known the victimizer. The findings also indicate that experiences of the past and beliefs about justice may incline some people to adopt conflict-reducing or conflict-promoting beliefs. Thus, identifying the specificities behind the justice concerns expressed by citizens in a postwar setting may not only hone our understanding of the nuances in these claims but clarify their role in terms of the politics of victimhood and blame in BiH. On the whole, this emphasizes the necessity that those affected by an armed conflict participate in the implementation of symbolic forms of justice in order for these to fit their specific expectations of redress. In the same vein, scholarship supporting such an assessment-based perspective is increasingly calling for the necessity to engage justice stakeholders in the design and implementation of TJ measures so as to empower them in these processes and better tailor justice responses to their needs (Robins and Wilson 2015). With the awareness that justice needs change over time and as a function of sociopolitical changes (David 2017), we argue that as such "from below" assessments may need to be carried out prior, during and after the implementation of TJ measures. Moreover, in order to gain a deeper understanding of the dynamic and experience-specific complexities of justice perceptions in postwar settings, these assessments should be carried out using mixed-method approaches, involving both qualitative and quantitative methodologies (Parmentier, Rauschenbach and Van Craen 2018).

Moreover, the findings highlight that support for nonjudicial dimensions does not preclude support for judicial mechanisms, as many respondents who value symbolic forms of justice tend also to support legal forms of accountability and truth. This evidences the contention of complementarity between judicial and nonjudicial forms of TJ. It also hints at the perceived value of trials in their potential to yield symbolic outcomes of empowerment and recognition for victims and survivors (Minow 1998). However, scholarship suggests that this may not be the case for all victims (Doak 2011; Stover 2005). Many respondents may value trials as a realm for personal truths to be told and acknowledged because they conceive of these as the only possible arena. Very few initiatives exist in BiH where non-divisive, pluralistic or non-exclusive forms of truth can be told and recognized (for exceptions, see Simić 2015). Trials being, until recently, the prevailing mechanism of justice practiced in BiH, these may thus simply represent the only perceived space of recognition for victims. Another envisaged, but not yet implemented, realm could be RECOM, a project seeking to establish a regional truth-finding commission involving several Western Balkans countries, including BiH, which is currently under consultation. Whether it will constitute a forum for victims is uncertain, as the purported objectives do not mention this explicitly. According to RECOM's statute, this

> extra-judicial body will be tasked with: investigating all allegations of war crimes and other serious human rights violations in connection with the war; listing the names of all war victims and victims of crimes pertaining to the war; and collecting the information about the camps and other centers of forced detention.[8]

Thus, victims' accounts are likely to be constrained by the commission's founding objectives, in addition to the often-highlighted practical constraints of time and resources (Doak 2011). More appropriate channels for the expression of personal truths and acknowledgment of suffering could be found in forms of symbolic justice, such as artistic, storytelling or memorialization initiatives. In addition to their potential for promoting an inclusive social dialogue about the past, they could allow for the expression of individual personal truths as well as the memorialization of diverse and meaningful experiences. Oral histories (Rauschenbach et al. 2016) and artistic initiatives (Simić 2015) constitute valuable channels where personal memories can be diffused and actively managed by their beholders. This provides the marginalized voices a valuable opportunity for agency in confronting hegemonic interpretations of the past. Memorialization initiatives, provided they are not divisive and nationally driven (an oft-highlighted issue, see Armakolas 2015; Moll 2013), may also be an important realm for the expression of truths and the acknowledgment of sufferings, particularly if they integrate individual and collective dimensions of recognition. This may help avoid the challenges these dimensions pose when implemented separately: collective memorialization may often embody a broad-ranging and formal acknowledgment of societal harm, while individualized initiatives are necessarily selective, intimate and exclusive (Hamber 2009).

The aim of this study was to explore grassroots symbolic justice perceptions within a sample of citizens of Bosnia-Herzegovina in order to assess their perceived potential in this particular TJ setting. More particularly, it examined whether the relative support for two different forms of symbolic recognition (acknowledgment of suffering and truth-telling) can be related to particular profiles of experiences and beliefs (in terms of reported war experiences and beliefs about the conflict and justice). We must, however, stress that our objective was never to develop a typology but rather to gain a better understanding of the nuances attached to justice needs through the exploration of response tendencies attached to different perceptions of symbolic forms of justice. We argue that our approach is likely to be applicable and of relevance beyond the case of BiH. In line with the growing understanding within TJ scholarship (see, for example, Duthie and Seils 2017) that justice needs are likely to be heterogeneous within and between transitional contexts, a similar methodology of analysis could be refined and be used for a more in-depth exploration of the complexity of justice perceptions in other post-war and collective violence contexts. As a final comment, we wish to stress the fact that our findings should be read against the backdrop of the frequent observation that citizens' justice and victimhood concerns in Bosnia and Herzegovina are also significantly determined by everyday postwar experiences of structural exclusion and inequality (Gordy 2015; Jansen 2007). In this perspective, some have suggested that encouraging functional forms of cooperation and solidarity with the aim of promoting economic and social benefits may also constitute a significant marker of inclusive justice (Haider 2011). Let us add that historical injustices suffered in relation to enduring social inequalities (e.g., social class or urban vs. rural) may also shape current struggles for symbolic justice (Sorabji 1993). Such structural injustices should be considered when responding to justice needs in BiH, as overlooking these may undermine the very objectives and expected benefits of symbolic recognition initiatives (Hamber 2009). Overall, we contend that the development of appropriate symbolic reparations should be thought of alongside concrete responses to the current, sometimes war-related (Begicevic 2016) social justice concerns dominating everyday Bosnian life.

Notes

1 Within the field of transitional justice, the term "post-conflict" is used to describe a transitional setting in which state-based, armed violence in the context of a war has ceased, which is the case for BiH. However, in order to avoid the sense that BiH has resolved its conflicts, this volume uses the term "postwar" instead.

2 We refer to "symbolic forms of justice" instead of "symbolic reparations" since we include truth-telling measures within the category of symbolic justice, which are not generally considered a type of symbolic reparation.

3 We use the term "victim" in a broad sense to include all people who were affected by the conflict, since it impacted all citizens of BiH directly or indirectly. See Spahić-Šiljak's chapter in this volume for a discussion about this term.

4 The questionnaire only included a measure of religious affiliation with the assumption that there is a correspondence between religious affiliation and ethnicity. While acknowledging that this correspondence is not without problems, it was assumed at the time that

> religion continues to be used as an indicator of the ethnicity of each individual and in the case of surveys, it is more commonly used in order to inquire about a person's ethnicity since the concept of "ethnicity" is not yet well interiorized by all individuals. This survey followed that same approach and thus we used the question on religious affiliation in order to find out to which ethnic group the respondents belonged.
>
> (Valiñas, Parmentier and Weitekamp 2009, 11)

Thus, we only have data on respondents' religious affiliation and cannot make valid claims about the impact of ethnicity in this chapter.

5 The computation into two mean scores was validated by carrying out a hierarchical cluster analysis using Ward's Method on these four items.

6 This question for this measure was formulated as follows: Is it important for people to tell their experiences about the war? The answer options were: Yes, but only the victims; Yes, but only the perpetrators: Yes, both victims and perpetrators; No, it is not important.

7 The justice beliefs considered are categorized into two dimensions: accountability and personal truth-telling. The first dimension comprises beliefs about moral and legal accountability as well as reasons for prosecuting perpetrators. The second dimension comprises beliefs related to personal truth-telling which focus on (1) whether people should tell their experiences of war to others and who should do so, and (2) the audiences in which such truth-telling should occur.

8 For more information on RECOM, see: www.recom.link/about-us-2/sta-je-rekom/.

References

Armakolas, Ioannis. 2015. "Imagining Community in Bosnia: Constructing and Reconstructing the Slana Banja Memorial Complex in Tuzla." In *War and Cultural Heritage*, edited by Marie Louise Stig Sørensen and Dacia Viejo-Rose, 225–250. New York: Cambridge University Press.

Arriaza, Laura J., and Naomi Roht-Arriaza. 2010. "Weaving a Braid of Histories: Local Post-Armed Conflict Initiatives in Guatemala." In *Localizing Transitional Justice: Interventions and Priorities After Mass Violence*, edited by Rosalind Shaw and Lars Waldorf, 205–227. Stanford: Stanford University Press.

Ashplant, Timothy G., Graham Dawson, and Michael Roper, eds. 2000. *The Politics of War Memory and Commemoration*. London: Routledge.

Barkan, Elazar, and Belma Becirbasic. 2015. "The Politics of Memory, Victimization and Activism in Postconflict Bosnia and Herzegovina." In *Historical Justice and Memory*, edited by Klaus Neumann and Janna Thompson. Madison: University of Wisconsin Press.

Begicevic, Alma. 2016. "Money as Justice: The Case of Bosnia and Herzegovina." *Oñati Socio-Legal Series* 6.3: 396–425.

Bell, Christine. 2009. "Transitional Justice, Interdisciplinarity and the State of the 'Field' or 'Non-Field'." *International Journal of Transitional Justice* 3: 5–27.

Bougarel, Xavier, Elissa Helms, and Ger Duijzings. 2007. *The New Bosnian Mosaic. Identities, Memories and Moral Claims in a Post-War Society*. Aldershot: Ashgate.

Božić, Gordana. 2017. "Diversity in Ethnicization: War Memory Landscape in Bosnia and Herzegovina." *Memory Studies* 1–21. https://doi.org/10.1177/1750698017714834.

Braun, Christian. 2014. "The Srebrenica-Potocari Memorial: Promoting Injustice?" In *Memorials in Times of Transition*, edited by Susan Buckley-Zistel and Stephanie Schäfer, 173–198. Cambridge: Intersentia Publishing Ltd.

Brown, Kris. 2013. "Commemoration as Symbolic Reparation: New Narratives or Spaces of Conflict?" *Human Rights Review* 14.3: 273–289.

Centre for Nonviolent Action. 2016. *War of Memories: Places of Suffering and Remembrance of War in Bosnia-Herzegovina*. Belgrade. Accessed 21 September 2018. https://nenasilje.org/publikacije/pdf/War_of_Memories.pdf.

Corkalo, Dinka, Dean Ajdukovic, Harvey Weinstein, Eric Stover, Dino Djipa, and Miklos Biro. 2004. "Neighbors Again? Inter-Community Relations After Ethnic Violence." In *My Neighbor, My Enemy: Justice and Community in the Aftermath of Mass Atrocity*, edited by Eric Stover and Harvey Weinstein, 143–161. Cambridge: Cambridge University Press.

Danieli, Yael. 2014. "Healing Aspects of Reparations and Reparative Justice for Victims of Crimes Against Humanity." In *Reparations for Victims of Crimes Against Humanity*, edited by Jo-Anne Wemmers, 7–21. London: Routledge.

David, Roman. 2017. "What We Know About Transitional Justice: Survey and Experimental Evidence." *Advances in Political Psychology* 38.1: 151–177.

De Greiff, Pablo. 2006. "Justice and Reparations." In *The Handbook of Reparations*, edited by Pablo De Greiff, 451–477. Oxford: Oxford University Press.

d'Estrée, Tamra. Pearson. 2006. "The Role of 'Voice' in Intergroup Conflict De-escalation and Resolution". In *The Psychology of Resolving Global Conflicts: From War to Peace*, edited by Mari Fitzduff and Chris Stout, 103–121. Westport: Praeger Security International.

Doak, Jonathan. 2011. "The Therapeutic Dimension of Transitional Justice: Emotional Repair and Victim Satisfaction in International Trials and Truth Commissions." *International Criminal Review* 11.2: 263–298.

Duthie, Roger, and Paul Seils, eds. 2017. *Justice Mosaics: How Context Shapes Transitional Justice in Fractured Societies*. New York: International Center for Transitional Justice.

Everitt, Brian, Sabine Landau, Morven Leese, and Daniel Stahl. 2011. *Cluster Analysis*, 5th ed., Chichester: Wiley.

Fattah, Ezzat. 1991. *Understanding Criminal Victimization: An Introduction into Theoretical Victimology*. Scarborough: Prentice Hall.

Ferguson, Neil, Mark Burgess, and Ian Hollywood. 2010. "Who Are the Victims? Victimhood Experiences in Postagreement Northern Ireland." *Political Psychology* 31.6: 857–886.

Fischer, Martina, and Ljubinka Petrović-Ziemer, eds. 2013. "Dealing with the Past in the Western Balkans: Initiatives for Peacebuilding and Transitional Justice in Bosnia-Herzegovina, Serbia and Croatia." Berghof Report No. 18, Berghof Foundation, Berlin.

Fletcher, Laurel E., and Harvey M. Weinstein. 2002. "Violence and Social Repair: Rethinking the Contribution of Justice to Reconciliation." *Human Rights Quarterly* 24.3: 573–639.

Gordy, Eric. 2015. "Prof. Eric Gordy on 2014 Bosnian Protests and Plenums." Direct Democracy and Active Citizenship, 27 July. Accessed 17 March 2020. http://www.artsrn.ualberta.ca/direct-democracy/?cat=28.

Graham, Brian, and Yvonne Whelan. 2007. "The Legacies of the Dead: Commemorating the Troubles in Northern Ireland." *Environment and Planning D* 25.3: 476–495.

Grandits, Hannes. 2007. "The Power of 'Armchair Politicians': Ethnic Loyalty and Political Factionalism Among Herzegovinian Croats." In *The New Bosnian Mosaic. Identities, Memories and Moral Claims in a Post-War Society*, edited by Xavier Bougarel, Elissa Helms, and Ger Duijzings, 101–122. Aldershot: Ashgate.

Guthrey, Holly L. 2015. *Victim Healing and Truth Commissions: Transforming Pain Through Voice in Solomon Islands and Timor-Leste*. Switzerland: Springer International Publishing.

Haider, Huma. 2009. "(Re)Imagining Coexistence: Striving for Sustainable Return, Reintegration and Reconciliation in Bosnia and Herzegovina." *The International Journal of Transitional Justice* 3.1: 91–113.

Haider, Huma. 2011. "Social Repair in Divided Societies: Integrating a Coexistence Lens into Transitional Justice." *Conflict, Security & Development* 11.2: 175–203.

Hamber, Brandon. 2000. "Repairing the Irreparable: Dealing with the Double-Binds of Making Reparations for Crimes of the Past." *Ethnicity and Health* 5.3/4: 215–226.

Hamber, Brandon. 2009. *Transforming Societies After Political Violence: Truth, Reconciliation, and Mental Health*. Dordrecht: Springer.

Hamber, Brandon, and Grainne Kelly. 2016. "Practice, Power and Inertia: Personal Narrative, Archives and Dealing with the Past in Northern Ireland." *Journal of Human Rights Practice* 8: 25–44.

Hamber, Brandon, and Richard A. Wilson. 2002. "Symbolic Closure Through Memory, Reparation and Revenge in Post-Conflict Societies." *Journal of Human Rights* 1.1: 35–53.

Hammack, Phillip L., and Andrew Pilecki. 2012. "Narrative as a Root Metaphor for Political Psychology." *Political Psychology* 33.1: 75–103.

Herman, Judith. 1992. *Trauma and Recovery: From Domestic Abuse to Political Terror*. London: Pandora.

Hewstone, Miles, Ed Cairns, Alberto Voci, Frances McLernon, Ulrike Niens, and Masi Noor. 2004. "Intergroup Forgiveness and Guilt in Northern Ireland: Social Psychological Dimensions of 'The Troubles'." In *Collective Guilt International Perspectives*, edited by Nyla R. Branscombe and Bertian Doosje, 193–215. Cambridge: Cambridge University Press.

Hronešová, Jessie. 2016. "Might Makes Right: War-Related Payments in Bosnia and Herzegovina." *Journal of Intervention and Statebuilding* 10.3: 339–360.

Human Rights Watch. 1992. "War Crimes in Bosnia-Herzegovina: A Helsinki Watch Report." New York. Accessed 1 October 2018. www.hrw.org/reports/pdfs/y/yugoslav/yugo.928/yugo928full.pdf.

Isaacs, Anita. 2009. "Truth and the Challenge of Reconciliation in Guatemala." In *Reconciliation(s): Transitional Justice in Post Conflict Societies*, edited by Johanna R. Quinn, 116–146. Montreal: Mc-Gill-Queen's University Press.

Janoff-Bulman, Ronnie. 1985. *Shattered Assumptions: Towards a New Psychology of Trauma*. New York: The Free Press.

Jansen, Stef. 2007. "Remembering with a Difference: Clashing Memories of Bosnian Conflict in Everyday Life." In *The New Bosnian Mosaic: Identities, Memories and Moral Claims in a Post-War Society*, edited by Xavier Bougarel, Elissa Helms, and Ger Duijzings, 193–210. Aldershot: Ashgate.

Lambourne, Wendy. 2009. "Transitional Justice and Peacebuilding After Mass Violence." *International Journal of Transitional Justice* 3.1: 28–48.

Mannergren Selimovic, Johanna. 2018. "Gendered Silences in Post-Conflict Societies: A Typology." *Peacebuilding*. doi:10.1080/21647259.2018.1491681.

Margarell, Lisa. 2007. "Reparations in Theory and Practice." In *Reparative Justice Series*. New York: International Centre for Transitional Justice.

Minow, Martha. 1998. *Between Vengeance and Forgiveness: Facing History After Genocide and Mass Violence*. Boston: Beacon Press.

Moll, Nicolas. 2013. "Fragmented Memories in a Fragmented Country: Memory Competition and Political Identity-Building in Today's Bosnia and Herzegovina." *Nationalities Papers* 41.6: 910–935.

Moon, Claire. 2012. "'Who'll Pay Reparations on My Soul?' Compensation, Social Control and Social Suffering." *Social & Legal Studies* 21.2: 187–199.

Naidu, Ereshnee. 2004. *Symbolic Reparations: A Fractured Opportunity*. Johannesburg: Centre for the Study of Violence and Reconciliation. Accessed 17 March 2020. http://www.csvr.org.za/docs/livingmemory/symbolicreparations.pdf.

Naidu, Ereshnee. 2014. "Memorialisation in Post-Conflict Societies in Africa: Potentials and Challenges." In *Memorials in Times of Transition*, edited by Susan Buckley-Zistel and Stephanie Schäfer, 29–46. Cambridge: Intersentia Publishing Ltd.

Naidu, Ereshnee, and John Torpey. 2012. "Reparations for Human Rights Abuses." In *Handbook of Human Rights*, edited by Thomas Cushman, 476–490. New York: Routledge.

Noor, Masi, Rupert Brown, Roberto Gonzalez, Jorge Manzi, and Christopher Lewis. 2008. "On Positive Psychological Outcomes: What Helps Groups with a History of Conflict to Forgive and Reconcile with Each Other?" *Personality and Social Psychology Bulletin* 34: 819–832.

Noor, Masi, Nurit Shnabel, Samer Halabi, and Arie Nadler. 2012. "When Suffering Begets Suffering: The Psychology of Competitive Victimhood Between Adversarial Groups in Violent Conflicts." *Personality and Social Psychology Review* 16.4: 351–374.

Office of the United Nations High Commissioner for Human Rights (OHCHR). 2008. *Rule of Law Tools for Post-Conflict States: Reparations Programmes*. Geneva: United Nations.

Parmentier, Stephan, Mina Rauschenbach, and Martin Van Craen. 2018. "New Epistemologies for Confronting International Crimes: Developing the IDP Approach to Transitional Justice". In *Understanding the Age of Transitional Justice: Crimes, Courts, Commissions, and Chronicling*, edited by Nancy Adler, 75–96. New Brunswick, NJ: Rutgers University Press.

Parmentier, Stephan, Marta Valiñas, and Elmar Weitekamp. 2009. "How to Repair the Harm After Violent Conflict in Bosnia? Results of a Population-Based Survey." *Netherlands Quarterly of Human Rights* 27.1: 27–44.

Quinn, Joanna R. 2009. "What of Reconciliation? Traditional Mechanisms of Acknowledgment in Uganda." In *Reconciliation(s): Transitional Justice in Post Conflict Societies*, edited by Joanna R. Quinn, 174–206. Montreal: Mc-Gill-Queen's University Press.

Quinn, Joanna R. 2010. *The Politics of Acknowledgment: Truth Commissions in Uganda and Haiti*. Vancouver: University of British Columbia.

Ramanathapillai, Rajmohan. 2006. "The Politicizing of Trauma: A Case Study of Sri Lanka." *Peace and Conflict: Journal of Peace Psychology* 12: 1–18.

Rauschenbach, Mina, Stef Scagliola, Stephan Parmentier, and Franciska de Jong. 2016. "The Perfect Data-Marriage: Transitional Justice Research and Oral History Life Stories." *Transitional Justice Review* 1.4: 7–58.

Riaño-Alcalá, Pilar, and Erin Baines. 2011. "The Archive in the Witness: Documentation in Settings of Chronic Insecurity." *International Journal of Transitional Justice* 5.3: 412–433.

Robben, Antonius, and Marcelo Suarez-Orozco. 2000. *Cultures Under Siege: Collective Violence and Trauma*. Cambridge: Cambridge University Press.

Robins, Simon, and Erik, Wilson. 2015. "Participatory Methodologies with Victims: An Emancipatory Approach to Transitional Justice Research." *Canadian Journal of Law and Society/Revue Canadienne Droit et Société* 30.2: 219–236.

Roht-Arriaza, Naomi. 2006. "The New Landscape of Transitional Justice." In *Transitional Justice in the Twenty-First Century: Beyond Truth Versus Justice*, edited by Naomi Roht-Arriaza, 1–16. Cambridge: Cambridge University Press.

Shaw, Rosalind, Lars Waldorf, and Pierre Hazan. 2010. *Localizing Transitional Justice: Interventions and Priorities After Mass Violence*. Stanford: Stanford University Press.

Simić, Olivera. 2015. "Stories We Tell: Documentary Theatre, Performance and Justice in Transition." In *Post-Communist Transitional Justice: Lessons from Twenty-Five Years of Experience*, edited by Lavinia Stan and Nadya Nedelsky, 252–275. Cambridge: Cambridge University Press.

Sorabji, Cornelia. 1993. "Ethnic War in Bosnia?" *Radical Philosophy* 63: 33–35.

Stover, Eric. 2005. *The Witnesses: War Crimes and the Promise of Justice in The Hague*. Philadelphia: University of Pennsylvania Press.

Subotic, Jelena. 2016. "Political Memory as an Obstacle to Justice in Serbia, Croatia and Bosnia-Herzegovina." In *Transitional Justice and Reconciliation: Lessons from the Balkans*, edited by Martina Fischer and Olivera Simić, 121–138. New York: Routledge.

Teitel, R. 2000. *Transitional Justice*. New York: Oxford University Press.

Valiñas, Marta, Stephan Parmentier, and Elmar Weitekamp. 2009. "Restoring Justice in Bosnia and Herzegovina: Report of a Population-Based Survey." Working Paper No. 31, Leuven Center for Global Governance Studies.

Van Camp, Tinneke, and Jo-Anne Wemmers. 2013. "Victim Satisfaction with Restorative Justice: More than Simply Procedural Justice." *International Review of Victimology* 19.2: 117–143.

van der Merwe, Hugo. 2008. "What Survivors Say About Justice: An Analysis of the TRC Victim Hearings." In *Truth and Reconciliation in South Africa: Did the TRC Deliver?* edited by Audrey Chapman and Hugo van der Merwe, 23–44. Philadelphia: University of Pennsylvania Press.

Vinitzky-Seroussi, Vered, and Chana Teeger. 2010. "Unpacking the Unspoken: Silence in Collective Memory and Forgetting." *Social Forces* 88.3: 1103–1122.

Winter, Jay, and Emmanuel Sivan. 1999. *War and Remembrance in the Twentieth Century*. Cambridge: Cambridge University Press.

12 Taking play seriously

Creative processing of trauma through expressive arts

Kathryn Mansfield

Practitioners in peacebuilding, expressive arts and trauma treatment emphasize the central importance of the creative act. How does one explore pathways for generating creativity in the midst of deep, serious and sometimes painful efforts to transform trauma? How do embodied acts like moving, creating rhythm, playing and art-creating make a difference amid chronic violence? How does confronting "stuckness" in the body-mind enable people to face chronic violence and injustice, or even relational or professional challenges? This chapter explores some structures, potential impacts and challenges in applying expressive arts theory and practice in learning environments focused on transforming trauma and building resilience.

According to psychiatrist Bessel van der Kolk, "Negative judgment of oneself or others causes minds and bodies to tense up, which renders learning impossible. In order to recover, people need to feel free to explore and learn new ways to move" (2015, xv–xvi). His message agrees with peacebuilder John Paul Lederach's emphasis on "the fundamental belief in and pursuit of the creative act" (2005, 5). Both resonate with the expressive arts' aim to shape "experience which takes us out of our immersion in everyday life and opens us up to a new vision of existence . . . to respond, with the full range of human resources, to what affects us" (Knill, Levine and Levine 2005, 73).

During the 2016 Sarajevo conference "Trauma, Memory and Healing in the Balkans and Beyond," participants joined in activities ranging from brief daily attunement to lengthier engagement in movement, play and creative processing. Taking a look at specific examples of activities and experiences of participants in the Sarajevo conference, this chapter lays out both (a) the theoretical case for why "play" – in the form of embodied, arts-based learning – merits serious attention, and (b) the practical ways embodied, arts-based learning can shape and inform learning environments that are designed to transform trauma and build resilience.

I came to the conference in several capacities. First, I came to present about Strategies for Trauma Awareness and Resilience (STAR), an educational program based at Eastern Mennonite University's (EMU) Center for Justice and Peacebuilding that has worked for over 15 years to build resilience amid trauma and violence. STAR trainings have been facilitated since 2002 in more than 20 countries, with thousands of learners from over 60 countries. Elements of the

STAR curriculum have been translated and contextualized into more than 10 languages, including Arabic, French, Haitian Creole, Portuguese, Somali, Spanish, and various South Sudanese languages. Second, I was part of the conference planning committee, and conference leadership suggested I facilitate some embodied, expressive arts-based learning sessions during our time in Sarajevo. These emerged from my field of doctoral study and another course I co-teach, then called "Body-Mind Practices for Building Resilience."

I am currently working as STAR Lead Trainer while completing my doctoral studies in Expressive Arts and Conflict Transformation. In both STAR and the Building Resilience course, facilitators invite participants to engage in embodied, expressive arts-based processes over multiple days of intensive learning. In STAR, embodied, arts-based learning complements lectures, group work, films and circle processes. In Building Resilience, expressive arts-based, embodied activity forms the primary mode of learning and inquiry. My work facilitating embodied, arts-based learning experiences began when I worked with an organization called Peace Games[1] in Boston, which engaged in playing games and asking questions with young people to help build peacemaking and justice competencies in schools affected by violence. Later, after completing a master's degree in International Peace Studies at Notre Dame's Kroc Institute in 2008, I was apprenticed to peacebuilder John Paul Lederach. He noted how dance seemed very important to me and asked me why I hadn't integrated it into my peacebuilding practice. This question led me to study healing dance and practice it with incarcerated women, members of my church community and the Catholic Worker community locally in Indiana, and with fellow peacebuilding apprentices from Argentina, Burma/Myanmar, Colombia, the Philippines, Thailand and the United States. After that, I lived in Kenya for three years working with Kenyan peacebuilders, with a strong focus on trauma awareness and resilience. Through a PhD program at the European Graduate School in Switzerland, I learned about a wealth of Expressive Arts possibilities and applications, where my fellow students/practitioners and teachers (from Canada, different parts of Europe, Hong Kong, Israel, Turkey, the United States, and Venezuela) shared their experiences within therapeutic and educational settings as well as nonviolent social change movements, peacebuilding programs and community development and healing processes. As part of my doctoral research, I studied Personal Embodiment for three months at the Tamalpa Institute in California, with students and teachers from various parts of Europe and North America, Argentina, Colombia, Korea, Palestine, and Peru. I joined STAR and EMU's Center for Justice and Peacebuilding in 2015.

I. Stuck

Most human beings have experienced the phenomenon of feeling "stuck." When it comes to trauma, memory and healing, one can name a few specific manifestations of this feeling.

Ia. Stuck with painful memory, structural harm and legacies of historical harm

In efforts to respond to trauma, there are many causes for feeling stuck. Individuals and groups are stuck in haunting memories of violence and victimization; in difficulty accessing justice, livelihood, healthcare or power; in a climate of daily abusive violations, from micro-aggressions to domestic violence or sexual abuse; in illness, poverty or hunger. Amid political violence and legacies of historic harms – such as genocide, enslavement, colonization and apartheid – individuals and groups are stuck with a sense of insecurity, vulnerability to violations at the hands of individuals and institutional structures and fear of persecution for truth-telling or advocating for change.

Ib. Stuck in chronic violence

In her work on chronic violence and human development, Tani Marilena Adams (2017) questions the idea of preventing violence and names violence as a chronic, systemic challenge rather than a discrete problem to be solved. She acknowledges the pervasive nature of violence and how it impacts people as individuals, in families and close relationships as well as larger societies and international systems in different ways over time. She calls for the need to create spaces for responding to that violence in ways that acknowledge the complexity of its impacts and that do not escalate and create new violence.

Ic. Stuck in rigid patterns

Thousands of efforts and programs exist to invite people to open themselves to more peaceful relationships in order to address past and present harms and build toward a life-giving future. These can range from educational peacebuilding institutes to faith-based or local activist efforts to social change movements to NGO peacebuilding programming. This work requires tremendous creativity – an ability to envision and enact new patterns of relationship in the midst or aftermath of grave harm. Yet in the face of political violence, creativity, openness and flexibility can be scarce, even as the gifts of resilience and ingenuity are called upon for daily survival. Renos K. Papadopoulos describes how individuals and groups, in hopes of limiting potential damage, struggle to maintain calm composure even as they feel tremendous emotions:

> [T]his forced response of artificially steely calmness and over-rationalism is not very different (in terms of its effects) from the emotional response that caused it in the first place: both are of a compulsive nature that does not allow for openness, reflection and elasticity. As a result, reactions to political violence are likely to limit the repertoire of flexible and creative responses by individuals and groups and to promote rigid and compulsive thinking and acting.
>
> (2005, 36)

In the effort to minimize explosive responses to painful events, many individuals and groups also quiet the possibilities for life-giving, generative, liberating processes for responding.

Id. Stuck in our heads

Many mechanisms and forums for peacebuilding ignore the body, the need to engage the senses and breath and the need to build creativity to transcend the grip of trauma. One learns from trauma studies that if people cannot release and integrate the trauma response of our body-mind, they keep operating in survival mode, not operating out of empathy (Levine 2015; Ogden, Minton and Pain 2006; Siegel 2012; van der Kolk 2014). The field further teaches that the life narrative a person carries is lodged in a different part of the brain than moment-to-moment self-awareness, which is the system that "can change the emotional brain" (van der Kolk 2014, 238). Yet peacebuilding practitioners and peace educators do so much of this work through dialogue and spoken word and written research and policy, which are limited by language and preexisting paradigms. In this chapter, I urge us to engage the body more. What happens when the body is engaged intentionally? What happens when learning environments and participants attend to momentary sensations?

Ie. Defining "Stuck"

Paolo Knill, a founding teacher in the field of expressive arts, writes:

> When we look at the phenomenology of the helpless situation, keeping the generalizing reduction of being at the limit or edge in mind, it is important to note that sometimes such an experience is marked by *the sense that nothing is there and nothing helps*, and sometimes by the sense *that too much is there and it is overwhelming*. Both characterizations bring an experience *of being stuck, an agitated immobility*.
>
> (Knill, Levine and Levine 2005, 78, emphasis mine)

In other words, the stuck situation either lacks choice/options or else overwhelms. One might add to this description a sense of mechanization, repetition or rigidity.

II. Trauma and resilience: some basics[2]

Feelings of being overwhelmed or helpless can arise amid daily stresses, yet in their extreme form they characterize responses to traumatic events. Peter Levine (1997) defines trauma as a situation in which one's capacity to respond to threat is overwhelmed. David Emerson characterizes trauma as "an extreme lack of choice" (2015, 63). Bessel van der Kolk expresses the experience of trauma as when one is unable to escape from harm, being immobilized or trapped, thwarted from the natural fight/flight response to danger (2014, 30; see also Good in this volume).

IIa. Potentially traumatic events

In STAR (Strategies for Trauma Awareness and Resilience) trainings, participants begin by exploring the myriad potential sources of a trauma response (Mansfield 2017). The trauma experience can manifest in the individual body as well as collectively in communities and societies. Trauma responses can result from individual experiences such as abuse, rape or even accidents, or collective violations such as mass violence, attacks, natural disasters, war, police brutality, mass incarceration or displacement. Trauma responses may emerge from single events or continuous, chronic situations, from natural or human-caused disaster, from harms experienced by prior generations or our own, lived experiences. Cultural or structural trauma (e.g., legal, social and institutional persecution and exclusion) can also elicit a trauma response. Cultural trauma may be interpreted in different ways, such as when one's culture has been targeted, so that one cannot openly live within/according to one's culture's language, norms, religion and place. Cultural trauma can also occur when cultural practices or beliefs themselves support grave harm (e.g., the cultural acceptance of gender-based violence, the acceptance of persecution of LGBTQ+ persons or other unquestioned/accepted cultural practices of exclusion, persecution or violence by dominant groups).

Trauma responses may result from what was done to people or from participating in doing harm – called perpetration-induced (or participatory) traumatic stress (MacNair 2002). As a caregiver, educator, professional helper, or even distant witness, even if one was not directly impacted by or involved in potentially traumatic events, one may experience secondary or shared trauma (Figley 2012; Nussbaum 2018; Tosone, Nuttman-Shwartz and Stephens 2012). Some may simply call this compassion.

Typically, communities cannot point to one of these sources of harm but rather experience harms intersectionally (Collins and Bilge 2016; Crenshaw 1989). For example, different members of a community facing natural disaster will likely experience trauma in different ways depending on race, gender, sexuality, age, ability and citizenship. These forces of social division and power relations – themselves potential sources of structural trauma – can interact to generate both powerful webs of resilience and more painful complexity in the overwhelming nature of traumatic experience.

IIb. Trauma response – and resilience

What do all these different types of events have in common? They can be sources of debilitating disruption in body, brain, beliefs and behavior – and they can also be sources of resilience. As Levine puts it, "Trauma has the potential to be one of the most significant forces for psychological, social, and spiritual awakening and evolution" (1997, 2).

When groups investigate why people can't "just get over it" in a STAR training, we emphasize that everyone has a different response to potentially traumatic events or "traumagenic" events, according to Anderson Hooker and Czajkowski (2013), although some form of physiological response seems to be universal. Unless the physical body has an opportunity to release the protective energy created by traumatic stress, that energy is stored in the body and can lead us to do harm against self and others. While we cannot assume that everyone who has been through extreme adversity is "traumatized," exploring common elements of the Trauma Experience (Figure 12.1) helps to de-stigmatize some of the experiences for which people often blame and question themselves, some of the spaces in which people often feel stuck.

After traversing these spaces, participants move deeper into the question of how pain is transferred when it is not transformed (Rohr 2016).[3] They look at how experiences within the victim cycle can spill into the aggressor cycle – how victims' pain and narratives can translate into aggressor narratives and actions to create new harms and more victims (see Figure 12.2). Learners unpack how individuals and communities can become stuck inside the cycles of violence, acting in on self and acting out against others.

STAR groups identify strategies for breaking free from these cycles of violence and ways to build healthy resilience as individuals and communities. A starting point, and one emphasized frequently during the STAR learning journey, is the need to integrate body-mind-spirit tools that help individuals and communities

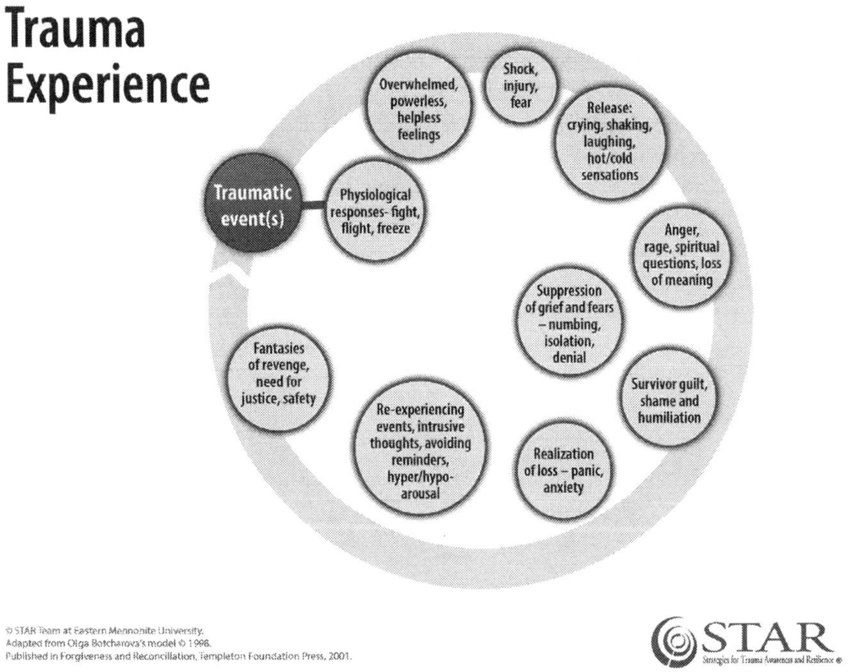

Figure 12.1 Trauma Experience (STAR 2019)

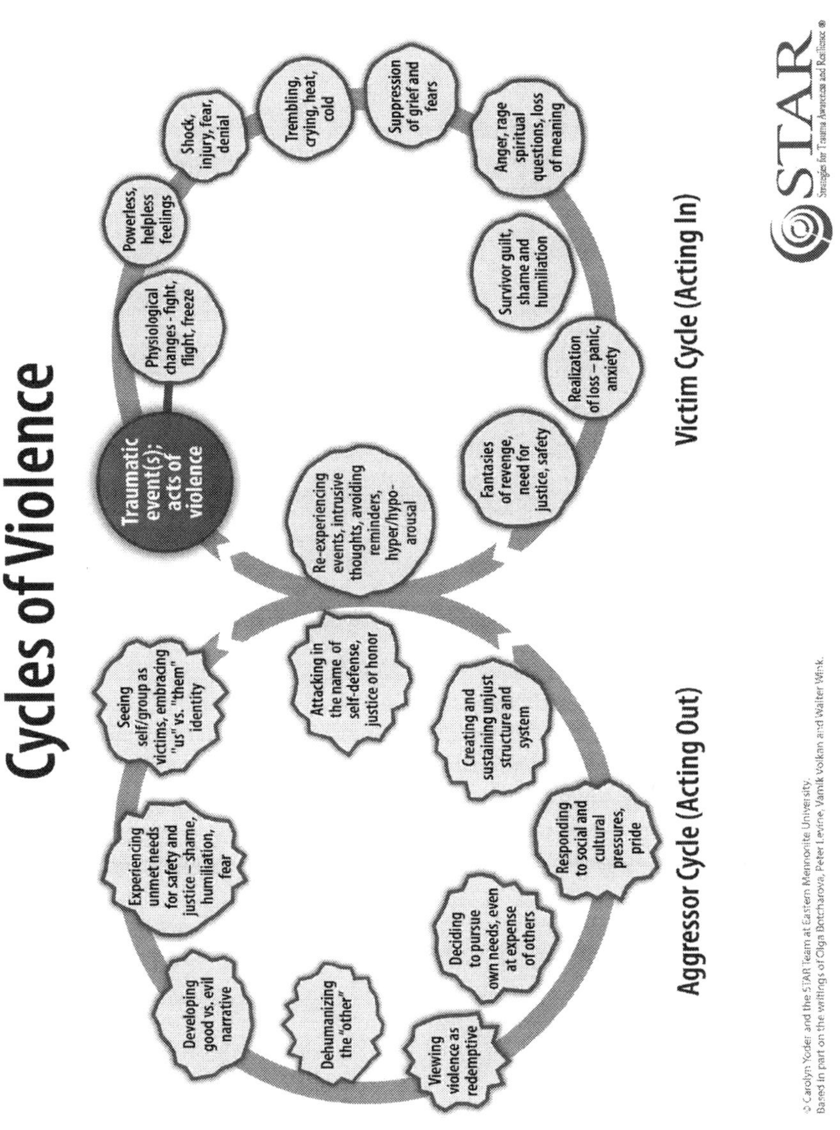

© Carolyn Yoder and the STAR Team at Eastern Mennonite University.
Based in part on the writings of Olga Botcharova, Peter Levine, Vamik Volkan and Walter Wink.

Figure 12.2 Cycles of Violence (STAR 2019)[4]

acknowledge feelings without becoming overwhelmed or driven to violence. Bessel van der Kolk advises:

> The challenge of recovery is to reestablish ownership of your body and your mind – of yourself. This means feeling free to know what you know and to feel what you feel without becoming overwhelmed, enraged, ashamed, or collapsed. For most people this involves (1) finding a way to become calm and focused, (2) learning to maintain that calm in response to images, thoughts, sounds, or physical sensations that remind you of the past, (3) finding a way to be fully alive in the present and engaged with the people around you, (4) not having to keep secrets from yourself, including secrets about the ways that you have managed to survive.
>
> (2014, 205–206)

IIc. Trauma and resilience in Bosnia and Herzegovina

In the discussions at the 2016 conference on Trauma, Memory and Healing in Sarajevo, Bosnia and Herzegovina, some presentations referred to people's attachment to particular narratives – or intentional omission of pieces of the story – about one's community or the communities who represented their enemies. The conference included a visit to Srebrenica/Potočari, where conference participants witnessed both tremendous resilience and ongoing trauma responses, along with stories that were transformative/transforming and stories that seemed stuck.

We were hosted by a group called Snaga Žene – women who have decided to work together across ethnic lines to build livelihood possibilities and open up multiethnic spaces for storytelling, healing and mutual care. The women's responses seemed life-giving as they served and enjoyed food together and told stories of how they had assisted each other in finding hope and care. Their painful stories were somehow transformed by the companionship and care they showed each other.

Before our delicious homemade meal with these women, we visited the Srebrenica/Potočari memorial site. On one side of the road we passed through a cemetery, a stone memorial listing names of the lost, and a prayer space. On the other side of the road, we walked through the abandoned factory-turned UN military base, where thousands took refuge and were later handed over to the enemy forces. The pain of the memories of the place was palpable. As our guide told the story of what happened to his family, it was hard to imagine breaking free of the sense of victimization and loss. Inside the massive factory space, now a memorial center, we gazed at photos and profiles of those held responsible for the genocide, of the process of collecting and identifying remains, of memorial services.

A brilliantly colored photo of a woman, her back to the lens and the sun shining through the forest in front of her, first attracted me with its beauty and wistfulness and warmth. Then I realized her feet were not touching the ground. She was hanging from that tree. Although the circumstances of her death were unclear, the overwhelming burden of her experiences was clear. I felt it all at once – nothing helps. And it is too much. It is overwhelming. As my eyes, body and mind adjusted from attraction to repulsion, I felt rigid. As I walked out of the factory, I became aware that a strong bodily pain I'd been carrying for a few days (as a result of an accident only days before) was imperceptible. My body was not feeling the sensation that had been with me for days and nights since my fall. I was disconnected.

III. Why play? Feeling, freedom, imagination and capacity to learn

Working to move away from violence toward inclusive peace and justice, a variety of educators and facilitators of social change have offered insight on the importance of sensation, feeling, imagination and embodying new patterns (brown 2017; generative somatics 2019; Lederach 2005; van der Kolk 2015). Facing racism and homophobia and addressing women of color, Audre Lorde wrote, "The white fathers told us, I think, therefore I am. The Black mother within each of us – the poet – whispers in our dreams, I feel, therefore I can be free" (1984, 38). Addressing one of those more mundane forms of pain and stuckness – the breakup – brown encourages, "[F]eel your feelings" (2017, 134). In the face of chronic violence and war, Lederach calls would-be peacebuilders to embrace complexity and creativity:

> The moral imagination requires the capacity to imagine ourselves in a web of relationships that includes our enemies; the ability to sustain a paradoxical curiosity that embraces complexity without reliance on dualistic polarity; the fundamental belief in and pursuit of the creative act; and the acceptance of the inherent risk of stepping into the mystery of the unknown that lies beyond the far too familiar landscape of violence.
>
> (2005, 5)

Psychiatrist van der Kolk names negative judgment as a force that impedes the possibility of learning new patterns: "Negative judgment of oneself or others causes minds and bodies to tense up, which renders learning impossible. In order to recover, people need to feel free to explore and learn new ways to move. Only then can nervous systems reorganize themselves and new patterns be formed" (2015, xv–xvi).

IIIa. Feeling, imagination and opening to new patterns – while working to transform trauma

So much of an academic conference revolves around theory, thought, language and not-very-embodied performance rituals: sitting (as part of an audience) or standing (as a speaker), sharing stories, theories, logic and questions. Yet responding to trauma is not typically a rational or linear process. So in planning this conference on Trauma, Memory and Healing, we talked about arts-based and body-engaging mechanisms – various forms of play – to complement the academic content and the visit to Srebrenica/Potočari.

If transforming trauma, social healing and breaking free from cycles of violence require creativity, curiosity and risk-taking; if freedom requires allowing ourselves to feel, and if learning requires we explore and move in new ways, then shouldn't the educational spaces around these concepts (transforming trauma, social healing and breaking free from cycles of violence) invite participants to embody those requirements as well? Is it not just good sense to draw more holistically on human experience and capacities? The discussion will now examine basic principles of expressive arts education and examples of engaging expressive arts and the physical body in educational efforts at transforming trauma and building resilience, some of which we tried to incorporate into the Sarajevo conference.

IIIb. How? Some core principles in expressive arts

Sally Atkins explains that "[A]rt making can be a method of inquiry, offering us the possibility to live the questions of life, to seek answers beyond the limitations of rational linear thinking" (Eberhart and Atkins 2014, 58). Her explanation emerges from the perspective of an expressive arts practitioner, while trauma expert Bessel van der Kolk explains how capacity for learning, for forming new patterns, requires exploration of "new ways of moving, breathing and engaging, and cannot be accomplished by prescribing specific actions geared at 'fixing'" (2015, xv–xvi). Meanwhile Lederach asserts that moral imagination is built on imaginative capacity, curiosity, creativity and risk-taking to move "beyond the far too familiar landscape of violence" (2005, 5). Expressive arts and body-based approaches can help people to seek answers beyond the rational and linear, beyond prescriptive, "fixing" orientations and without creating new violence (Eberhart and Atkins 2014; Knill, Levine and Levine 2005; Lederach 2005; Levine and Levine 2011).

In their *Sourcebook in Expressive Arts Therapy*, Atkins and Duggins Williams (2007, 21–25) summarize eight principles of practice when engaging in expressive arts activities. These principles connect with work to build resilience in the midst or aftermath of traumatic events.

1) Have clear purpose and intention

Clarity around intention "is one of many important differences that separate expressive arts therapy from arts and crafts class" (Atkins and Williams 2007, 21). In engaging expressive arts in building resilience amid ongoing or recent trauma, the intention is not just to create something interesting or beautiful (though that might happen). Intentions might include to exercise the imagination, to deepen a capacity for curiosity, questioning and creativity or to rebuild a sense of safety and connection within oneself and with other people.

2) Prepare materials and physical space

Space and materials matter – can people hear each other well if they need to communicate verbally? Does space allow for movement, if movement is involved?

Does space allow one to spread out with art supplies, if that is required? Are the materials intimidating or inviting? How do participants become sensitized to/familiar with the materials? Does the space feel vulnerably exposed or safely enclosed?

3) Attend carefully to use of time and space, prioritizing safety and support

While Atkins and Williams speak into "the therapist's responsibility to keep the time and to hold the psychological space" (2007, 22), the same can apply to the educator's responsibility in the learning space. Both circle processes (Pranis 2005; Boyes-Watson and Pranis 2014) and arts-based learning/sharing spaces require significant responsibility from the facilitator, including attention to detail and presence. In circle-keeping, a facilitator invites participants to sit in a circle and allows each person in the circle the opportunity to speak and listen, in turn. Circles are used in many spaces to address conflict, healing, justice, decision-making and celebration needs, among others. Likewise, in expressive arts spaces, a facilitator attends to the setting of guidelines, ritualized opening and closing and careful, adaptive holding of presence throughout the expressive arts experience. One must be cautious about moving too fast into or out of the arts-based activity. While these cautions apply to expressive arts, they are also critical in work to transform trauma, regardless of the mode of engagement. For example, in STAR trainings some participants have so valued the opportunity to speak openly about traumatic events that have been part of their lives that they feel they must provide those storytelling spaces for others. However, if one hosts a simple two-hour workshop among people who do not know each other well, one likely does not have enough time to create a safe container of relationship and possibilities for follow-up.

Furthermore, in work to develop new patterns, one may ultimately explore spaces that are *not* safe – with "safe" in this case meaning familiar or well-known (though admittedly people who have gone through potentially traumatic events may find danger all too familiar or well known!). A supportive environment that allows people to play, imagine and explore unknown territory will, like a safe space for telling stories, require substantial building of trust and relationship. A simple step toward safety is for the facilitator to acknowledge and invite multiple possibilities for participation – for example, stating to participants that one can participate by observing if one does not want to participate in the center of arts-based or embodied activity.

4) Value low skill/high sensitivity

In expressive arts exploration, one may find people who are highly skilled in a particular mode of art-making within the group of participants; however, their expertise is less important to the process than their sensitivity to the topic, material, time and space (Knill, Levine and Levine 2005, 98–99). This valuing of sensitivity over skill is something we can also learn from in research on trauma and resilience; learning facilitators would be wise to place developing theory as a distant second to holding trauma situations with extreme sensitivity and care.

5) Engage intermodal transfers – layering different art modes

While one person may be comfortable drawing and another at home with dance and movement, and yet another skilled with spoken word and poetry and another adept at sculpting, most humans have at least one realm where we encounter a sense of "I-can't-do-this." By shifting from one mode of art to another, "everyone can benefit from the experience of being a beginner or being awkward and uncomfortable at something" (Atkins and Williams 2007, 23). Persevering through this discomfort can translate to recognizing new internal resources for developing new patterns.

6) Experience "getting lost" – "decentering"

The process involved in expressive arts invites "losing a sense of time and space" (Atkins and Williams 2007, 24), what might be explained as allowing oneself to focus completely on the act of art-making or object of awareness. The term "decentering" is also used frequently to describe the process of moving away from the everyday concerns or areas of awareness into an imaginative, playful or ritual space (Knill, Levine and Levine 2005, 83–85). At a practical level, one might experience this as a refreshing change of scene, yet in terms of expressive arts theory, the idea of moving into the liminal space of play, imagination or ritualized action – away from the everyday – is a critical stage of the generative process. In working with trauma in body, mind and spirit, careful engagement of this process can provide space for release of trauma energy and reconnecting with feelings in ways that logic and language cannot.

7) Value the power of image and metaphor

Images and metaphoric discoveries, as well as bodily sensations, often emerge from arts-based exploration. Lederach writes, "Metaphors are like a living museum of conflict resources. They usually lead me toward an aesthetic appreciation of the context, the process, and the challenges of change" (2005, 72). Valuing images, metaphors and bodily sensations, and not skipping too fast to interpreting, understanding or judging them, can provide fodder for learning and transformation.

8) Aesthetic response with care, respect and authenticity

Witnessing and responding to someone else's art can take many forms, yet a shared value in expressive arts practice is that "judgment and critical analysis are avoided" (Atkins and Williams 2007, 25). Rather than offering praise or critique or interpretation, a witness may respond with silence, sound, words or even her own artistic creation (e.g., drawing, dance, song), or a description of her sensory experience taking in the work. The goal of response is for the creator "to feel heard and seen without judgment" (Ibid.). This kind of response offers a space to practice embracing complexity, one of the practices Lederach recommends for building moral imagination.

IIc. What? Putting principles into practice

How have expressive arts and body-mind awareness practices been part of forums for transforming trauma? This chapter explores some examples of visual art creation spaces, practices for daily attunement and workshops that engage people in decentering amid learning about trauma and resilience.

Visual art spaces

At the conference in Sarajevo, we created a wall for artistic response in a corner of the space where breaks were held. We invited participants to make use of this space between presentations as a space to post questions or visual artwork responses to what they were hearing. The intention was a space where people could create a small drawing in hopes that a small mosaic of our collective artistic responses would take shape. We shared three prompts as invitations, given that we were asking for something slightly different than an academically critical response (Halprin 2003):

- *Physical: I see . . . I hear . . . I sense in my body . . . I taste. . .*
- *Emotional: I feel. . .*
- *Mental: I remember . . . I imagine (associations, thinking, reflecting – more than analyzing)*

As supplies, we provided pastels, chalk, small pieces of paper and glue and a backdrop of brown paper (about 1 meter tall by 2.5 meters wide) on which people could paste their (roughly 10 cm^2) drawings. The outcome from this effort was that not many participants engaged in this space, perhaps because this was not a practice to which they are accustomed, perhaps because we did not reemphasize the invitation or perhaps because no time was explicitly designated for engaging in this way. Furthermore, we did not provide time and space for participants to become sensitized to the space or to the art materials; the introduction to the process was done in another room rather than in the art-making space. This was an important learning: if one is too abrupt in introducing an arts-based process and does not provide some intentional expanse for people to cross into a playful, alternative mode of inquiry and expression, the process may not bear much fruit. Greater attention to the principles of clarity of purpose, careful preparation of materials and space and attending to a sense of safety in the space (Atkins and Williams 2007) may have yielded a richer experience.

In STAR Level II trainings, typically held at Eastern Mennonite University, participants return after applying learning from STAR Level I for a deepening of knowledge and time to plan how they will bring trauma-informed and resilience-oriented practices into their own spaces. A common activity includes mandala-making. Participants create mandalas using pastels during 20–30 minutes or more for silent reflection and drawing time. On the following day, we engage in a circle process where one by one participants are invited to describe the process of creating their mandala and then receive aesthetic feedback from the others in the circle. In response, several participants offer an aesthetic response, using the language, "If this were my drawing, I would see –" (exercise instructions developed by Helen Hudson, LCSW of Harrisonburg, VA).

Figure 12.3 includes a series of mandalas created by participants in a recent STAR Level II training at EMU. In this circle, participants who had been mostly silent throughout the training opened up to share how they were touched by others' artistic expression. Engaging in art-making and aesthetic response elicited fuller engagement.

Attunement to breath, bodily sensation and surroundings

Each morning during the Sarajevo conference we took a few minutes with the early arrivers to focus on our breath and attune to our own bodies, each other and the space. One participant commented that she had never experienced this at any academic conference and that it was very helpful to her. A conference organizer

Figure 12.3 Mandalas from a STAR Training

found the time "focusing . . . useful personally, starting the day . . . in a centered space where I was aware of my body and the other people around my body breathing. . . . These are helpful to use in a group setting."[5]

In another setting, a course on Body-Mind Practices for Building Resilience included participants from six countries: Colombia, France, Iran, Palestine, the United Kingdom and the United States. To start each morning of the five-day workshop, my co-facilitator, Katia Ornelas (from Mexico), guided a breathing exercise and body scan. Each day closed with a trauma-sensitive yoga practice. Multiple participants commented on how they noticed sensations in their bodies they had been ignoring and how they were surprised by how quickly the group connected.

In addition to the daily breathing and yoga practices, this group took a half-hour silent walk through a local forest on an exceptionally windy day. Following the walk, participants tuned into specific senses (touch, sound and sight) to develop their own haiku observations.[6] Participants counted this time outside in fully embodied, non-conversational observation mode as a highlight of the course.

Short workshops: play and stuckness

During the Sarajevo conference, two workshops invited participants into embodied practice to complement the day's academic content. Each workshop occupied between 60 and 90 minutes; attendance was optional.

WORKSHOP 1: "PLAY TO DEVELOP NEW PATTERNS"

The ideas framing the first workshop included Augusto Boal's question, "What is a sectarian but a person – of the left or right – who has mechanized all their thoughts and responses?" (2002, 30) and van der Kolk's assertion that developing new patterns "can only be done by investigating new ways of moving, breathing, and engaging, and cannot be accomplished by prescribing specific actions geared at 'fixing'" (2015, xv–xvi). My goal as facilitator was to explore de-mechanization, both in terms of bodily movement and cultural norms, as a possible foundation for developing new patterns on the first day of the conference.

The session began with a slow-motion race (the one who finishes last wins) and asked people what they noticed physically, emotionally and in terms of memories or imaginations that rose up. Then the whole group (of about 30) attuned to the space and our bodies, moving around and exploring the space with different qualities of movement: speed (fast vs. slow), weight (heavy vs. light), flow (bound and free) and direction (moving directly toward a focus object, then wandering indirectly around the space).[7]

After this warm-up, participants engaged in an activity entitled "Coming Out of the Jar," created by Martha Rossi (Atkins and Williams 2007, 40). The title comes from a kindergarten teacher's likening of placing children in school for the first time to placing butterflies into jars. In the exercise, after sharing a movement or sound they liked to do when they were children, participants are given instructions to deliberately disobey the instructions of the "teacher," to play with coming out of the jar. Instructions ranged from "be still" and "be quiet" to "girls, walk modestly" and "boys, go first" to "don't use your mother tongue" and "be careful what you say to new people" and "don't notice your emotions."

WORKSHOP 2: "STUCKNESS, SENSING AND SENSE OF HUMOR"

On the second day, a group of ten gathered to explore being stuck. Framing thoughts included Knill's description of the phenomenology of being stuck (2005, 78), Papadopoulos' observation that political violence can promote "rigid and compulsive thinking and acting" (2005, 36) and Emerson's assertion that "to be traumatized is to live in a body with which you have an unreliable and unpredictable relationship" (2015, 54).

We oriented to the space and each other, again engaging various movement qualities (e.g., speed, directness) and adding rounds of movement with the instruction to notice another person but without them knowing, and then with the instruction to notice and let them know. Then, in pairs, participants conversed about situations in which they have felt stuck. After sharing experiences, they were invited to create a "cartoon image," using their own bodies, illustrating the phenomenon of stuckness. After each group shared their "body sculpture" and the other groups observed and responded, we completed the process by inviting each person to share a movement embodying breaking free.

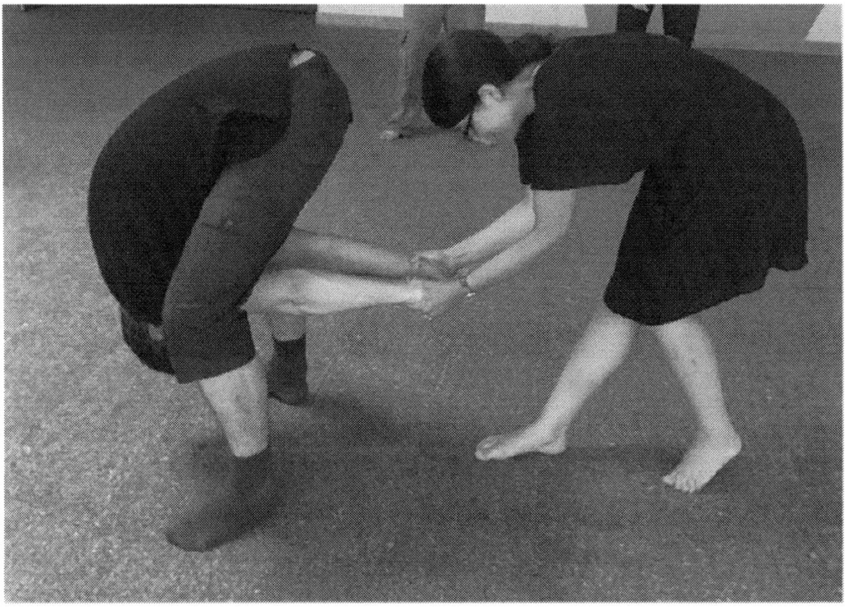

Figure 12.4 Participants T. Lotter and R.A. Aúz García illustrate feeling "stuck" (used with permission).

IIId. So what? Responses to expressive arts activities at the Sarajevo conference

Interviews with the conference organizers revealed different levels of response to the expressive arts workshops. Organizer Julianne Funk saw the value in these spaces' capacity to build interpersonal connections and understandings among participants and to add an unusual experiential component to an academic conference. She reflected, "I immediately feel like a child when we play, which feels a little bit awkward . . . makes me feel connected to these professional conference participants, watching them play, being comfortable connecting to them in a way – being [like] children [with people] you're normally professional with was oddly welcome, desirable."[8]

The other lead organizer, Zilka Spahić Šiljak, summarized the workshops as an "interesting and revealing experience, simply to work with our bodies, discovering through the motion of our bodies how much we are stuck with certain emotions, fears, norms, and most of the time we are not aware of it."[9] She continued, "[T]his was a really good way to become conscious of all of these layers of emotions and norms that govern our lives, that are important, but also somehow . . . limit us to express what we feel and what we would like to do but cannot or shouldn't, or are not supposed to, do."

A Sarajevo resident working globally in academic, governmental and nongovernmental initiatives, Spahić Šiljak has worked in her own society and others to transform conflicts and explore identity politics. She holds a PhD in gender studies, and her scope of work includes addressing cutting-edge issues involving human rights, politics, religion, education and peacebuilding. Reflecting on the expressive arts sessions, she talked about the common practice, "especially [among] those who live in post-conflict societies," of suppressing emotions.

> It's important to express our emotions . . . anger, fear, but we are not trained how to express them properly. So many of us [are] engaged in peacebuilding – let's see this argument, that argument – but we neglect the emotional part. Through these workshops I realized how much this was important. This was my feeling – I realized how much I have inside my body and my conscience. We need to work more on that.

When asked if training in Nonviolent Communications (NVC) might provide the needed strategies for expressing emotions, she responded that they had gone through NVC training, but it was more "about how to communicate with words" and did not provide adequate means for sensing emotions in the physical body. She continued:

> These exercises make us think more deeply about our own experiences – we are all stuck about our own traumas and sufferings – direct and indirect, what we may have been through in the war. It takes time to absorb everything – and to work through these traumatic experiences once you realize how much

> you have inside your body, inside your muscles. I thought at that time there is trauma in every muscle, every nerve in my body. Before that, just running to accomplish, to provide, just dispersing around all kinds of activities. Once you are part of these [expressive arts] activities, you see "my entire body is full of these emotions – I'm realizing how much I need to work on myself." I think it would be good to include this kind of exercises more in our work.

She also remarked that the conference camera person had said to her, "[I]t look[s] like a game the children play on the playground, not very important." "But it was the opposite," she said, "it was quite important – it took us on a journey inside ourselves, helped us discover what we had in order to work on it and be able to help others."

She also described an impact on her leadership and organizational interactions: "In our own team, our organization, I noticed I was much more attentive to the emotions of other people – not that I wasn't before – but I started to have a more mature approach to it." She suggested that such activities would help with team-building and empowerment: "It gives you more understanding, it empowers you to not only better understand but to really be there for your colleagues, no matter what. I was there for them no matter what before, but after the conference I started thinking more deeply about it." She summarized the experience: "This was simply empowering. To help me, to give more lights to what's going on."

IV. Play: feel, engage, create and find resources

Trauma and resilience live side by side. In the STAR curriculum, we explore how physical and mental vulnerability to traumagenic or potentially traumatic events can be particularly strong when people have little or no awareness of what happens in their bodies during stress or trauma, or have awareness but now claim to be numb or immune so that they can keep going (Fawcett 2003, 25). So to be in a position to cultivate resilience, one may start with deepening awareness of what is going on in one's body, mind and spirit in the midst and aftermath of traumatic events. With such awareness, one can find healthier connections to others to generate community resilience and nonviolent possibilities for breaking free of cycles of violence.

When simply engaging in a logical, intellectual exploration to understand and respond to trauma, one is likely to get stuck for multiple reasons. First, in their overwhelming nature, traumagenic events tend to defy logic and intellect. Second, trauma response lives in the lower brain – within instinctual drives, memories and emotions – often disconnected from the centers of logic and language in the brain. No matter what decisions we make with the mind, untransformed trauma may be alive and well in our bodies, potentially leading to poor health and unpredictable, harmful behaviors. Third, a purely intellectual study does not access the full range of resources of the body, mind and spirit.

Engaging in play means engaging the full capacities of the body, mind and spirit in ways to which people are often unaccustomed as adults. Moving and breathing in new ways can reduce negative tension in individual bodies and in relationships, which can open space for learning. Responding with creativity and noticing how that feels, rather than responding with critical analysis and ignoring our bodies and emotions, would be a shift in practice for academics and for many peacebuilders. What might peacebuilders learn if we allowed ourselves to play, engage with the fullness of our humanity and create together? According to the theory and practical experiences documented in this chapter, we might be better equipped to generate resources for transforming trauma and building resilience in our selves and our communities.

Notes

1 Now Peace First.
2 This section draws heavily upon the 2019 manual for Strategies for Trauma Awareness and Resilience (STAR) Level I training and Yoder's *Little Book of Trauma Healing* (2005). STAR is a program, based at Eastern Mennonite University's Center for Justice and Peacebuilding, that facilitates training and education to equip practitioners from many fields whose work and lives are impacted by traumatic events. See www.emu.edu/star for more information.
3 Rohr's (2016) precise words: "If we do not transform our pain, we will most assuredly transmit it."
4 Cycles of Violence and other visual aids are available at www.emu.edu/cjp/star/toolkit/.
5 J. Funk, personal communication, December 6, 2016.
6 Haiku poetry is a short form that typically involves a total of seventeen syllables, 5–7–5. John Paul Lederach has written about haiku in multiple places, most recently in *The Year in Haiku* (2015), where he explores the value of haiku for peacebuilding. Our exercise drew directly on exercises he has led in efforts at peacebuilding leadership development.
7 These movement qualities are based on Rudolf Laban's Movement Analysis.
8 J. Funk, personal communication, December 6, 2016.
9 Z. Spahić Šiljak, personal communication, November 30, 2016: all subsequent quotes from Dr. Spahić Šiljak are from this interview.

References

Adams, Tani Marilena. 2017. "How Chronic Violence Affects Human Development, Social Relations, and the Practice of Citizenship: A Systemic Framework for Action." Woodrow Wilson International Center for Scholars, Washington, DC. Accessed 17 July 2017. www.wilsoncenter.org/sites/default/files/chronic_violence_final_by_tani_adams.pdf.
Atkins, Sally, and Lesley Duggins Williams. 2007. *Sourcebook in Expressive Arts Therapy*. Blowing Rock, NC: Parkway Publishers.
Boal, Augusto. 2002. *Games for Actors and Non-Actors*. 2nd ed. New York: Routledge.
Boyes-Watson, Carolyn, and Kay Pranis. 2014. *Circle Forward*. St. Paul: Living Justice Press.
brown, adrienne m. 2017. *Emergent Strategy: Shaping Change, Changing Worlds*. Chico: AK Press.
Collins, Patricia Hill, and Sirma Bilge. 2016. *Intersectionality*. Malden, MA: Polity Press.
Crenshaw, Kimberlé. 1989. "Demarginalizing the Intersection of Race and Sex: Black Feminist Critique of Antidiscrimination Doctrine, Feminist Theory and Antiracist Politics." *University of Chicago Legal Forum* 140: 139–167.

Eberhart, Herbert, and Sally Atkins. 2014. *Presence and Process in Expressive Arts Work: At the Edge of Wonder*. London and Philadelphia: Jessica Kingsley Publishers.
Emerson, David. 2015. *Trauma-Sensitive Yoga in Therapy: Bringing the Body into Treatment*. New York: W.W. Norton & Company.
Fawcett, John, ed. 2003. *Stress and Trauma Handbook: Strategies for Flourishing in Demanding Environments*. Monrovia, CA: World Vision International.
Figley, Charles R., ed. 2012. *Encyclopedia of Trauma: An Interdisciplinary Guide*. Thousand Oaks, CA: Sage.
generative somatics. 2019. "What Is a Politicized Somatics?" Accessed 20 January 2020. https://generativesomatics.org/wp-content/uploads/2019/10/Copy-of-What-is-a-politicized-somatics.pdf.
Halprin, Daria. 2003. *The Expressive Body in Life, Art and Therapy: Working with Movement, Metaphor and Meaning*. London: Jessica Kingsley Publishers.
Hooker, David A., and Amy Potter Czajkowski. 2012. "Transforming Historical Harms." Accessed 15 May 2016. http://comingtothetable.org/wp-content/uploads/2013/10/01-Transforming_Historical_Harms.pdf.
Knill, Paolo, Ellen G. Levine, and Stephen K. Levine. 2005. *Principles and Practice of Expressive Arts Therapy: Toward a Therapeutic Aesthetics*. London: Jessica Kingsley Publishers.
Lederach, John Paul. 2005. *The Moral Imagination: The Art and Soul of Building Peace*. New York: Oxford University Press.
Lederach, John Paul. 2015. *The Year in Haiku*. Self-published.
Levine, Ellen G., and Stephen K. Levine, eds. 2011. *Art in Action: Expressive Arts Therapy and Social Change*. London and Philadelphia: Jessica Kingsley Publishers.
Levine, Peter. 1997. *Waking the Tiger – Healing Trauma*. Berkeley: North Atlantic Books.
Levine, Peter. 2015. *Trauma and Memory: Brain and Body in a Search for the Living Past*. Berkeley: North Atlantic Books.
Lorde, Audre. 1984. *Sister Outsider: Essays and Speeches*. Berkeley: The Crossing Press.
MacNair, Rachael. 2002. *Perpetration-Induced Traumatic Stress: The Psychological Consequences of Killing*. Lincoln: Praeger/Greenwood Publishing Group.
Mansfield, Kathryn. 2017. "Strategies for Trauma Awareness and Resilience Programme: Experiential Education Towards Resilience and Trauma Informed People and Practice." *Intervention* 15.3: 264–277.
Nussbaum, Trina Trotter. 2018. "Self-Care May Not Be Enough: Secondary Traumatic Stress and Organizations: A Multiple Methods Study." Master's thesis, Eastern Mennonite University.
Ogden, Pat, Kekuni Minton, and Clare Pain. 2006. *Trauma and the Body: A Sensorimotor Approach to Psychotherapy*. New York: W.W. Norton & Company.
Papadapoulos, Renos K. 2005. "Political Violence, Trauma and Mental Health Interventions." In *Art Therapy and Political Violence: With Art, Without Illusion*, edited by Debra Kalmanowitz and Bobby Lloyd, 35–59. London: Routledge.
Pranis, Kay. 2005. *Little Book of Circle Processes*. Intercourse, PA: Good Books.
Rohr, Richard. 2016. "Transforming Our Pain." Center for Action and Contemplation, 26 February. https://cac.org/transforming-our-pain-2016-02-26/.
Siegel, Daniel. 2012. *The Developing Mind*. 2nd ed. New York: Guilford Press. (Original work published 1999.)
Strategies for Trauma Awareness and Resilience (STAR). 2019. *Training Manual*. Harrisonburg, VA: Eastern Mennonite University.

Tosone, Carol, Orit Nuttman-Shwartz, and Tricia Stephens. 2012. "Shared Trauma: When the Professional is Personal." *Clinical Social Work Journal* 40.2: 231–239.
van der Kolk, Bessel. 2014. *The Body Keeps the Score: Brain, Mind and Body in the Healing of Trauma*. New York: Penguin Books.
van der Kolk, Bessel. 2015. "Foreword." In *Trauma and Memory: Brain and Body in a Search for the Living Past*, edited by Peter Levine, xi–xviii. Berkeley: North Atlantic Books.
Yoder, Carolyn. 2005. *Little Book of Trauma Healing*. Intercourse, PA: Good Books.

13 Conclusion

Lessons from Bosnia and Herzegovina

Marie E. Berry

Violence has tragically unfolded in many places since the war in Bosnia came to an end in 1995. As this book goes to press, violence rages in Syria and more than four million Syrians are displaced across the world; hundreds of thousands of Rohingya have fled state-sanctioned mass killing in Myanmar and a humanitarian catastrophe is unfolding in Yemen. As we know from Bosnia and Herzegovina, the impacts of these wars will continue to be felt for years and decades to come, stretching long past ceasefires and formal peace agreements. Indeed, all around us are the legacies of past wars. We see these legacies in the exodus of people from El Salvador, Honduras and Guatemala as they seek safety from pervasive violence in their communities and homes decades after Cold War-era conflicts engulfed their homelands. We see them in the heightened rates of substance abuse, intimate partner violence and homelessness among those who have served in active-duty combat missions. We see them in generations of people growing up displaced from their homelands – Palestinians, Somalis, Eritreans, Afghans and so many others whose lives have been spatially and temporally disrupted by the outbreak of war.

There are positive stories, too. After five decades of war in Colombia, a peace agreement was signed in 2017, and the first stages of demobilization and transitional justice are being implemented. In Nepal, a ten-year-long Maoist insurgency led to democratization, and recent efforts to implement transitional justice mechanisms have received much support. The year 2018 marked the formal end of war between Ethiopia and Eritrea, 20 years after it started. And in places with some of the bloodiest recent memories of war – such as Cambodia or Rwanda – there has been no resurgence of military conflict.

Yet even these more promising trends do not mask the fact that the legacies of violence live on long after the bullets stop flying. At the core of this book is the belief that there can be no sustainable peace without working to heal trauma that results from violence. Without addressing trauma directly, it can become "stuck" – both in individuals as well as in our social institutions and broader societies. Better addressing trauma in societies rocked by violence will be an essential component of learning how to more successfully build durable, inclusive and positive peace. And this work has never been more urgent as we are reminded daily of the extent to which violence, past or present, continues to shape our social world.

The successes and failures of peacebuilding work in Bosnia and Herzegovina provide a blueprint for much of this essential learning. As the first war to unfold on the European continent since World War II, the violent breakup of Yugoslavia captured the attention of people across the globe. Rather than dismissing the violence as far away, out of sight from Western institutions and political elites, the war unfolded in front of global audiences as part of the 24-hour news cycle. Many watched in horror as Sarajevo, a cosmopolitan, global city that had hosted the 1984 Winter Olympic games less than a decade prior, was subjected to a three-and-a-half-year horrific and bloody siege. When reporting revealed that thousands of Bosnians were being held in concentration camps eerily similar to those from the Nazi Holocaust, there was a broad sense of global urgency that intervention was necessary. With the internationally brokered Dayton Accords bringing the conflict to an official end, myriad international actors from NATO to the UN to the US played critical roles in orchestrating the country's transition to stability.

Given the scale of international attention on Bosnia and the host of actors involved with bringing the war to an end, Bosnia and Herzegovina experienced many internationally led efforts to build peace and promote justice. The International Criminal Tribunal for the former Yugoslavia was founded in The Hague in 1993 with a mandate to address war crimes that took place in the Western Balkans in the 1990s. Multinational organizations, including the Organization of Security and Cooperation in Europe (OSCE) and the United Nations, implemented programs that prioritized security, instituted political reforms and revamped economic policy. An essential prerequisite for these reforms to be successful were elections – promoting democratic electoral processes became the chief component of the international community's plan to bring peace to the Balkans. Elections were seen as the vehicle through which international actors could support the "right" domestic actors, helping them gain positions of political power from which they could work in conjunction with international actors to build peace (Woodward 1999). Bosnia became known as "the single largest post-Cold War international effort to confront and constrain intrastate conflict and promote reconstruction" (Andreas 2004, 30).

What was missing from these efforts?

As the authors in this book illustrate, there were major shortcomings to the international community's peacebuilding efforts in Bosnia and Herzegovina. In many cases, the priorities of international actors were disconnected from the needs of locals. Moreover, donor priorities often changed radically – in the first few years after the Dayton Accords, for instance, priorities changed quickly between democracy promotion, refugee resettlement and repatriation, justice and good governance. Rarely in these efforts was there a deep consideration of healing and peacebuilding to address the trauma of war in individuals, families, institutions, communities and in the country as a whole.

The authors in the book make clear that the postwar rebuilding toolkit, as deployed by international actors during the peacebuilding process in Bosnia and

Herzegovina, is in dire need of an overhaul. Their chapters illustrate how more trauma-informed, culturally embedded, locally owned and creative ways of thinking about building peace will be needed to bring about sustainable, positive peace. Several themes from these discussions can serve to inform other peacebuilding efforts, highlighting both what worked and what did not in the Bosnian case.

Theme 1: *Sustainable peacebuilding requires individual and social healing* - addressing trauma is an essential part of building peace after war

The authors in the book all coalesce around the firm belief that trauma interventions are necessary for building peace. Such interventions may enable individual people to move forward emotionally and physically after war, as they may also enable entire societies to engage in the process of addressing trauma that can reemerge in future conflicts. In situations of complex trauma, such as after armed conflict, the authors argue that trauma healing must be a core part of a multidisciplinary peacebuilding framework.

Nancy Good and Julianne Funk's chapter (2) offers a powerful summary of what trauma is and is not. In the aftermath of war, there is often a tendency to equate trauma with posttraumatic stress disorder (PTSD), a diagnostic term that reflects perhaps one end of a trauma spectrum. Deepening our understanding of trauma is necessary in order to design more effective peacebuilding and transitional justice interventions after war, as Good and Funk's notes. This will require better understanding trauma as something affecting individuals and societies; as something that is both debilitating and also potentially generative of emotional and spiritual growth; as something requiring holistic and multifaceted approaches to remedy, including approaches focused on the body, and not only the psyche. The framework offered in this chapter should guide practitioners and advocates from all fields who are invested in designing more effective interventions to cultivate healing and peacebuilding after violence.

Kristina Hook's chapter (3) further emphasizes the interrelatedness of trauma recovery and peacebuilding. Reviewing the existing literature that emphasizes an integrated approach to these topics, she explains sociocultural and biological anthropological findings, which jointly establish the societal and physical effects of trauma over multiple generations. This raises the stakes at play: without addressing trauma's enduring effects, we see it reverberate among those who did not even experience the war firsthand. Postwar societies face alarmingly high rates of conflict recurrence (Collier, Hoeffler and Söderbom 2004), and Hook further emphasizes that unaddressed trauma can fuel the political co-option of particular conflict narratives, deepening social divides and narrowing the consideration of who constitutes a victim vs. a perpetrator.

Barry Hart's chapter (4) outlines a practical framework for integrating support for psychosocial trauma into peacebuilding processes. The Peacebuilding Wheel is a model for the way that diverse actors with different backgrounds can work together to move societies forward after conflict. Designed to be used by NGO and INGO programs working to build peace, toward conflict transformation and for transitional justice, the model offers a chance to visualize the multifaceted processes required to move the wheel forward. Building toward a more stable and peaceful society requires the eventual (inter)action of *all* sections of the wheel, with each spoke providing an entry point.

Taken together, these chapters urge us to acknowledge the complexity of different experiences, needs and trauma after war and elaborate ways of doing so in the future.

Theme 2: *Multiperspectivity and multidirectionality* - acknowledging and giving space to the complexity of wartime trauma

John Paul Lederach and other peacebuilders have emphasized the importance of embracing complexity in the work of post-violence conflict transformation. In his book *The Moral Imagination* (2003), Lederach identifies "*the* great challenge of peacebuilding: how to build creative responses to patterns of self-perpetuating violence in a complex system made up of multiple actors, with activities that are happening at the same time" (Lederach 2003, 33). To break the code of this complexity, Lederach determined four "core 'essences' of peacebuilding" (Ibid., 34), elements that allow us to break out of violence. These include a vision of interrelatedness; a desire to understand others from their own point of view and to think "outside the box"; an embrace of creativity and a willingness to take great risks in the pursuit of peace. This framework goes beyond saying that all conflicts are complex by reclaiming the need for flexibility, creativity and boldness of ideas as necessary to build peace after violence.

Throughout this book, the authors also draw our attention to the importance of acknowledging and giving space to this complexity of wartime trauma and experiences. Stephanie Edwards's chapter (6) calls for us to begin this focus in how we construct memories of war. Memories that are multidirectional, which look beyond the divisive, competing memories often shaped by national political elites and toward a more communal memory that acknowledges shared pain will be necessary for people throughout the former Yugoslavia to reshape their narrative of division toward one of nonviolent relations. In Zilka Spahić Šiljak's chapter (8), we see how women, often reduced to characterizations as "victims," in reality possess tremendous complexity, resilience and power. Giving women room to narrate their own stories, with more open vocabulary that allows for multiple experiences, will better capture and thereby affirm women's complex identities.

In much the same way, Alma Jeftić (5) talks about the needed for multiperspectivity in the way that we craft collective memories and narratives about the war. Since the Council of Europe recommended suspending teaching about the war years in 2000,[1] three different narratives of the war period have emerged and been passed along to younger generations through school systems as well as through peers, the media and dominant political discourse. When memories differ and even clash, it can reinforce divisions between groups and lead to strong expressions of in-group solidarity. To counter these dominant narratives and begin to forge more constructive and inclusive narratives, Jeftić talks about the need to create curricular innovations – extra classes, summer schools and/or workshops – that explicitly adopt a focus on multiperspectivity and discuss the mechanisms through which divergent narrative memories have taken shape.

The chapter by Mina Rauschenbach, Stephan Parmentier and Maarten Van Craen (11) echoes many of these points and applies the importance of complexity and multiperspectivity to the transitional justice field. Focusing on the limits of the tools conventionally seen as "core" to the transitional justice toolkit – such as truth commissions or trials – they emphasize the need for complexity in centering more localized and community-driven forms of justice that are attuned to the inequalities and legacies of marginalization that exist in society. Symbolic forms of justice are essential, they argue, in part because they better address the complex spiritual and embodied experiences of trauma and the heterogeneity of needs of those affected – not all individuals impacted by the same events heal from trauma in the same way. In contexts fractured by ethnicity, class and other axes of difference, the justice arena is not neutral; it can become a site of contestation and power struggles, reinforcing exclusion and inequality. An emphasis on the symbolic forms of justice may better serve the complex needs of a fractured society than our mainstream transitional justice approaches.

Edita Čolo Zahirović's chapter (7) proposes another specific intervention along these lines. Drawing from the *My World, My Words* Public Speaking Event program orchestrated by Catholic Relief Services and Caritas in Bosnia and Herzegovina after the war, she describes how storytelling became a way of exposing youth and other war survivors to different narratives in a way that fostered personal relationships and helped individualize people from different sides of the conflict. She describes how regardless of their ethnic and religious backgrounds, participants "developed friendships, helped each other find jobs, collected money to support those with less, found strength within each other and jointly visited places which they had previously considered triggers for their traumatic experience" (110, this volume). Structured storytelling became a vehicle for personal transformation for participants and also promoted interethnic trust, peace and collaboration across ethnic lines.

This call for explicit attention to narratives of conflict has implications for other countries rocked by violence. Where competing narratives of victimhood emerge, international actors often attach to a single narrative that clearly fits their broader understanding of a conflict as learned through media, political elites or other sources. Often narratives can flatten the complexity of people's experiences in a way that can obscure some people's suffering while elevating the suffering of others. I've written elsewhere about how this can create *hierarchies of victimhood*, which present new barriers to rebuilding social trust and community after armed conflict (Berry 2017; see also Helms 2013; Krystalli 2019). For women in Bosnia and Herzegovina, the international media's attention to the "epidemic of rape" during the war helped to create moral economies of victimhood, where "raped women" were given status as the ultimate victims in a way that obscured other experiences of suffering. It was too frequently assumed that women who had survived sexual violence wanted to receive services and support on the basis of their status as a "rape victim" instead of some other identity. Moreover, because the dominant discourse of the war featured Serbs as the aggressors, the focus on raped women was directed at Bosniak and Croat women. This attention obscured the experiences of Serb women who had been subjected to harm and sexual violence by perpetrators on all sides of the conflict. International actors were frequently complicit in this process: they uncritically adopted the narratives of particular political elites or the "victims" groups who most effectively leveraged their experiences into moral and political capital. Elevating and thereby legitimating particular conflict narratives had the effect of erasing complex experiences.

The authors in the book make it clear that to be effective, peacebuilding, transitional justice and humanitarian interventions must, at their core, center multiple experiences and complexity. Rethinking the categories of victimhood used to offer interventions, alongside ways to embrace multiple truths in processes of truth-telling, will support – rather than undermine – the process of building more communal, equitable and cohesive societies after violence.

Theme 3: Embodied healing through the arts – drawing in creativity and changing the cycle

The authors in this book also make clear that we need to look beyond formal peacebuilding interventions toward more innovative, creative spaces and forums for healing. Jessica Smith critically notes that many who have lived through war have been the subjects of stories rather than the storytellers themselves. This powerful point deprives entire postwar societies of their agency to determine the narratives that describe their own experiences. As the chapters by Smith, Mansfield and others show, the arts – whether photography, theater, or what I've called a "gendered aesthetic of beauty" – can contribute to meaning-making, self-reflection and the cultivation of resilience after war. They can also help move energy or emotions seen as "stuck" through the body, as Mansfield notes in her discussion of how trauma can linger.

The arts are a vehicle through which the direction of stories can be changed. Jessica Smith's chapter (10) begins by asking a core question: what does it mean for women to be "empowered" in the aftermath of war? Her answer lies in the stories of women. Using a narrative lens, she argues, helps us rethink interventions aimed at "empowering" women as it views stories as linked to emotional and cognitive development. Narrative praxis can help participants tell their stories – participants can discover new things about themselves and their experiences that can structure their understanding of their past. Smith suggests that arts-based methods, such as photovoice, can assist with this process by facilitating self-reflection and meaning-making. Critically, photovoice – or the capturing of everyday lived experienced through structured photography projects – can promote marginalized voices and experiences, reinforcing the goal of centering complexity in peacebuilding interventions.

Smith's photovoice project in Bosnia and Herzegovina was both a research methodology as well as an intervention – an innovation that also holds promise for other scholars considering research in violence affected contexts. Arts-based methods allowed for research participants to find spaces for growth and power in the process of participating in research; as one of her research participants put it, taking pictures of herself and then seeing her photo displayed in a gallery allowed her to tell the public how she prefers "to be seen by others in the future" (155, this volume).

The arts may also offer something particularly powerful to persons living with trauma. Kathryn Mansfield (12) closes this volume with an important call to focus on embodied forms of trauma healing and peacebuilding. "Why do we not engage the body more?" Mansfield asks, and "what happens when we do?" In her chapter, she outlines a model of how to integrate expressive arts therapy and practice into learning environments focused on transforming trauma and building resilience. Using the Strategies for Trauma Awareness and Resilience (STAR) program trainings, Mansfield explains how trauma can be moved from the body through physical movement. Critically, expressive arts and body-based approaches offer something beyond talk therapy and more rational approaches – they do not aim to "fix" but rather can support transformation. These workshops include art-making, breath work, trauma-sensitive yoga practices, silent forest walks and a series of games and play activities that work to de-program participants' bodies, minds and even cultural norms. Expressive arts and body-based approaches can help to seek answers beyond the rational and linear, beyond prescriptive, "solution" orientations and without creating new forms of violence.

Moving forward: lessons from Bosnia and Herzegovina

What do all of these lessons from the Bosnian case suggest for peacebuilders working in other conflict affected places? While the lessons are multifaceted, my own reading of the author's chapters suggests a few concrete takeaways:

1. Addressing individual and collective trauma is critical for healing and peacebuilding after war;
2. To address trauma, we need to better understand its effects on our "Bodies, Brains, Beliefs, and Behavior" (Good 2009), and to think more creatively about how to address it;
3. Systems that fail to capture the complexity of experiences, inequalities and perspectives in conflict-affected contexts risk creating new divisions between communities and undermine longer-term prospects of peace and resilience;
4. Narrative and stories are powerful ways of transforming trauma, and the arts offer a way of deepening narrative praxis;
5. The body matters: engaging in body-aware and embodied strategies for healing will be essential in building more durable peace after armed conflict.

When I first traveled to Bosnia and Herzegovina in 2010, I heard several Bosnians sigh that every four decades their country experiences a war. The Herzegovinian uprising in 1875 was followed by the first Balkan war in 1912, followed by World War I and then World War II; just over four decades later, the recent war began in 1992. Many things have changed in Bosnia and the world since the early 1990s, and there are reasons to be optimistic that the days of armed conflict are in Bosnia's past. But this fear of the potential for future violence must be taken seriously in order to prevent it from ever becoming a reality. This means that trauma-focused peacebuilding work after war is not only essential for healing the wounds of the past but for preventing new wounds in the future.

We may also find that the more holistic, trauma-centered peacebuilding approaches help societies more effectively heal from structural violence as well; in seemingly "peaceful" countries like the United States or Canada, legacies of settler colonialism, indigenous genocide and enslaved labor continue to structure individual and community experiences today. The lessons from Bosnia discussed in this book encourage us to consider how we might better heal these past wounds by centering the multifaceted voices of marginalized communities, creating space for individuals and groups to re-narrate their stories and engaging in embodied, arts-based trauma healing. One thing that becomes clear by looking at the Bosnian case is that there is no clear "end date" to war; violence morphs, and embeds itself in bodies, institutions and systems more broadly. As such, Western democracies must reckon with their own traumatic legacies to truly build equitable and just societies that reflect our democratic ideals.

The need for this work has never been more urgent. While there is now a strong global commitment to ending wars and helping communities recover in their aftermath, we are increasingly faced with evidence that our strategies for doing both leave much to be desired. The rates of conflict reoccurrence and the persistent effects of war suggest a moral imperative for renewed attention to designing more effective, equitable and durable peacebuilding interventions. We need to build on the lessons from Bosnia and Herzegovina in Syria, Myanmar, South Sudan, Yemen and so many other places affected by war in recent years. Such a paradigm shift will be necessary to transform the trauma of the past in order to prevent its transfer in the present and future.

Note

1 [1] "Recommendation 1454 (April 2000) Education in BiH," Council of Europe.

References

Andreas, Peter. 2004. "The Clandestine Political Economy of War and Peace in Bosnia." *International Studies Quarterly* 48.1: 29–51.

Berry, Marie E. 2017. "Barriers to Women's Progress After Atrocity: Evidence from Rwanda and Bosnia-Herzegovina." *Gender & Society* 31.6: 830–853.

Collier, Paul, Anke Hoeffler, and Måns Söderbom. 2004. "On the Duration of Civil War." *Journal of Peace Research* 41.3: 253–273.

Good, Nancy. 2009. "The 4 Bs in Traumatic Stress and Resilience: Body, Brain, Beliefs, Behavior." Workshop material used in traumatic stress workshops, The KonTerra Group, Washington, DC.

Helms, Elissa. 2013. *Innocence and Victimhood: Gender, Nation, and Women's Activism in Postwar Bosnia-Herzegovina*. Madison, WI: University of Wisconsin Press.

Krystalli, Roxani. 2019. "Narrating Violence: Feminist Dilemmas and Approaches," in *Handbook on Gender and Violence*, edited by Laura J. Shepherd, 173–188. Cheltenham, UK: Edward Elgar.

Lederach, John Paul. 2003. *The Moral Imagination: The Art and Soul of Building Peace*. New York: Oxford University Press.

Woodward, Susan L. 1999. "Transitional Elections and the Dilemmas of International Assistance to Bosnia and Herzegovina." In *Three Dimensions of Peacebuilding in Bosnia: Findings from USIP-Sponsored Research and Field Projects*, edited by Steven Riskin. Washington, DC: US Institute of Peace.

Index